Environmental and Energy Policy
and the Economy

Environmental and Energy Policy and the Economy

Edited by
Matthew J. Kotchen, *Yale University and NBER,*
  United States of America
James H. Stock, *Harvard University and NBER,*
  United States of America
Catherine D. Wolfram, *University of California, Berkeley,*
  and NBER, United States of America

The University of Chicago Press
Chicago and London

NBER Environmental and Energy Policy and the Economy, Number 2, 2021

Published annually by The University of Chicago Press.
www.journals.uchicago.edu/EEPE/

Subscriptions: Individual subscription rates are $63 print + electronic and $30 e-only ($15 for students). Institutional print + electronic and e-only rates are tiered according to an institution's type and research output: $101 to $213 (print + electronic), $88 to $185 (e-only). For additional information, including back-issue sales, classroom use, rates for single copies, and prices for institutional full-run access, please visit www.journals.uchicago.edu /EEPE/. Free or deeply discounted access is available in most developing nations through the Chicago Emerging Nations Initiative (www.journals.uchicago.edu/ceni/).

Please direct subscription inquiries to Subscription Fulfillment, 1427 E. 60th Street, Chicago, IL 60637-2902. Telephone: (773) 753-3347 or toll free in the United States and Canada (877) 705-1878. Fax: (773) 753-0811 or toll-free (877) 705-1879. E-mail: subscriptions @press.uchicago.edu.

Standing orders: To place a standing order for this book series, please address your request to The University of Chicago Press, Chicago Distribution Center, Attn. Standing Orders/Customer Service, 11030 S. Langley Avenue, Chicago, IL 60628. Telephone toll free in the U.S. and Canada: 1-800-621-2736; or 1-773-702-7000. Fax toll free in the U.S. and Canada: 1-800-621-8476; or 1-773-702-7212.

Single-copy orders: In the U.S., Canada, and the rest of the world, order from your local bookseller or direct from The University of Chicago Press, Chicago Distribution Center, 11030 S. Langley Avenue, Chicago, IL 60628. Telephone toll free in the U.S. and Canada: 1-800-621-2736; or 1-773-702-7000. Fax toll free in the U.S. and Canada: 1-800-621-8476; or 1-773-702-7212. In the U.K. and Europe, order from your local bookseller or direct from The University of Chicago Press, c/o John Wiley Ltd. Distribution Center, 1 Oldlands Way, Bognor Regis, West Sussex PO22 9SA, UK. Telephone 01243 779777 or Fax 01243 820250. E-mail: cs-books@wiley.co.uk.

The University of Chicago Press offers bulk discounts on individual titles to Corporate, Premium, and Gift accounts. For information, please write to Sales Department—Special Sales, The University of Chicago Press, 1427 E. 60th Street, Chicago, IL 60637 USA or telephone 1-773-702-7723.

This book was printed and bound in the United States of America.

ISSN: 2689-7857
E-ISSN: 2689-7865
ISBN-13: 978-0-226-80237-4 (pb.:alk.paper)
ISBN-13: 978-0-226-80254-1 (e-book)

Environmental and Energy Policy and the Economy

Relation of the Directors to the Work and Publications of the NBER

1. The object of the NBER is to ascertain and present to the economics profession, and to the public more generally, important economic facts and their interpretation in a scientific manner without policy recommendations. The Board of Directors is charged with the responsibility of ensuring that the work of the NBER is carried on in strict conformity with this object.

2. The President shall establish an internal review process to ensure that book manuscripts proposed for publication DO NOT contain policy recommendations. This shall apply both to the proceedings of conferences and to manuscripts by a single author or by one or more coauthors but shall not apply to authors of comments at NBER conferences who are not NBER affiliates.

3. No book manuscript reporting research shall be published by the NBER until the President has sent to each member of the Board a notice that a manuscript is recommended for publication and that in the President's opinion it is suitable for publication in accordance with the above principles of the NBER. Such notification will include a table of contents and an abstract or summary of the manuscript's content, a list of contributors if applicable, and a response form for use by Directors who desire a copy of the manuscript for review. Each manuscript shall contain a summary drawing attention to the nature and treatment of the problem studied and the main conclusions reached.

4. No volume shall be published until forty-five days have elapsed from the above notification of intention to publish it. During this period a copy shall be sent to any Director requesting it, and if any Director objects to publication on the grounds that the manuscript contains policy recommendations, the objection will be presented to the author(s) or editor(s). In case of dispute, all members of the Board shall be notified,

and the President shall appoint an ad hoc committee of the Board to decide the matter; thirty days additional shall be granted for this purpose.

5. The President shall present annually to the Board a report describing the internal manuscript review process, any objections made by Directors before publication or by anyone after publication, any disputes about such matters, and how they were handled.

6. Publications of the NBER issued for informational purposes concerning the work of the Bureau, or issued to inform the public of the activities at the Bureau, including but not limited to the NBER Digest and Reporter, shall be consistent with the object stated in paragraph 1. They shall contain a specific disclaimer noting that they have not passed through the review procedures required in this resolution. The Executive Committee of the Board is charged with the review of all such publications from time to time.

7. NBER working papers and manuscripts distributed on the Bureau's web site are not deemed to be publications for the purpose of this resolution, but they shall be consistent with the object stated in paragraph 1. Working papers shall contain a specific disclaimer noting that they have not passed through the review procedures required in this resolution. The NBER's web site shall contain a similar disclaimer. The President shall establish an internal review process to ensure that the working papers and the web site do not contain policy recommendations, and shall report annually to the Board on this process and any concerns raised in connection with it.

8. Unless otherwise determined by the Board or exempted by the terms of paragraphs 6 and 7, a copy of this resolution shall be printed in each NBER publication as described in paragraph 2 above.

Contents

Introduction

Matthew J. Kotchen, *Yale University and NBER,* United States of America

James H. Stock, *Harvard University and NBER,* United States of America

Catherine D. Wolfram, *University of California, Berkeley, and NBER,* United States of America

Welcome to the second volume of *Environmental and Energy Policy and the Economy* (*EEPE*). The six papers published in this issue were first presented and discussed in May 2020 via an online conference hosted by the National Bureau of Economic Research (NBER) that included participants from academia, government, and nongovernmental organizations. Although the annual conference was originally scheduled to take place at the National Press Club in Washington, DC, the novel coronavirus forced us to convert the conference to an online format. Participants missed out on the opportunity for face-to-face interaction, but we made up for it with a larger than expected number of participants. The agenda also featured a presentation by Ted Halstead, chairman and CEO of the Climate Leadership Council, on "A Climate Solution Where All Sides Can Win."

The broad aim of the *EEPE* initiative is to spur policy-relevant research and professional interactions in the areas of environmental and energy economics and policy. This is inspired by growing concerns about environmental and energy issues and by the significant economic consequences of policy making in this area. At the time of this writing, much of the world is focused on the immediate challenges of responding to and managing the spread of COVID-19. But alongside these concerns, and sometimes closely connected, remain issues of environmental and energy policy. The papers included in the volume contribute original research to many of the important topics.

In the first paper, Robert Pindyck provides a systematic overview of what we know and don't know about climate change. When it comes to formulating policy, he discusses the importance of forecasting economic growth, emissions intensity per unit of output, atmospheric dissipation of emissions, climate temperature sensitivity, economic impacts of temperature change, abatement costs, and discounting. Given the uncertainties

Environmental and Energy Policy and the Economy, volume 2, 2021.

at each stage, he considers how the potential for learning might affect climate policy responses and argues that the insurance value of mitigating climate change is likely to be significant.

Shaikh Eskander, Sam Fankhauser, and Joana Setzer offer insights from the most comprehensive data set on climate change legislation and litigation across all countries of the world over the past 30 years. The trends are important because of the way that any one country, including the United States, inevitably looks to others as a way of calibrating its own climate policies. They find that climate legislation peaked worldwide between 2009 and 2014, well before the Paris Agreement; climate change legislation is less of a partisan issue than commonly assumed; legislative activity decreases in times of economic difficulty; and the courts in most countries other than the United States tend to rule in favor of greater climate protections.

The growing financial risks to coal-reliant communities is the topic addressed in the paper by Adele Morris, Noah Kaufman, and Siddhi Doshi. In communities where coal production constitutes a large share of the local economy, government revenues are at increasing risk due to shifts in the energy sector and the prospects for climate policies, both of which are not favorable to coal. The paper provides a clear example of how greater attention to the distribution consequences of environmental and energy policy is important. Not only are distributional concerns important on their own, but they also play a critical role in the political economy that defines the space of feasible policies. Morris and coauthors shine a light on how expected trends in the coal industry will have significant implications on the local public finances of coal-reliant communities, and policy makers would be well advised to begin thinking through policy responses.

Joseph Aldy, Matthew Kotchen, Mary Evans, Meredith Fowlie, Arik Levinson, and Karen Palmer consider the treatment of cobenefits in benefit-cost analyses of federal clean air regulations. Cobenefits are benefits that arise when compliance with a regulation leads to benefits that are not directly tied to a regulation's intended target. The topic has become increasingly important with recent actions by the US Environmental Protection Agency (EPA) to change the way it treats cobenefits in regulatory impact analyses. Aldy and coauthors assemble and make available a comprehensive data set on the benefits and costs of all economically significant Clean Air Act rules issued by the EPA over the period 1997–2019. The data set allows an examination of the role cobenefits have played over time and complements the paper's theoretical analysis, which demonstrates how cobenefits are simply a semantic category of benefits that are standard to include in benefit-cost analyses.

Tatyana Deryugina, Nolan Miller, David Molitor, and Julian Reif provide a detailed analysis of the geographic and socioeconomic heterogeneity in the benefits of reducing particulate matter air pollution. Their paper takes advantage of comprehensive data on Medicare recipients across the United States to develop a vulnerability index to air pollution. Although the estimates are useful for understanding the heterogeneous impacts of policies that affect pollution, the results point to a further implication for the design of air quality regulations. Because they find that vulnerability is negatively correlated with the average pollution level within a region, policies that base air quality regulations on current pollution levels alone may fail to target regions with the most to gain by reducing exposure.

In the last paper, Oliver Browne, Ludovica Gazze, and Michael Greenstone use detailed data on residential water consumption to answer an important question: Do conservation policies work? During a period of drought in California from 2011 to 2017, they consider a series of conservation policies that were implemented in the city of Fresno. After disentangling the effects of the different policies, they estimate price elasticities of the demand for water based on price schedule changes, the effect of allowing a reduced number of watering days, and the impact of public announcements calling for greater water conservation. The first two are found to have significant effects, whereas the public announcements did not. The paper also provides a discussion of the challenges that arise when seeking to estimate the impact of interventions over a period when multiple policies are changing.

Finally, we are grateful to all of the authors for their time and effort in helping to make the second year of *EEPE* a success. We are grateful to Jim Poterba, president and CEO of the NBER, for continuing to support the initiative, and to the NBER's conference staff, especially Rob Shannon, for making the organization a pleasure, including the transition to an online conference. Helena Fitz-Patrick's help with the publication is also invaluable and greatly appreciated. Lastly, we would like to thank Evan Michelson and the Alfred P. Sloan Foundation for the financial support that has made the *EEPE* initiative possible.

Endnote

Author email addresses: Kotchen (matthew.kotchen@yale.edu), Stock (James_Stock @harvard.edu), Wolfram (wolfram@haas.berkeley.edu). For acknowledgments, sources of research support, and disclosure of the authors' material financial relationships, if any, please see https://www.nber.org/books-and-chapters/environmental-and-energy-policy -and-economy-volume-2/introduction-environmental-and-energy-policy-and-economy -volume-2.

What We Know and Don't Know about Climate Change, and Implications for Policy

Robert S. Pindyck, *Sloan School of Management, Massachusetts Institute of Technology, and NBER,* United States of America

Executive Summary

There is a lot we know about climate change, but there is also a lot we don't know. Even if we knew how much CO_2 will be emitted over the coming decades, we wouldn't know how much temperatures will rise as a result. And even if we could predict the extent of warming that will occur, we can say very little about its impact. I explain that we face considerable uncertainty over climate change and its impact, why there is so much uncertainty, and why we will continue to face uncertainty in the near future. I also explain the policy implications of climate change uncertainty. First, the uncertainty (particularly over the possibility of a catastrophic climate outcome) creates insurance value, which pushes us to earlier and stronger actions to reduce CO_2 emissions. Second, uncertainty interacts with two kinds of irreversibilities: CO_2 remains in the atmosphere for centuries, making the environmental damage from CO_2 emissions irreversible, pushing us to earlier and stronger actions and reducing CO_2 emissions requires sunk costs, that is, irreversible expenditures, which pushes us away from earlier actions. Both irreversibilities are inherent in climate policy, but the net effect is ambiguous.

JEL Codes: Q5, Q54, D81

Keywords: environmental policy, climate change, integrated assessment models, climate impact, social cost of carbon, CO_2 emissions abatement, damage functions, climate sensitivity, uncertainty, irreversibilities, insurance

I. Introduction

There is a lot we know about climate change, but there is also a lot we don't know. Even if we knew exactly how much carbon dioxide (CO_2) and other greenhouse gases (GHGs) the world will emit over the coming decades, we wouldn't be able to predict with any reasonable precision how much the global mean temperature will rise as a result. Nor would we be able to predict other aspects of climate change, such as rises in sea levels and increases in the frequency and intensity of storms, hurricanes, and droughts. And even if we were able to predict the extent of climate change that will occur over the coming decades, we can say very little about its likely impact—which in the end is what matters. The fact is that we face considerable uncertainty over climate change, and as we'll see, that uncertainty has crucial implications for policy.

Despite the uncertainty, the debate over climate policy is usually framed in deterministic terms. We start with some scenario regarding GHG emissions, perhaps under "business as usual" or under some emission abatement policy, and then make and discuss projections of temperature change through the end of the century. Sometimes those projections include high, medium, and low alternatives, but without much basis for how and why those alternatives differ as they do. We then talk in broad terms about the likely impacts of those temperature changes—reductions in agricultural output, reduced productivity generally, greater damage from more intense storms and droughts, and perhaps displacements of populations if rising sea levels inundate low-lying areas. We sometimes try to translate those impacts into percentage reductions in gross domestic product (GDP), which is necessary if we want to come up with a number for the social cost of carbon (SCC). We know that those impacts are very difficult—perhaps impossible—to predict because climate change happens slowly, over decades, and we don't know the extent of adaptation that will occur in response.

And despite all the uncertainty, we evaluate climate change policies in terms that suggest a high level of precision is possible. As I have argued elsewhere, this is particularly true when we use complex integrated assessment models (IAMs) to make outcome and impact projections, evaluate alternative policies, and estimate the SCC.[1] But as I will argue, it is the uncertainty over climate change and its impact that is critical to policy formulation, and that should be the focus of analysis and discussion.

To get a sense of why the uncertainties are so important, consider the irreversibilities that are an inherent part of climate policy (and environmental policy more generally). It has been long understood that environmental damage can be irreversible, which can lead to a more "conservationist" policy than would be optimal otherwise. Thanks to Joni Mitchell, even noneconomists know that if we "pave paradise and put up a parking lot," paradise may be gone forever. And because the value of paradise to future generations is uncertain, the benefit from protecting it today should include an option value, which pushes the cost-benefit calculation toward protection. But there is a second kind of irreversibility that works in the opposite direction: protecting paradise over the years to come imposes sunk costs on society. If paradise includes clean air and water, protecting it could imply sunk cost investments in abatement equipment and an ongoing flow of sunk costs for more expensive production processes. This kind of irreversibility would lead to policies that are less "conservationist" than they would be otherwise.

Which of these two irreversibilities applies to climate policy? Both. Given that they work in opposite directions, which one is more important? We don't know.[2] Because CO_2 can remain in the atmosphere for centuries, and ecosystem destruction from climate change can be permanent, there is clearly an argument for taking early action. But the costs of reducing CO_2 emissions are largely sunk, which implies an argument for waiting.[3] Which type of irreversibility will dominate depends in part on the nature and extent of the uncertainties involved, and will be explored in this paper.

There is another reason why the uncertainties over climate change are so important, and it has to do with "tail risk." If climate change turns out to be moderate, and its impact turns out to be moderate, we may not have too much to worry about. But what if climate change and its impact turn out to be catastrophic—the far right tail of the outcome distribution. It is that possibility, even if the probability is low, that might drive us to quickly adopt a stringent emission abatement policy. In effect, by reducing emissions now we would be buying insurance. But how much of a premium should we be willing to pay for such insurance? The answer depends in part on society's degree of risk aversion, which is complex and hard to evaluate. As I will show, however, the risk premium could be considerable.

This paper has two main parts. First, I lay out what we know, don't know, and sort of know about climate change and discuss why we don't know certain things and the nature of the uncertainties. One of the two more important uncertainties pertains to the extent of warming (and other aspects of climate change) that will occur given current and expected future GHG emissions. The second uncertainty pertains to the economic impact of any climate change that might occur, an impact that depends critically on the possibility of adaptation. Although various estimates are available, we simply don't know how much warmer the world will become by the end of the century under the Paris Agreement, or under any other agreement. Nor do we know how much worse off we will be if the global mean temperature increases by 2°C or even 5°C.

In fact, we may never be able to resolve these uncertainties (at least over the next few decades). It may be that the extent of warming and its impact are not just unknown but also unknowable—what King (2016) refers to as "radical uncertainty," or extreme Knightian uncertainty.[4] And as King (2016, 131) puts it (in a very different context), "The fundamental point about radical uncertainty is that if we don't know what the future might hold, we don't know, and there is no point pretending otherwise."[5] But even though we may never resolve these uncertainties, we can characterize them and better understand them.

That leads to the second part of this paper, which deals with the implications of uncertainty for climate policy. In a risk-neutral world with no irreversibilities, only the expected values of outcomes should matter, not the degree of uncertainty over those outcomes. But macroeconomic and financial market data suggest that society (or at least the people that make up society) is far from risk-neutral, so that there is likely to be a significant insurance value to reducing GHG emissions now. Likewise, we know that there are two types of irreversibilities at play, which work in opposite directions. In formulating climate policy, what is the insurance value of GHG emission reductions, and what is the net effect of the relevant irreversibilities? This paper addresses those questions.

In the next three sections, I lay out the steps through which emissions of CO_2 (and other GHGs) accumulate in the atmosphere, how increases in the atmospheric CO_2 concentration affect the global mean temperature (and regional temperatures), how temperature increases affect sea levels as well as other aspects of climate, and how changes in climate can in turn have economic and social impacts (i.e., "damages"). I will characterize in general terms the state of our knowledge with respect to each of these steps, that is, the extent of our uncertainty. For two of these steps— how rising GHG concentrations affect climate and how climate change causes damages—the uncertainty is huge.

I will also refine the statement that "the uncertainty is huge." I will try to characterize these uncertainties in terms of probability distributions that have come out of recent studies in climate science and economics. I will address the question of whether those distributions have "fat tails" (and whether that matters). I will also review the evidence on how these uncertainties are changing over time. (As I will explain, between the 2007 and 2014 Intergovernmental Panel on Climate Change [IPCC] reports, uncertainty over how changes in the atmospheric CO_2 concentration affect temperature has actually increased.) This is important because it addresses the value of waiting for new information rather than taking immediate action now.

I will then turn to the implications of uncertainty for policy. First, how does climate change uncertainty interact with the two opposing irreversibilities outlined above? I will address this question using a simple two-period example. Second, I will explain how climate change uncertainty creates an insurance value of early action. But readers hoping that I can tell them exactly how large that insurance value is will be disappointed. The reason is that there is a catch-22 at work here: the very uncertainties over climate change that create a value of insurance prevent us from determining how large that value is with any precision. On the other hand, we can get a rough sense of how important that insurance value is, and determine whether it is something we should take into account. As we will see, it is indeed something we should take into account.

II.   Some Climate Change Basics

To keep things simple, I will ignore methane and other non-CO_2 GHGs in this paper and focus only on CO_2, which is by far the greatest driver of climate change. Yes, the warming potential of a ton of atmospheric methane is about 25 times the warming potential of a ton of CO_2, but far fewer tons of methane are emitted each year, and methane stays in the atmosphere only for a decade or so, whereas CO_2 stays there for centuries. As a result, methane accounts for less than 10% of the total warming effects of GHG emissions.

It will be useful to go over the basic mechanisms by which CO_2 emissions originate and accumulate in the atmosphere, how increases in the atmospheric CO_2 concentration leads to climate change, how climate change in turn leads to impacts, and how those impacts can be evaluated in economic terms. We also want to know how emissions can be reduced, and at what cost. We could think about this in terms of a projection of climate damages over the coming century under "business as usual," in which nothing is done to reduce emissions, and under alternative emission reduction policies. The steps would be as follows:

1. **GDP Growth:** GHG emissions are generated by economic activity. If all economic activity stopped—no production, no consumption—emissions caused by humans would likewise stop. So the first step in projecting CO_2 emissions is to project GDP growth over the coming century. Not easy! Projecting GDP growth for different countries or regions over the next 5 years is hard enough. (For example, no one anticipated the deep worldwide recession caused by the COVID-19 pandemic.) And now think about projecting GDP growth over the next 50 years. Tough job, and clearly subject to considerable uncertainty.

2. **CO_2 Emissions:** Marching ahead, let's assume we have a reasonable projection of GDP growth (by region) through the end of the century. We would use this information to make projections of future CO_2 emissions under "business as usual," that is, no emission reduction policy, or under one or more abatement scenarios. To do this, we might relate CO_2 emissions to GDP and then use our projections of future GDP. But this is problematic, in part because the relationship between CO_2 emissions and GDP has been changing, and is likely to continue to change in ways that are not entirely predictable. (The impact of the COVID-19 pandemic is an example of how the relationship between CO_2 emissions and GDP can change suddenly and unpredictably.) Note that CO_2 emissions are measured in billions of metric tons, called gigatons (Gt) for short.

3. **Atmospheric CO_2 Concentration:** Suppose we have projections of CO_2 emissions through the end of the century. We could use those projections to project future atmospheric CO_2 concentrations, accounting for past and current emissions as well as future emissions. The key fact is that 1 Gt of CO_2 emitted into the atmosphere increases the CO_2 concentration by 0.128 parts per million (ppm).[6] There is some uncertainty here, because the CO_2 dissipation rate—in the range of 0.0025–0.0050 per year on average—depends in part on the total concentrations of CO_2 in the atmosphere and in the oceans. But relative to other uncertainties, translating emissions to concentrations can be done with reasonable accuracy.

4. **Temperature Change:** Now we come to the hard part. We would like to make projections of the average global mean temperature change likely to result from higher CO_2 concentrations. That means we need a number for *climate sensitivity*—the increase in the global mean temperature that would eventually result from a doubling of the atmospheric CO_2 concentration. OK, so what's that number? Unfortunately, we don't know the true value of climate sensitivity. The "most likely" range (according to the IPCC) is from 1.5°C to 4.5°C, and if we include what the IPCC considers "less likely" but possible values, the range would run from 1.0°C to 6.0°C. Even 1.5°C–4.5°C is a huge range, and it implies a huge range for temperature change. On top of that uncertainty, what is the time lag between an increase in the CO_2 concentration and its impact on temperature? Something like 10–40 years, but again, that is a wide range.

5. **Impact of Climate Change:** But let's march ahead and assume we know how much the temperature will increase during the coming decades

(and how much sea levels will rise, etc.) and try to project the economic impact of such changes in terms of lost GDP and consumption. Now we are in truly uncharted territory. Most IAMs make such projections by including a "damage function" that relates temperature change to lost GDP, but those damage functions are not based on any economic (or other) theory or much in the way of empirical evidence. They are essentially arbitrary functions, made up to describe how GDP goes down when temperature goes up. To make matters worse, "economic impact" should include indirect impacts, such as the social, political, and health impacts of climate change, which might somehow be monetized and added to lost GDP. Here, too, we are in the dark. Basically, we know very little about what the true damage function looks like. The bottom line: projecting the impact of climate change is the most speculative part of the analysis.

6. **Abatement Costs:** To evaluate a candidate climate policy, we must compare the benefits of the policy to its costs. What are the benefits? A reduction in climate-induced damages; for example, a reduction in the loss of GDP that would otherwise result from climate change. But as I just said, projecting the impact of climate change is highly speculative. And what about the costs of a candidate climate policy, that is, the costs of abating GHG emissions by various amounts, both now and throughout the future. A small amount of abatement (say, reducing CO_2 emissions by 5% or 10%) is fairly easy, but a large amount (say, cutting emissions in half) is likely to be quite costly. But how costly? We're not sure, in part because we have had no experience cutting emissions by half or more. Also, we expect that abatement costs will fall over the coming decades, but by how much? Answering that question requires projections of technological change that might reduce future abatement costs, and technological change is hard to predict. Once again, we face considerable uncertainty.

7. **Valuing Current and Future Losses of GDP:** Finally, let's assume that we could somehow determine the annual economic losses (measured in terms of lost GDP) resulting from any particular increase in temperature. Let's also assume that we know the increases in temperature that would result from "business as usual" and under some abatement policy. And suppose we also know the annual cost (again in terms of lost GDP) of that abatement policy. How would we compare the benefits from the policy to its costs? We would need to know the discount rate that would let us compare current losses of GDP (from the cost of abating emissions) with the future gains in GDP from the reduction in damages resulting from the abatement policy.[7] The discount rate (in this

case the social rate of time preference, because it measures how society values a loss of GDP and hence consumption in the future versus today) is critical: a low discount rate (say around 1%) makes it easier to justify an immediate stringent abatement policy; a high rate (say around 5%) does the opposite. So what is the "correct" discount rate? There is no clear number on which economists agree. The US government's Interagency Working Group used three discount rates to estimate the SCC, 2.5%, 3.0%, and 5.0%, although Stern (2015) argues that the "correct" discount rate is about 1.1%. The problem is that 1.1% and 5% will give wildly different estimates of the SCC.

To summarize, there are aspects of climate change—CO_2 emissions and concentrations—where we have a reasonable amount of knowledge and can make reasonable projections. Yes, there is uncertainty, especially when projecting out 50 or more years. But at least we can pinpoint the nature of the uncertainty, and to some extent bound it. And then there are aspects of climate change—changes in temperature, and most notably, the economic impact of those changes—where we know very little. I turn now to a more detailed discussion of what we know and don't know, why we don't know certain things, and the extent of the uncertainty.

III.   What We Know (or Sort of Know)

We understand fairly well some parts of the climate change process. There is uncertainty over the specific numbers, but at least we can estimate those numbers and come up with reasonable bounds.

A.   What Drives CO_2 Emissions?

How much carbon will be burned over the coming decades, and how much CO_2 will be emitted? Putting aside efforts at emissions abatement for now, the answer depends in part on economic activity. As economic activity grows, CO_2 emissions will grow as well. But the answer also depends on the relationship between GDP and CO_2 emissions, and that relationship is neither simple nor fixed. Over the past 50 years or so, the amount of CO_2 emitted per dollar of GDP has declined steadily—in the United States, in Europe, in China, in almost all countries. This ratio, CO_2 emitted per dollar of GDP, is called carbon intensity.

Carbon intensity has been declining for several reasons: (a) The composition of GDP has been changing. Compared with 50 years ago, services have become more important than manufacturing, and services use less energy and therefore emit less CO_2 than manufacturing. (b) Technological improvements in the way we produce and utilize goods and services have resulted in the use of less energy, and thus lower emissions of CO_2. For example, cars, trucks, and buses are much more fuel efficient than they were 50 years ago, as are home and commercial heating and cooling systems. (c) Energy itself is becoming "greener." Energy generation from renewables (especially wind and solar) has been growing, and the share of energy coming from fossil fuels, especially coal, has been falling.

Carbon intensity and its components can be measured and understood as follows:

1. **Energy Intensity:** The amount of energy consumed per dollar of GDP. We measure energy consumption in quadrillions of BTUs (10^{15} BTUs, denoted as quads), and GDP in billions of US dollars.[8] So the unit of measurement for energy intensity is quad BTUs/$ billion.

2. **Energy Efficiency:** Sometimes referred to instead as CO_2 efficiency, this is the amount of CO_2 emitted from the consumption of 1 quad of energy. If, for example, the energy is generated from wind or solar, little or no CO_2 will be emitted, but a large amount is emitted if the energy is from coal. For energy efficiency, we measure CO_2 emissions in megatons (Mt, millions of metric tons), so the unit of measurement is Mt of CO_2/quad BTUs.

3. **Carbon Intensity:** The amount of CO_2 emitted per $ billion of GDP. Carbon intensity is simply the product of energy intensity and energy efficiency:

$$\text{Carbon Intensity} = \text{Mt } CO_2/\$ \text{ billion}$$
$$= (\text{quads}/\$ \text{ billion}) \times (\text{Mt } CO_2/\text{quad})$$

Decomposing carbon intensity into its two components is useful because the drivers of energy intensity and energy efficiency can be quite different.

What does this decomposition of carbon intensity tell us? It says that if we want to predict CO_2 emissions over the coming decades (with or without some abatement policy), we would have to (1) predict GDP growth, (2) predict changes in energy intensity, and (3) predict changes in energy efficiency. And we'd have to do this for every major country, or at least different regions of the world, because GDP growth, energy intensity, and energy efficiency are likely to evolve very differently in different countries and regions.

What has happened to carbon intensity and its components over the past 40 or 50 years, and what is likely to happen in the future? Briefly:

1. **Energy Intensity:** Figure 1 shows the evolution of energy intensity since 1980 for the world, and for the United States, Europe, India, and China. For the United States and Europe, energy intensity has declined steadily, largely due to gradual changes in the composition of GDP and the ways in which GDP is produced and consumed. Compared with 1980, services are now a larger share of GDP, and the production of services uses less energy than the production of manufactured goods. In addition, we now use less energy to produce and utilize goods and services; cars and trucks have become more fuel efficient, as have household appliances and home and commercial heating and cooling systems. In China, energy intensity has declined sharply, in part because the Chinese GDP was so low in 1980. But there has been little or no decline

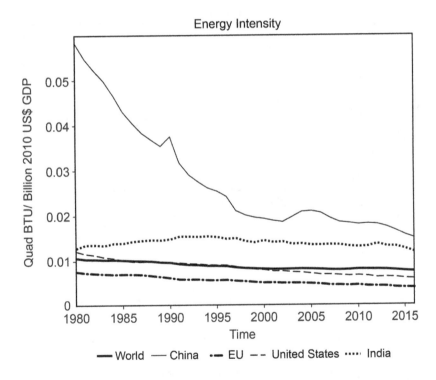

Fig. 1. Energy intensity for the world, and for the United States, European Union (EU), India, and China. Energy intensity is measured in quad (10^{15}) British thermal units (BTUs) per billion 2010 US dollars of gross domestic product (GDP). Sources: World Bank, US Energy Information Agency.

in energy intensity in India and other large developing countries. For the world as a whole, reductions in energy intensity have been quite limited; a decline from 0.011 in 1980 to about 0.0075 quads/$ billion today.

2. **Energy Efficiency:** Even if energy intensity remains constant, we would see a reduction in carbon intensity if we could achieve a significant improvement in energy efficiency. Figure 2 shows the evolution of energy efficiency since 1980 for the world, and for the United States, Europe, India, and China. Both Europe and (to a lesser extent) the United States have had improvements in energy efficiency, in part because energy production is becoming "greener." Energy generation from renewables has been growing, and the share of energy coming from fossil fuels, especially coal, has been falling. But alas, energy efficiency in China and India is now about where it was in 1980—around 70 Mt CO_2/quad BTU in China and around 80 Mt CO_2/quad BTU in India—and well above the levels in the

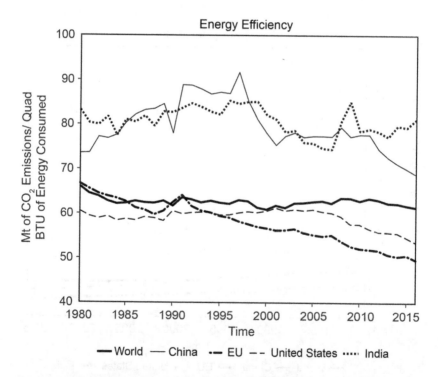

Fig. 2. Energy efficiency for the world, and for the United States, European Union (EU), India, and China. Energy efficiency is measured in megaton (Mt) of CO_2 emissions per quad British thermal unit (BTU) of energy consumed, so a *reduction* in energy efficiency implies an improvement, that is, a reduction in the amount of CO_2 generated from the use of energy. Source: US Energy Information Agency.

United States and Europe. Energy efficiency has followed a similar pattern in other large developing countries. The net result: on a worldwide basis, energy efficiency has remained roughly constant (at about 60 Mt CO_2/quad BTU).

3. **Carbon Intensity:** What matters in the end is the product of energy intensity and energy efficiency, namely carbon intensity. It has followed a path that is very similar to energy intensity, because energy efficiency hasn't changed much. As illustrated in figure 3, for the world as a whole there has been a gradual decline in carbon intensity from about 0.69 Mt CO_2/\$ billion in 1980 to 0.50 Mt CO_2/\$ billion in 2000, but after 2000 just a minimal decline, to about 0.46 Mt CO_2/\$ billion in 2018.

What does a decline in worldwide carbon intensity from 0.69 Mt CO_2/\$ billion in 1980 to about 0.46 Mt CO_2/\$ billion in 2018 imply for

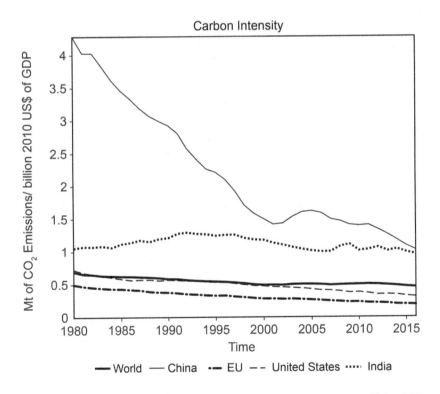

Fig. 3. Carbon intensity for the world, and for the United States, European Union (EU), India, and China. Carbon intensity is the product of energy intensity and energy efficiency, and is measured in megaton (Mt) of CO_2 emissions per billion 2010 US dollars of gross domestic product (GDP).

worldwide CO_2 emissions? If world GDP had remained constant over that time period, CO_2 emissions would have declined by about a third. But (fortunately) world GDP has grown substantially. Measured in 2010 constant US dollars, it nearly tripled, going from about $28 trillion in 1980 to about $80 trillion in 2018. And that's why global CO_2 emissions have increased so much.[9]

What does this tell us about future CO_2 emissions? On one level it paints a rather grim picture. Worldwide, carbon intensity has been declining very slowly, only by about 1% per year, but world GDP has been growing at an average rate of about 3% per year. So there are only two ways that CO_2 emissions can decline in the future: (1) a decline in world GDP or (2) a decline in worldwide carbon intensity. A decline in world GDP is not a happy thought, and we certainly wouldn't want to engineer a global recession as a means of reducing CO_2 emissions. So that leaves us with the second option—a decline in carbon intensity. Do we have any good reasons to expect this to occur? Both energy intensity and energy efficiency can both be affected by government policy. The adoption of strong CO_2 abatement policies seems quite likely in Europe, but less so in the United States, and much less so in key countries such as China, India, Indonesia, and Russia. And the free-riding problem reduces the political feasibility of strong abatement policies in many countries.

Where does this leave us with regard to future CO_2 emissions? If we could predict the growth of GDP around the world and predict the changes in energy intensity and energy efficiency, and thus the changes in carbon intensity, we could come up with at least a rough prediction of future CO_2 emissions. And we would want to make that rough prediction under "business as usual" and under one or more CO_2 abatement policies. Yes, lots of uncertainty, but relatively manageable.

B. What Drives the Atmospheric CO_2 Concentration?

Remember that CO_2 emissions do not directly cause increases in temperature. Instead, warming is caused by increases in the atmospheric CO_2 concentration. Of course increases in the CO_2 concentration are the result of CO_2 emissions, so if we want to make predictions about increases in temperature, we need to determine how any particular path for emissions affects the future path of the CO_2 concentration.

Isn't the current atmospheric CO_2 concentration just the sum of past emissions, minus any dissipation? Roughly, but not precisely. The problem is that some atmospheric CO_2 is absorbed by the oceans, and some of the CO_2 in the oceans can reenter the atmosphere. How much goes each way? That depends on a variety of factors, including the amounts of CO_2 both in the atmosphere and in the oceans, and the ocean temperature. So even if we had precise projections of CO_2 emissions over the next several decades, our projection of the atmospheric CO_2 concentration would be subject to some uncertainty. Nonetheless, compared with some of the other uncertainties we face, this one is not too bad. Given a predicted path for CO_2 emissions, we can predict the atmospheric CO_2 concentration reasonably well, using the fact that 1 Gt of CO_2 emissions adds 0.128 ppm to the atmospheric CO_2 concentration. Adding up past CO_2 emissions and subtracting dissipation:

$$M_t = (1 - \delta)M_{t-1} + E_t, \tag{1}$$

where E_t is emissions in year t, M_t is the concentration, and δ is the dissipation rate. And what is the correct value for the dissipation rate? Estimates generally range from 0.0025 to 0.0050 per year. Fitting equation (1) to data on CO_2 emissions and the CO_2 concentration yields an estimate of $\delta = .0035$ per year.[10] So once again, although there is some uncertainty, it is relatively manageable.

IV. What We Don't Know

Now we come to the hard part. We would like to make projections of the average global temperature changes likely to result from higher CO_2 concentrations. And then given projections of how much the temperature will increase during the coming decades (and how much sea levels will rise, etc.), what matters is the impact of those changes. If we had reason to believe that higher temperatures and higher sea levels will cause little damage, it would be hard to argue that we should devote resources today on preventative measures. On the other hand, if the likely damages are extreme, then we certainly should act quickly to reduce emissions and prevent climate change. Thus it is important to determine the likely economic impact of warming, rising sea levels, and other measures of climate change in terms of lost GDP and consumption. Unfortunately, when it comes to the impact of climate change we are very limited in what we know, and thus for the most part we can only speculate.

Why is it so difficult to pinpoint climate sensitivity, or at least narrow the range of estimates? Why can't we predict the likely impact of climate change on the economy? I turn now to these questions.

A. Climate Sensitivity

Recall that climate sensitivity is defined as the temperature increase that would eventually result from a doubling of the atmospheric CO_2 concentration. The word "eventually" means after the world's climate system reaches a new equilibrium. It would take a very long time, however, for the climate system to completely reach a new equilibrium, around 300 years or more. However, the climate system will get quite close to equilibrium in a few decades. How many decades depends in part on the size of the increase in the CO_2 concentration—the larger the increase, the longer is the time lag—and even for a given increase, there is some uncertainty over the time lag. But generally 10–40 years is a reasonable range, and 20 years is a commonly used number.[11]

I said that there is a great deal of uncertainty over the true value of climate sensitivity. Three questions come up. First, just how much uncertainty is there? Second, has research in climate science during the past few decades resulted in more precise estimates of climate sensitivity? In other words, has the uncertainty been reduced, and if so, by how much? And third, why is there so much uncertainty over climate sensitivity? I address each of these questions in turn.

How Much Uncertainty Is There?

Over the past 2 decades, there have been a large number of studies by climate scientists on the magnitude of climate sensitivity. Virtually all of those studies conclude by providing a range of estimates, often in the form of a probability distribution. From the probability distribution we can determine the probability that the true value of climate sensitivity is above or below any particular value, or within any interval; for example, above 4.0°C, or between 2.0°C and 3.0°C. Thus each study gives us an estimate of the nature and extent of uncertainty, according to that study. But there is considerable dispersion across studies, and that dispersion gives us further information regarding the extent of the uncertainty.

To explore this dispersion, I used information from the roughly 130 studies of equilibrium climate sensitivity assembled by Knutti, Rugenstein, and Hegerl (2017). Most of these studies provide a "best" (most likely) estimate of climate sensitivity, as well as a range of "likely" (i.e., probability greater than 66%) values. Although Knutti et al. (2017) surveyed a few earlier studies, I included only those from 1970 through 2017. I also located and added nine additional studies published in 2017 and 2018.[12]

For each study, I used both the low end of the range of likely values (which I refer to as "minimum estimates") and the high end ("maximum estimates"), as well as the "best" (most likely) estimate. To see how views about climate sensitivity might have changed over time, I divided the studies into two groups based on year of publication: pre-2010 and 2010 onward. Figure 4 shows a histogram with the "best" estimates from these studies.

From the figure, note that the bulk of the studies (115 of the 131) have "best estimates" between 1.5°C and 4.5°C, which is the "most likely" range according to the IPCC. But this is still a wide range, and 16 studies have "best estimates" outside this range (as low as 0.5°C and as high as 8°C). We can also get a sense of how views about climate sensitivity changed by comparing the pre-2010 studies with those published from 2010 onward. Both the mean and standard deviation are somewhat higher for the more recent studies: 2.77 and 1.03, respectively for the pre-2010 studies, and 2.87 and 1.11, respectively, for the later studies.

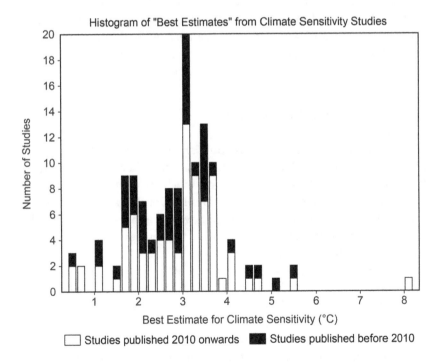

Fig. 4. Histogram of best estimates of climate sensitivity from 131 studies, of which 47 were published prior to 2010 and 84 from 2010 onward. The studies are from Knutti et al. (2017), supplemented by nine additional studies published in 2017 and 2018, and listed in footnote 12.

Figure 5 shows histograms for the low end of the range of likely values reported by these studies ("minimum estimates") and the high end ("maximum estimates"). The bulk of the "minimum estimates" are in the range of 0.5°C–4.0°C, with only three estimates above this range. The bulk of the "maximum estimates" are in the range of 3.0°C–7.0°C, but there are 13 estimates above this range, with seven estimates at 10°C–15°C.

Figure 5 tells us that there is a huge amount of uncertainty over climate sensitivity. If we ignore the outliers and simply consider the bulk of the "minimum" and "maximum" estimates, we get a range of 0.5°C–7.0°C. Remember that this is a range of "likely" (i.e., probability greater than 66%) values, and excludes more extreme values that are unlikely but still possible.

Climate scientists have conducted numerous studies that try to estimate climate sensitivity. The individual studies show large ranges of "likely" values, and that range becomes much greater once we account for the dispersion across the different studies. The bottom line: We are quite certain that climate sensitivity is a positive number, but at this point we simply don't know its actual value. And that's unfortunate, because climate sensitivity is a critical determinant of the temperature increases we can expect over the coming decades.

Has the Uncertainty Been Reduced?

Climate scientists have been busy, publishing hundreds of papers that directly or indirectly relate to climate sensitivity. There is little question that our understanding of the physical mechanisms that underlie climate sensitivity has improved considerably over the past couple of decades. Doesn't this mean that we are now better able to pinpoint the magnitude of climate sensitivity, that is, that our uncertainty over its true value has been reduced?

Unfortunately, the answer is no. In fact, if anything the extent of the uncertainty has grown. This is suggested by the earlier (pre-2010) and later (2010 onward) "best estimates" in the set of studies shown in figure 4; although the distributions are skewed right, the standard deviation is higher for the more recent studies (1.13 vs. 1.03).

The increase in uncertainty has also been demonstrated in a paper by Freeman, Wagner, and Zeckhauser (2015), who compared the survey of climate sensitivity studies in the 2007 IPCC report with the updated survey in the 2014 report. In the 2007 report, the IPCC surveyed 22 peer-reviewed

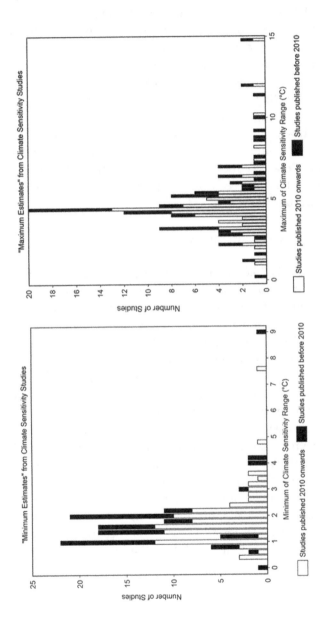

Fig. 5. Histograms of minimum and maximum estimates of climate sensitivity from 143 studies, of which 54 were published prior to 2010 and 89 from 2010 onward. The studies are from Knutti et al. (2017), supplemented by nine additional studies published in 2017 and 2018, and listed in footnote 12.

published studies of climate sensitivity and estimated that the "most likely" range is from 2.0°C to 4.5°C.[13] But then in the 2014 report, that "most likely" range widened, to 1.5°C–4.5°C. Furthermore, the implied standard deviation increased. These results are in part good news, because the bottom of the range became lower (1.5°C instead of 2.0°C). But there is also some bad news, because the estimated uncertainty became greater.

This increase in uncertainty does not mean that climate scientists have not been working diligently, or have otherwise done a bad job. Their work has indeed given us a better understanding of the physical mechanisms through which increases in the atmospheric CO_2 concentration affect temperature. But a better understanding of those physical mechanisms need not mean reduced uncertainty over the magnitude of climate sensitivity. Instead it can simply provide clarity over why there is so much uncertainty.

Why Is There So Much Uncertainty over Climate Sensitivity?

The basic problem is that the magnitude of climate sensitivity is determined by crucial feedback loops, and the parameter values that determine the strength (and even the sign) of those feedback loops are largely unknown, and for the foreseeable future may even be unknowable. This is not a shortcoming of climate science; on the contrary, climate scientists have made enormous progress in understanding the physical mechanisms involved in climate change. But part of that progress is a clearer realization that there are limits (at least currently) to our ability to pin down the strength of the key feedback loops.

The problem is easiest to understand in the context of the simple (but widely cited) climate model of Roe and Baker (2007). It works as follows. Let S_0 represent climate sensitivity in the absence of any feedback effects (i.e., without feedback effects, a doubling of the atmospheric CO_2 concentration would cause an initial temperature increase of $\Delta T_0 = S_0 \,°C$). But as Roe and Baker explain, the initial temperature increase ΔT_0 "induces changes in the underlying processes . . . which modify the effective forcing, which, in turn, modifies ΔT." Thus the actual climate sensitivity is given by

$$S = \frac{S_0}{1-f},$$

where f (with $0 \leq f \leq 1$) is the total feedback factor.[14] So if $f = 0.95$, then $S = 20 \times S_0$.

Of course this is an extremely simplified model of the climate system. A more complete and complex model would incorporate several feedback effects; here they are all being rolled into one. Nonetheless, this simple model allows us to address the key problem: Climate sensitivity is very sensitive to the magnitudes of the feedback effects, which in this simplified model comes down to the value of f. But we don't know the value of f. Roe and Baker point out that if we knew the mean and standard deviation of f, denoted by $\bar{f}$ and σ_f respectively, and if σ_f is small, then the standard deviation of S would be proportional to $\sigma_f/(1-\bar{f})^2$. This implies that uncertainty over S is greatly magnified by uncertainty over f, and becomes very large if f is close to 1.

For example, suppose our best estimate of f is 0.95, but we believe that could be off by a factor of 0.03, that is, f could be as low as 0.92 or as high as 0.98. In that case, S could be as low as $(1/.08) \times S_0 = 12.5 \times S_0$ or as high as $(1/.02) \times S_0 = 50 \times S_0$. But $50 \times S_0$ is four times as large as $12.5 \times S_0$, so this seemingly small uncertainty over f creates a huge amount of uncertainty over climate sensitivity.

To illustrate the problem further, Roe and Baker assume that f is normally distributed (with mean $\bar{f}$ and standard deviation σ_f) and derive the resulting distribution for S, climate sensitivity. Given their choice of $\bar{f}$ and σ_f, the resulting median and 95th percentile are close to the corresponding numbers that come from averaging across the standardized distributions summarized by the IPCC.[15]

This Roe-Baker distribution has become well-known and widely used, but it may well understate our uncertainty over climate sensitivity. The reason is that we don't know whether the feedback factor f is in fact normally distributed (and even if it is, we don't know its true mean and standard deviation). Roe and Baker simply assumed a normal distribution. In fact, in an accompanying article in the journal *Science*, Allen and Frame (2007) argued that climate sensitivity is in the realm of the "unknowable," and that the uncertainty will remain for decades to come.

B. The Impact of Climate Change

When assessing climate sensitivity, we at least have scientific results to rely on, and we can argue coherently about the probability distributions that are most consistent with those results. When it comes to predicting the impact of climate change, however, we have much less to go on, and the uncertainty is far greater. In fact, we know very little about the impact that higher temperatures and rising sea levels would have on the economy and on society more generally.

Why is it so difficult to estimate how climate change will affect the economy? One problem is that we have very few data on which to base empirical work. True, we do have data on temperatures in different locations and in different periods of time, and we can try to relate changes in temperature to changes in GDP and other measures of economic output. In fact there have been some empirical studies that made use of weather data for a large panel of countries over 50 or more years.[16] And there have been many more studies that explore how changes in temperature and rainfall affect agricultural output.[17]

But all of these studies suffer from a fundamental problem: they relate changes in *weather* to changes in GDP or agricultural output, and weather is not the same as climate. The weather in any location (temperature, rainfall, humidity, etc.) changes from week to week and month to month, but the climate—which determines the average temperature and rainfall that we can expect in any particular week or month—changes very slowly (if at all). An unexpectedly hot summer might indeed reduce that year's wheat or corn harvest, but the impact of a gradual change in climate (in which average expected temperatures rise) might have a very different (and probably lower) impact because farmers will shift what and where they plant. Finally, the observed changes in temperature used in these studies are relatively small—not the 4°C or more of warming that many people worry about.

A second problem is that there is little or nothing in the way of economic theory to help us understand the potential impact of higher temperatures. We have some sense of how higher temperatures might affect agriculture, and indeed, most of the empirical work that has been done is focused on agriculture. But we also know that losses of agricultural output in some regions of the world (e.g., near the equator) might be offset by increased output in other regions (e.g., northern Canada and Russia). Furthermore, agriculture is a small fraction of total economic output: 1%–2% of GDP for industrialized countries and 3%–20% of GDP for developing countries. Beyond agriculture, it is difficult to explain, even at a heuristic level, how higher temperatures will affect economic activity.

A third problem is that climate change will occur slowly, which allows for adaptation. This is not to say that adaptation will eliminate the impact of climate change—it will only reduce the impact. But we don't know by how much it will reduce the impact. As a result, adaptation is another complicating factor that makes it very difficult to estimate the extent of the losses we should expect.

It may be that the relationship between temperature and the economy is not just something we don't know, but something that we cannot know, at least for the time horizon relevant to the design and evaluation of climate policy. As discussed earlier, some researchers have come to the conclusion that climate sensitivity is in this category of the "unknowable," and it may be that the impact of climate change is in that same category. On the other hand, we may start learning more about the impact of climate change, perhaps not in the next few years, but in the next few decades. With more time, and most important with more data related to higher temperatures, it is likely that we will be better able to estimate impacts. For now, however, we need to recognize that our ability to predict the impact of climate change is extremely limited.

C. A Catastrophic Outcome

It may turn out that over the coming decades climate change and its impact will be mild to moderate. Given all of the uncertainties, this might happen even if little is done to reduce GHG emissions. And if we were certain that this will be case, it would imply that we can relax and stop worrying about climate change.

But we are not certain that the outcome will be so favorable. There is a possibility of an extremely unfavorable outcome, one that we could call catastrophic. Such an outcome would entail a major decline in human welfare from whatever climate change occurs. The IAMs that have been used to make projections have little or nothing to tell us about such outcomes. This is not surprising; the damage functions in these models, which are ad hoc, are calibrated to give small damages for small temperature increases and cannot tell us very much about the kinds of damages we should expect for temperature increases of 5°C or more. And that's unfortunate, because it is the possibility of a catastrophic outcome that really drives the SCC and matters for climate policy.

For climate scientists, a "catastrophic outcome" usually means a high temperature outcome. How high? There is no fixed rule here. Almost all would agree that a 5°C or 6°C increase by 2100 would be in the realm of the catastrophic, and might result if the climate system reaches a "tipping point" as the CO_2 concentration keeps increasing. Putting aside the difficulty of estimating the probability of that outcome, what matters in the end is not the temperature increase itself but rather its impact.

Would that impact be "catastrophic," and might a smaller (and more likely) temperature increase, perhaps 3°C or 4°C, be sufficient to have a catastrophic impact? Again, opinions vary. Some have argued that even a 2°C temperature increase would be catastrophic. For example, Carbon-Brief, an interactive collection of 70 peer-reviewed climate studies that show how different temperatures are projected to affect the world, suggests that 2°C of warming could reduce global GDP by 13%. (The website is https://www.carbonbrief.org.)

Why does the possibility of a catastrophic outcome matter so much for climate policy? Because even if it has a low probability of occurring, the possibility of a severe loss of GDP (broadly interpreted) can justify a large carbon tax (or equivalent emission abatement policy). A mild to moderate outcome, on the other hand, is something to which society can respond, in part through adaptation, at a relatively low cost. This means that to a large extent climate policy has to be based on the (small) likelihood of an extreme outcome.

So how likely is a catastrophic outcome, and how catastrophic might it turn out to be? How high can the atmospheric CO_2 concentration be before the climate system reaches a "tipping point," and temperatures rise rapidly? We don't know. We don't know where a "tipping point," if there is one, might lie, and what the impact of a large temperature increase might be. Furthermore, is difficult to see how answers to these questions will become clear in the next few years, despite all of the ongoing research on climate change. We may know much more in the next 20 years, but in the short term, the likelihood and impact of a catastrophic outcome may simply be in the realm of the "unknowable."

V.   The Policy Implications of Uncertainty

The uncertainties discussed above make the design and analysis of climate policy very different from most other problems in environmental economics. Most environmental problems are amenable to standard cost-benefit analysis. Determining the limits to be placed on sulfur dioxide emissions from coal-burning power plants is a good example. These emissions can harm the health of people living downwind, and they also cause acidification of lakes and rivers, harming fish, and other wildlife. We would like to limit these emissions, but doing so is costly because it would raise the price of the electricity produced by the power plant. On the other hand, the benefit of reducing emissions is a reduction in the health problems that they cause, as well as less damage to lakes and rivers.

So how should we decide the extent to which power plant emissions should be reduced? The standard way that economists approach the problem is to compare the cost of any particular emission reduction to the resulting benefit and consider reducing emissions further if the cost is less than the benefit. Of course there will be uncertainties over the costs and benefits of any candidate policy, but the characteristics and extent of those uncertainties will usually be well understood and comparable in nature to the uncertainties involved in other public and private policy or investment decisions. Economists might argue about the details of the analysis, but at a basic level, we're in well-charted territory and we think we know what we're doing. If we come to the conclusion that a policy to reduce sulfur dioxide emissions by some amount is warranted, that conclusion will be seen—at least by most economists—as defensible and reasonable.

But this is not the case with climate change. Climate policy is controversial in part because the uncertainties are so large and thus complicate the policy arguments. There is considerable disagreement among both climate scientists and economists over the likelihood of alternative climate outcomes, especially catastrophic outcomes. There is also disagreement over the framework that should be used to evaluate the potential benefits from an abatement policy, including the discount rate to be used to put future benefits in present value terms. These disagreements make climate policy much less amenable to standard cost-benefit analysis.

So what should we do? Is there a way to properly account for this uncertainty in our models of climate change? How should we handle the possibility of a catastrophic outcome? And how can we account for the insurance value of early action, and the conflicting irreversibilities inherent in climate policy? I don't pretend to provide complete answers to all of these questions, but in what follows I lay out some ways to think about the problem.

A.   The Value of Climate Insurance

Uncertainty over climate change creates insurance value in two ways, and it is important to keep them clear:

1. First, it occurs through the "damage function," that is, the loss of GDP resulting from any particular temperature increase. Although the impact of any increase in temperature is highly uncertain, it is very likely that the damage function is a convex function of temperature, that is, it becomes increasingly steep as the temperature change becomes larger. Put

another way, going from 3°C of warming to 4°C is likely to cause a much larger reduction in GDP than going from 1°C to 2°C. As the temperature increase becomes larger, adaptation becomes more difficult, so the damage from an additional 1°C of warming becomes larger.

2. The second way that uncertainty creates insurance value is through social risk aversion. Risk aversion refers to a preference for a sure outcome rather than a risky outcome, even if that risky outcome has the same expected value as the sure outcome. We do not know what the "correct" social welfare function is, but we expect it to exhibit at least some risk aversion. This means that society as a whole would pay to avoid the risk of a very bad climate outcome.

The Damage (or Loss) Function

To understand how uncertainty, combined with a convex damage function, creates a value of insurance, we'll use a very simple example. We will consider a single point in the future, say the year 2050, and we will ignore the issue of discounting future costs and benefits. For purposes of this illustrative example, I will assume that the percentage loss of GDP resulting from a temperature increase T is given by

$$L(T) = 1 - \frac{1}{(1 + .01T^2)}. \tag{2}$$

Equation (2) says that $L(0) = 0$, that is, with no temperature increase, there would be no loss of GDP. It also says that $L(2) = .04$, that is, a 2°C temperature increase would result in a loss of 4% of GDP, $L(4) = 14$, that is, a 4°C temperature increase would result in a loss of 14% of GDP, $L(6) = .26$, that is, a 6°C temperature increase would result in a 26% loss of GDP, and so on. Note that each additional 2°C increase in temperature results in a larger and larger additional loss.

What does this tell us? First, suppose we know for certain that in 2050 the global mean temperature will have increased by 2°C. And using equation (2), suppose we know that this 2°C temperature increase will cause a 4% drop in GDP, compared with what GDP would be without the higher temperature. Ignoring social risk aversion for now, what percentage of GDP should we be willing to sacrifice to avoid this temperature increase? Up to 4%. Hopefully, we could avoid the temperature increase at a cost that is less than 4% of GDP (perhaps by developing and making use of new energy-saving technologies). But if we had to, we'd be willing to sacrifice up to 4% of GDP.

Now, suppose there is uncertainty over the temperature increase. We think that the temperature might not increase at all, or that it might increase by 4°C, with each outcome having a 50% probability. The expected value of the temperature increase is $(0.5)(0) + (0.5)(4) = 2°C$, that is, the same as it was in the first case. But now there is uncertainty. How does this change things?

How bad would a 4°C temperature increase be in terms of its impact on GDP? Would it reduce GDP by 8%, that is, twice the 4% drop we said would occur with a 2°C temperature increase? No, we just saw that the impact would be much larger; the damage caused by higher temperatures will rise more than proportionally. Why? Because 4°C of warming is more likely to cause substantial increases in sea levels (e.g., by melting the Antarctic ice sheets), substantial damage to crops, and so forth. We don't know what the impact would be, but using equation (2) we will assume it causes a 14% drop in GDP. In this case, what percentage of GDP should we be willing to sacrifice to avoid the possibility of a 4°C temperature increase?

To answer this, consider the expected size of the impact on GDP. It is $(0.5)(0) + (0.5)(14) = 7%$ of GDP. That says that we should be willing to sacrifice up to 7% of GDP to avoid the 50% chance of a 4°C temperature increase. (Once again, hopefully we can avoid the temperature increase at a cost that is less than 7% of GDP, but if we had to, we'd be willing to sacrifice up to that amount.)

Let's take this one more step. Suppose there is a 75% probability that there will be no temperature increase, and just a 25% chance of an 8°C temperature increase. And suppose that an 8°C temperature increase would be close to catastrophic and, consistent with equation (2), result in a 40% loss of GDP. The expected value of the temperature increase is still 2°C, but the expected impact of this temperature gamble is now $(0.75)(0) + (0.25)(40) = 10%$ of GDP. That says that we should be willing to sacrifice up to 10% of GDP to avoid a 25% chance of an 8°C temperature increase.

These calculations are summarized in table 1. What's going on here is fairly simple: In terms of its impact on GDP, a 4°C temperature increase is more than twice as harmful as a 2°C temperature increase. So even though there is only a 50% chance of the 4°C increase happening, we would sacrifice a lot to avoid the risk. And an 8°C temperature increase is much more than four times as harmful as a 2°C temperature increase.

Table 1
Possible Temperature Outcomes and Economic Impacts

Maximum T Possible	Probability Max T Occurs	Probability of $T = 0$	% Loss of GDP if Max T Occurs	Expected Loss of GDP (%)
2°C	1	0	4	4
4°C	.5	.5	14	7
8°C	.25	.75	40	10

Note: Impacts are based on the (hypothetical) loss function $L(T) = 1 - [1/(1 + .01T^2)]$, which gives the percentage loss of GDP resulting from a temperature increase T. Note that in each case the expected temperature change is 2°C. GDP = gross domestic product; Max = maximum.

So we would be willing to pay a lot to avoid a very bad outcome, even if that outcome has only a small chance of occurring. For example, how much would we be willing to pay for the first row of table 1 instead of the third row, that is, for a certain temperature increase of 2°C rather than a 75% chance of no temperature increase and a 25% chance of an 8°C increase? From the last column of the table, we would be willing to give up 10% – 4% = 6 % of GDP. Quite a lot!

This is the essence of insurance: we are willing to pay, sometimes a lot, to avoid a very bad outcome, even if that outcome is very unlikely. So we insure our homes against major damage from fire, storms, or floods, we buy medical insurance to cover the cost of a major hospitalization, and we buy life insurance even if we are healthy and expect to live many more years. This framework suggests that we should be willing to pay a considerable amount for insurance against a very bad (even if unlikely) climate outcome.

The Social Welfare Function

These simple calculations suggest that we should be willing to sacrifice quite a bit of GDP (and hence quite a bit of consumption) to insure against the risk of a very bad climate outcome. But we have understated the value of insurance. We focused on the expected loss of GDP but implicitly assumed that a 10% loss of GDP is exactly twice as bad as a 5% loss. In fact, a 10% loss of GDP might be more than twice as bad as a 5% loss. The reason has to do with how people value more (or less) income and consumption.

Suppose your annual disposable (after-tax) income is $60,000. Suppose this income is increased to $70,000, so you now have an additional

$10,000 to spend on things. That might make you very happy. But now suppose your starting income is $160,000, and we add an extra $10,000, for a total of $170,000. The extra $10,000 will still make you happy, but probably not as much as it would if your starting income was only $60,000. We call this a "declining marginal utility of income"; the value (in terms of the satisfaction it provides) of an additional $10,000 of income is lower the higher your starting income is.

This declining marginal utility of income corresponds to risk aversion. You would probably refuse a lottery in which you had a 50-50 chance of winning $10,000 or losing $10,000. The reason is that (for most people) the value of winning $10,000 is less than the lost value of losing $10,000. How much would you have to be paid to agree to take part in that lottery? Is it $2,000, or $3,000? The higher the amount you'd have to be paid, the greater is your risk aversion.[18] You can think of this amount you'd have to be paid as an insurance premium.

How risk averse is society as a whole? That's a complicated question because society is made up of different people with different attitudes toward risk. Financial market data tell us that investors in the aggregate seem to have substantial risk aversion, but not everyone is an investor, and averting climate change is not the same as investing in the stock market.[19]

So what does this tell us about climate policy? If risk aversion for society as a whole is substantial, that would push us further toward a stringent emissions abatement policy. Apart from that, it shows us why the uncertainties over climate change are so important, and in particular why in this modeling framework society should be willing to sacrifice a substantial amount of GDP to avoid the risk of an extremely bad climate outcome. In effect, by reducing emissions now we would be buying insurance. And the value of that insurance could be considerable.

You might be thinking "Well, this is nice. But exactly how large is the value of climate insurance? To what extent does it push us toward early action, and by how much more should we reduce CO_2 emissions if we want to properly account for the insurance value?" Sorry, but I can't provide those numbers. You may be disappointed with that answer, but remember, we don't know much about the actual loss function (the loss function used to generate table 1 is completely hypothetical), nor do we know the extent of social risk aversion. All we can say at this point is that the value of insurance is likely to be substantial, and will push policy toward earlier and more stringent emission abatement.

B. The Effects of Irreversibilities

Environmental damage can sometimes be irreversible, which can lead to a more "conservationist" policy than would be optimal otherwise. If the value of environmental amenities to future generations is uncertain, the benefit from protecting the environment today should include an option value, which accounts for the possibility that future generations will deeply regret irreversible environmental damage. This option value pushes the cost-benefit calculation toward protection.[20]

But environmental protection requires irreversible expenditures, that is, imposes sunk costs on society. This could include sunk cost investments in abatement equipment and an ongoing flow of sunk costs for alternative and perhaps more expensive production processes. If the future value of the environment is uncertain, this would lead to policies that are less "conservationist" than they would be otherwise. Why? Because future generations might find it less valuable than we currently expect, in which case they will regret the irreversible expenditure that we made on preservation.

Given that these two irreversibilities work in opposite directions, which one is more important? We don't know. Because CO_2 can remain in the atmosphere for centuries, and ecosystem destruction from climate change can be permanent, there is clearly an argument for taking early action. But the costs of reducing CO_2 emissions are largely sunk, which implies an argument for waiting.[21] Which type of irreversibility will dominate depends in part on the nature and extent of the uncertainties involved, as we will see.

Before proceeding, it is important to be clear about the nature of "learning" and its connection to climate change uncertainty. Over the next 2 decades, it is likely that our understanding of climate change and its impact will improve considerably. Although so far our uncertainty over climate sensitivity has not decreased (and as discussed above, has actually increased somewhat), more data combined with advances in climate science are likely to reduce the uncertainty. And more data will likely improve our understanding and ability to predict climate change impacts. But at the end of the 2 decades there will still be a good deal of uncertainty as we look toward the next 2 decades. It's a bit like forecasting the price of oil. We don't know what the price will be 5 years from now, but we will find out when the 5 years are up. Then what? As we look out to the next 5 years, there will again be uncertainty. Nonetheless, the ongoing uncertainty creates option value, in this case pushing us away from investing in the development of new oil reserves or related projects.[22]

Now let's return to climate change policy. The implications of the two conflicting irreversibilities described above can be understood with a simple numerical example.

A Numerical Example

Suppose we must decide whether to spend money now to reduce CO_2 emissions, and then we will decide again in the future, say 40 years from now. We'll assume that at each time there are only two choices: spend nothing on abatement ($A = 0$) or spend 6% of GDP on abatement ($A = .06$). If today we spend nothing ($A_1 = 0$), there will be 10 units of CO_2 emissions that will accumulate in the atmosphere. So, denoting emissions now by E_1 and the atmospheric concentration by M_1, we will have $E_1 = M_1 = 10$. On the other hand, if we do spend 6% of GDP to abate emissions ($A_1 = .06$), emissions will be reduced by 80%, so that $E_1 = M_1 = 2$. Finally, we will assume that CO_2 emissions are partly irreversible: 50% of the today's emissions will dissipate over the next 40 years, so if we emit 10 units of CO_2 today, only 5 units will remain.

To keep this simple, we will also assume that today's emissions cause no damage to the economy now; any damage will occur only in the future. Also, right now we don't know how much damage atmospheric CO_2 will cause in the future: there is a 50% chance that atmospheric CO_2 will cause no damage (the "good" outcome) and a 50% chance it will cause significant damage (the "bad" outcome). Of course 40 years from now there will still be uncertainty over climate change impacts another 40 years out—there will always be uncertainty about future events and impacts. But for purposes of this very simple example, we will only be concerned with decisions now and 40 years from now. The abatement and outcome possibilities are summarized in table 2 and also illustrated in figure 6.

Suppose there is no abatement now ($A_1 = 0$), so 10 units of CO_2 are emitted. How much abatement would we want in the future? The answer depends on the economic impact, which by then we will know. If the impact is zero (the "good" outcome), then there is no reason to abate, so we will have $A_2 = 0$. (This outcome is not shown in the table.) But if the "bad" outcome occurs (an 8% loss of GDP), we will want to abate emissions, that is, set $A_2 = .06$. As table 2 shows, with the "bad" outcome and $A_2 = 0$, the loss of GDP will be 31%, but with $A_2 = .06$,

Table 2

Example Illustrating the Trade-off between Immediate Emissions Abatement versus
Waiting for Information about Impact of Warming

% GDP for Abatement, A_1	$M_1 = E_1$	% GDP for Abatement, A_2	$M_2 = (1 - \delta) M_1 + E_2$	"Bad Outcome" Loss of GDP
$A_1 = 0$	10	$A_2 = 0$	$5 + 10 = 15$	31%
$A_1 = 0$	10	$A_2 = .06$	$5 + 2 = 7$	**17%**
		Expected Loss if $A_1 = 0$: $(.5)(.17) + (.5)(.06) = 11.5\%$		
$A_1 = .06$	2	$A_2 = 0$	$1 + 10 = 11$	25%
$A_1 = .06$	2	$A_2 = .06$	$1 + 2 = 3$	**8%**
		Expected Loss if $A_1 = .06$: $(.5)(.08) + (.5)(.06) = 7\%$		

Note: There are two periods, "now" and, say, 40 years from now. A_1 is expenditure on abatement now, as percentage of GDP, and A_2 is expenditure 40 years from now. We denote emissions by E and the amount in the atmosphere by M. If $A_1 = 0$, there will be 10 units of emissions (E_1), which will accumulate in the atmosphere (so $M_1 = 10$), but half will dissipate over the next 40 years ($\delta = .5$). If $A_1 = .06$ (6% of GDP is spent on abatement), emissions will be reduced by 80%, so that $E_1 = M_1 = 2$. Damages occur in 40 years, and depend only on the CO_2 in the atmosphere at that time, $M_2 = (1 - \delta)M_1 + E_2$. With equal probability the impact could be "good," in which case there is no loss of GDP, or "bad," in which case the loss of GDP is $1 - [1/(1 + .03M)]$, and is shown in the last column. Whatever the value of A_1, if the impact turns out to be "bad," it is best to abate, that is, set $A_2 = .06$, so that the loss of GDP is only 17% (and shown in bold). Also shown is the expected loss of GDP if $A_1 = 0$ (11.5%) and if $A_1 = .06$ (7%). Because the difference ($11.5 - 7 = 4.5$) is less than the 6% cost of abatement, it is better not to abate now, but instead wait and abate in the future only if we learn the impact is "bad." GDP = gross domestic product.

the loss of GDP will only be 17%. Abatement will cost 6% of GDP, but we will save $(31 - 17) = 14\%$ of GDP, so the investment in abatement is clearly warranted, and the 17% is shown in bold.

Why not set $A_1 = .06$ at the outset, before we learn whether the impact will be "bad" or "good"? Because spending 6% of GDP on abatement is an irreversible expenditure, which we will regret if it turns out the impact is "good." But to see whether the potential regret is large enough, we have to see what happens if we do set $A_1 = .06$ at the outset. As table 2 shows, with $A_1 = .06$, only 2 units of CO_2 will be emitted, and of those 2 units, only 1 will remain after 40 years. If we then learn that the impact is "good," there will be no reasons to abate, so we will set $A_2 = 0$. But if the impact is "bad," it will be best to abate, so we will set $A_2 = .06$.

Now let's come back to the initial decision regarding A_1. What is the expected loss of GDP if we set $A_1 = 0$? As shown in table 2, there is a 50% chance that the impact will turn out to be "bad," in which case we will set $A_2 = .06$ (which costs 6% of GDP) and lose 17% of GDP. So the expected loss if $A_1 = 0$ is $(0.5)(.17) + (0.5)(.06) = 11:5\%$. Also shown is

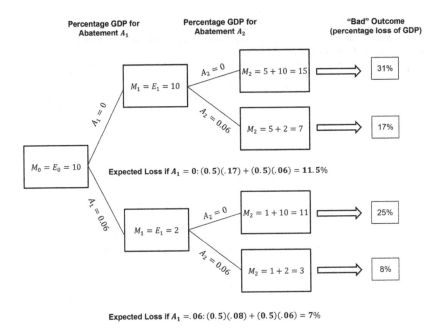

Fig. 6. Trade-off between immediate emissions abatement versus waiting. This figure provides another way of looking at the information in table 2.

the expected loss of GDP if $A_1 = .06$, which turns out to be 7%. Because the difference $(11.5 - 7 = 4{:}5\%)$ is less than the 6% cost of abatement, it is better not to abate now but instead to wait and abate in the future only if we learn the impact is "bad."

To summarize, we have assumed that CO_2 emissions are only partly irreversible, that is, 50% of today's emissions will dissipate over the next 40 years. The cost of abatement (6% of GDP), however, is completely irreversible; it is a sunk cost that can never be recovered. In this case, given that the impact of CO_2 is uncertain and will only be known in the future, it is better to wait, rather than spend 6% of GDP now on abatement. In this case the abatement cost irreversibility outweighs the environmental irreversibility.

Revising the Example

But now let's change one of the key assumptions. This time we will assume that there is no dissipation of CO_2 once it enters the atmosphere. This means setting $\delta = 0$ so that $M_2 = M_1 + E_2$. The results are shown in table 3 and also illustrated in figure 7.

Table 3

Modified Example Illustrating the Trade-off between Immediate Emissions Abatement versus Waiting for Information

% GDP for Abatement, A_1	$M_1 = E_1$	% GDP for Abatement, A_2	$M_2 = (1 - \delta)M_1 + E_2$	"Bad Outcome" Loss of GDP
$A_1 = 0$	10	$A_2 = 0$	$10 + 10 = 20$	37.5%
$A_1 = 0$	10	$A_2 = .06$	$10 + 2 = 12$	**26.5%**
		Expected Loss if $A_1 = 0$: $(.5)(.265) + (.5)(.06) = 16\%$		
$A_1 = .06$	2	$A_2 = 0$	$2 + 10 = 12$	26.5%
$A_1 = .06$	2	$A_2 = .06$	$2 + 2 = 4$	**11%**
		Expected Loss if $A_1 = .06$: $(.5)(.11) + (.5)(.06) = 8.5\%$		

Note: Everything here is the same as in table 2, except the dissipation rate, δ, is 0. Whatever the value of A_1, if in the future the impact turns out to be "bad," it is best to abate, that is, set $A_2 = .06$, yielding the GDP loss shown in bold. Also shown is the expected loss of GDP if $A_1 = 0$ (16%) and if $A_1 = .06$ (8.5%). Now the difference ($16 - 8.5 = 7.5\%$) is greater than the 6% cost of abatement, so it is optimal to abate immediately. Because emissions are now completely irreversible, we are pushed toward early action. The sunk (irreversible) cost of abatement remains, pushing us toward waiting, but now the environmental irreversibility dominates. GDP = gross domestic product.

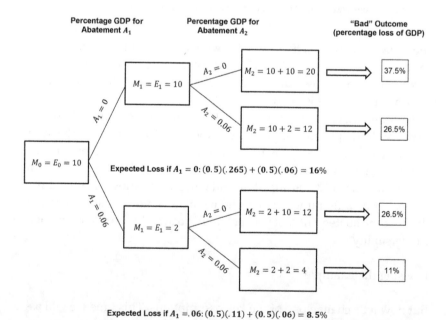

Fig. 7. Modified example of trade-off between immediate emissions abatement versus waiting. This figure provides another way of looking at the information in table 3.

Because we have now assumed that any CO_2 emitted into the atmosphere stays there forever, the loss of GDP under the "bad" outcome will be greater, whatever the abatement policy happens to be. (Compare the last column of table 3 with the last column of table 2.) As in the previous example, whatever the value of A_1, if in the future the impact turns out to be "bad," it is best to abate, that is, set $A_2 = .06$.

What is the optimal abatement policy today? As before, we find out by calculating the expected loss of GDP if we set $A_1 = 0$, and the expected loss if we set $A_1 = .06$. If $A_1 = 0$ the expected loss of GDP is 16%, and if $A_1 = .06$ the expected loss is 8.5%. Now the difference $(16 - 8.5 = 7.5\%)$ is greater than the 6% cost of abatement, so it is optimal to abate immediately. The uncertainty is the same as before, but because emissions are now completely irreversible (there is no dissipation), we are pushed toward early action. The sunk (irreversible) cost of abatement remains, pushing us toward waiting, but now the effect of the environmental irreversibility dominates.

To further illustrate, these effects of irreversibility, let's make another modification to the numbers in table 3. As in the table, we will assume that there is no dissipation, that is, whatever CO_2 is emitted in the beginning will remain in the atmosphere over the 40 years. However, we will make one simple change: we now assume that positive abatement requires an expenditure of 8% of GDP rather than 6%. In other words, in table 3 and figure 7, replace $A_1 = .06$ with $A_1 = .08$ and $A_2 = .06$ with $A_2 = .08$. Now we can once again calculate the expected loss if $A_1 = 0$ and the expected loss if $A_1 = .08$. Doing so, we will find that the expected loss is 17% if $A_1 = 0$ and 9% if $A_1 = .08$. The difference, $17 - 9 = 8\%$, is just equal to the 8% cost of abatement. In this case the effects of the two irreversibilities just balance out, so we would be indifferent between abating now and not abating now.

Emissions Abatement: Hold Back or Accelerate?

These numerical examples were simply designed to illustrate the opposing effects of the two irreversibilities that are an inherent aspect of climate policy. But now you might be thinking that the examples are interesting, but what do they tell us about the real world? Which of these two irreversibilities is more important when it comes to actual climate policy? Should we hold back on emissions abatement because of the sunk cost, or should we accelerate abatement because of the irreversible environmental damage caused by emissions? And by how much should we hold back or accelerate? Sorry, but I can't answer these questions. Why not? Because we simply don't know enough about the climate system and about the impact of varying amounts of climate change.

In the numerical examples I assumed that CO_2 emissions could be reduced by 80% at a cost of 6% (or 8%) of GDP. But we don't actually know how much it would cost (in terms of a percentage of GDP) to reduce emissions by 80%. What we do know is that the cost would be sunk, that is, irreversible, which would lead us to hold back, and the greater the cost the more we would want to hold back. And although we know that CO_2 can remain in the atmosphere for centuries, we don't know what effect it would have on temperature, or what the impact of a higher temperature would be on GDP and other measures of social welfare. (I simply assumed a relationship between the amount of CO_2 in the atmosphere and the percentage reduction in GDP.) These uncertainties, combined with the near-permanence of atmospheric CO_2, would lead us to accelerate abatement.

The balance between these two irreversibilities is also affected by the degree of social risk aversion for the economy as a whole. The sunk cost of abatement can be estimated, at least roughly. But the effect of CO_2 emissions on temperature and the impact of temperature on GDP are highly uncertain. Coming back to our discussion of climate change insurance, these uncertainties would amplify the effect of the environmental irreversibility, and thereby push us toward accelerated abatement.

VI. Conclusions

Unfortunately, many of the books, articles, and press reports that we read make it seem that we know a lot more about climate change and its impact than is actually the case. Likewise, commentators and politicians often make statements of the sort that if we don't take immediate action and sharply reduce CO_2 emissions, the following things will happen, as though we actually know what will happen. Rarely do we read or hear that those things *might happen*; instead we're told they *will happen*.

This shouldn't come as a surprise. We humans prefer certainty to uncertainty, we feel uncomfortable when we don't know what lies ahead, and many people have trouble understanding concepts involving probabilities. Most people prefer to hear or read statements of the sort "By 2050 the temperature will rise by X°C, sea levels will rise by Y meters, and as a result GDP will fall by Z%," as opposed to "There is a 10% chance that temperature will rise by X°C." Many people ignore the fact, or find it hard to accept, that even if we could accurately predict future GHG emissions, we don't know—and at this point can't know—by how much the temperature or sea levels will rise. And even if we could accurately predict how much the temperature and sea levels will rise, we don't know what the impact would be on GDP or other measures of economic and social welfare. The simple fact is that the "climate outcome," by which I mean the extent of climate change and its impact on the economy and society more generally, is far more uncertain than most people think. This is reflected in the wide variation in expert opinion, as I have shown here in the context of climate sensitivity and I have shown in Pindyck (2019) in the broader context of the SCC.

Our uncertainty over climate change and its impact has important implications for policy. Some would argue that, with so much uncertainty, we should wait and see what happens rather than try to sharply reduce emissions right away. After all, if we don't know how much the climate will change, and we don't know what the impact of climate change will be, why take costly actions now? There is something to that argument, because those costly actions are largely irreversible. But there is another irreversibility that works in the opposite direction, and that is the environmental damage itself; CO_2 emissions remain in the atmosphere for centuries. Which of these two irreversibilities dominates? Unfortunately, we just don't know enough about the climate system to say. (I provided some illustrative numerical examples, but they are just examples.)

There is another reason why uncertainty need not lead us to delay action: with uncertainty, especially the kind of uncertainty we face in the climate sphere, we need insurance. The kind of uncertainty I am talking about is the possibility of a catastrophic outcome, that is, tail risk. I have explained that "climate insurance" is valuable for two reasons. First, although we can't specify the damage function in any detail, we do know that the incremental damage (in terms of lost GDP) from an extra 1°C of warming increases sharply with the total amount of warming. That was the basis for the simple examples in tables 2 and 3. Second, most people exhibit substantial risk aversion, so it is reasonable to think that the social welfare function (representing society as a whole) should also exhibit risk aversion.

So what, exactly, is the value of "climate insurance?" I can't say, because there is a catch-22 at work here: the very uncertainties over climate change that create a value of insurance prevent us from determining exactly how large that value is. This may disappoint some readers, who perhaps were hoping that I would state just how much CO_2 emissions should be reduced. On the other hand, the simple numerical examples we explored suggest that the insurance value is likely to be large. And what is most important, the very fact that there is an insurance value is a reason why the correct policy response to uncertainty is not to sit back and wait to see what happens.

Endnotes

Author's email address: Pindyck (rpindyck@mit.edu). This paper was prepared for the NBER Conference on Environmental and Energy Policy and the Economy. My thanks to Miray Omurtak for her outstanding research assistance, and to Henry Jacoby, Chris Knittel, Matthew Kotchen, Bob Litterman, Sergey Paltsev, Dick Schmalensee, Andrei Sokolov, Rob Stavins, Jim Stock, Gernot Wagner, and the late Marty Weitzman for helpful comments and suggestions. For acknowledgments, sources of research support, and disclosure of the author's material financial relationships, if any, please see https://www .nber.org/books-and-chapters/environmental-and-energy-policy-and-economy-volume -2/what-we-know-and-dont-know-about-climate-change-and-implications-policy.

1. For a discussion of the flaws in IAMs that make them unsuitable for policy analysis, see Pindyck (2013a, 2013b, 2017). The US government's Interagency Working Group used three IAMs to estimate the SCC; see Interagency Working Group on Social Cost of Carbon (2013), and for a discussion of the Working Group's methodology and the models it used, see Greenstone, Kopits, and Wolverton (2013). For a different point of view on the value of IAMs, see Nordhaus (2014) and Weyant (2017).

2. A number of studies have explored this question in a theoretical setting; see, e.g., Kolstad (1996), Ulph and Ulph (1997), and Pindyck (2000). These studies illustrate the fundamental problem, but they don't tell us how to formulate climate policy.

3. There are other arguments for waiting or starting slowly: technological change may reduce abatement costs in the future, and the fact that the "unpolluted" atmosphere is an exhaustible resource implies that the SCC should rise over time (as the atmospheric CO_2 concentration rises).

4. For explanations of why "radical uncertainty" is likely to apply to climate change, see, e.g., Allen and Frame (2007) and Roe and Baker (2007). Heal and Millner (2014) also describe some of the uncertainties inherent in climate change and their implications for policy.

5. I would argue that the IAMs and related models used for policy analysis pretend otherwise, insofar as their projections understate the extent of uncertainty.

6. In 2018, global CO_2 emissions were about 36 Gt, so that year's emissions increased the atmospheric CO_2 concentration by about $(36)(0.128) = 4.61$ ppm.

7. We might also want to specify a social welfare function, i.e., the loss of social utility resulting from a loss of GDP (and hence from a loss of consumption). If GDP and consumption are very high, the loss of utility resulting from a 5% loss of GDP would be smaller than if GDP and consumption were low.

8. One BTU (British thermal unit) is the amount of heat energy required to raise the temperature of 1 lb of water by 1°F. In the metric system, the unit of energy is the calorie, which is the amount of heat required to raise the temperature of 1 g of water by 1°C. One BTU is approximately 252 cal.

9. The connection between GDP growth and climate change is also discussed by Stock (2019), who describes statistical approaches to estimating the relationship.

10. For example, emissions in 1961 were 9 Gt, which added $(9)(0.128) = 1.15$ ppm of CO_2 to the 315 ppm already in the atmosphere. Dissipation in 1961 was $(.0035)(315) = 1.10$ ppm, so the net increase was 0.05 ppm, making the 1961 concentration $315 + 0.05 = 315.05$.

11. Climate scientists often distinguish between "equilibrium climate sensitivity," which is climate sensitivity as I have described it above, and "transient climate response,"

which is the response of global mean temperature to a gradual (1% per year) increase in the CO_2 concentration. See National Academy of Sciences (2017, 88–95) for a discussion. I will simply use the term "climate sensitivity," and treat the time lag (10–40 years) as the time it takes for the climate system to get close to equilibrium.

12. All of the studies that Knutti et al. (2017) examined are listed in their paper. The nine additional studies that I added are Brown and Caldeira (2017), Krissansen-Totton and Catling (2017), Andrews et al. (2018), Cox, Huntingford, and Williamson (2018), Dessler and Forster (2018), Lewis and Curry (2018), Lohmann and Neubauer (2018), Skeie et al. (2018), and Keery, Holden, and Edwards (2018).

13. Intergovernmental Panel on Climate Change (IPCC 2007) also provides a detailed and readable overview of the physical mechanisms involved in climate change, and the state of our knowledge regarding those mechanisms. Each of the individual studies included a probability distribution for climate sensitivity, and by putting the distributions in a standardized form, the IPCC created a graph that showed all of the distributions in a summary form. This is updated in IPCC (2014).

14. In the notation of Roe and Baker (2007), λ_0 is climate sensitivity without feedback effects, and λ is climate sensitivity accounting for feedback effects.

15. Adding a displacement parameter θ, the Roe-Baker distribution is given by:

$$g(S; \bar{f}, \sigma_f, \theta) = \frac{1}{\sigma_f \sqrt{2\pi z^2}} \exp\left[-\frac{1}{2} \left(\frac{1 - \bar{f} - 1/z}{\sigma_f} \right)^2 \right],$$

where $z = S + \theta$. Fitting to the distributions summarized by the IPCC, the parameter values are $\bar{f} = 0.797$, $\sigma_f = .0441$, and $\theta = 2.13$. This distribution is fat-tailed, i.e., declines to zero more slowly than exponentially. Weitzman (2009, 2014) has shown that parameter uncertainty can lead to a fat-tailed distribution for climate sensitivity, and that this implies a relatively high probability of a catastrophic outcome, which in turn suggests that the value of abatement is high. Pindyck (2011) shows that a fat-tailed distribution by itself need not imply a high value of abatement.

16. For example, Dell, Jones, and Olken (2012) found that the impact of higher temperatures is largely on the growth rate of GDP, as opposed to its level, and is mostly significant in poor countries. See Dell et al. (2014) for an overview of this line of research.

17. For overviews, see Auffhammer et al. (2013) and Blanc and Schlenker (2017).

18. A utility function translates income, or wealth or consumption, into units of well-being (or satisfaction). For a textbook explanation, see Pindyck and Rubinfeld (2018). A commonly used utility function is

$$u(y) = \frac{1}{1 - \eta} y^{1-\eta},$$

where y is income and η is called the coefficient of relative risk aversion. In this case marginal utility, i.e., the benefit of an additional dollar of income, is $du/dy = y^{-\eta}$. Marginal utility declines with the level of income, and the larger η is the faster it declines. Thus the larger is η, the greater is the insurance premium you would require to take part in a lottery for which there is a 50–50 chance of winning or losing $10,000.

19. Based on financial market data, and data on consumption and savings, the coefficient of relative risk aversion for society as a whole seems to be in the range of 2–5, which is substantial.

20. One of the earliest studies to analyze this implication of irreversible environmental damage is Arrow and Fisher (1974).

21. There are other arguments for waiting or starting slowly: technological change may reduce abatement costs in the future, and the fact that the "unpolluted" atmosphere is an exhaustible resource implies that the SCC should rise over time (as the atmospheric CO_2 concentration rises).

22. For a textbook treatment of option value, including its application to the development of oil reserves, see Dixit and Pindyck (1994). For an application to environmental policy, see Pindyck (2000).

References

Allen, Myles R., and David J. Frame. 2007. "Call Off the Quest." *Science* 318:582–83.

Andrews, Timothy, Jonathan M. Gregory, David Paynter, Levi G. Silvers, Chen Zhou, Thorsten Mauritsen, Mark J. Webb, Kyle C. Armour, Piers M. Forster, and Holly Titchner. 2018. "Accounting for Changing Temperature Patterns Increases Historical Estimates of Climate Sensitivity." *Geophysical Research Letters* 45 (16): 8490–99.

Arrow, Kenneth J., and Anthony C. Fisher. 1974. "Environmental Preservation, Uncertainty, and Irreversibility." *Quarterly Journal of Economics* 88 (2): 312–19.

Auffhammer, Maximilian, Solomon M. Hsiang, Wolfram Schlenker, and Adam Sobel. 2013. "Using Weather Data and Climate Model Output in Economic Analyses of Climate Change." *Review of Environmental Economics and Policy* 7:181–98.

Blanc, Elodie, and Wolfram Schlenker. 2017. "The Use of Panel Models in Assessments of Climate Impacts on Agriculture." *Review of Environmental Economics and Policy* 11 (2): 258–79.

Brown, Patrick T., and Ken Caldeira. 2017. "Greater Future Global Warming Inferred from Earth's Recent Energy Budget." *Nature* 552 (7683): 45.

Cox, Peter M., Chris Huntingford, and Mark S. Williamson. 2018. "Emergent Constraint on Equilibrium Climate Sensitivity from Global Temperature Variability." *Nature* 553 (7688): 319.

Dell, Melissa, Benjamin F. Jones, and Benjamin A. Olken. 2012. "Temperature Shocks and Economic Growth: Evidence from the Last Half Century." *American Economic Journal: Macroeconomics* 4:66–95.

———. 2014. "What Do We Learn from the Weather? The New Climate-Economy Literature." *Journal of Economic Literature* 52 (3): 740–98.

Dessler, A. E., and P. M. Forster. 2018. "An Estimate of Equilibrium Climate Sensitivity from Interannual Variability." *Journal of Geophysical Research: Atmospheres* 123 (16): 8634–45.

Dixit, Avinash K., and Robert S. Pindyck. 1994. *Investment under Uncertainty*. Princeton, NJ: Princeton University Press.

Freeman, Mark C., Gernot Wagner, and Richard Zeckhauser. 2015. "Climate Sensitivity Uncertainty: When Is Good News Bad?" *Philosophical Transactions A* 373:1–15.

Greenstone, Michael, Elizabeth Kopits, and Ann Wolverton. 2013. "Developing a Social Cost of Carbon for Use in U.S. Regulatory Analysis: A Methodology and Interpretation." *Review of Environmental Economics and Policy* 7 (1): 23–46.

Heal, Geoffrey, and Antony Millner. 2014. "Uncertainty and Decision Making in Climate Change Economics." *Review of Environmental Economics and Policy* 8 (1): 120–37.

Interagency Working Group on Social Cost of Carbon. 2013. *Technical Support Document: Technical Update of the Social Cost of Carbon for Regulatory Impact Analysis*. Washington, DC: US Government.

IPCC (Intergovernmental Panel on Climate Change). 2007. *Climate Change 2007*. Cambridge: Cambridge University Press.

———. 2014. *Climate Change 2014*. Cambridge: Cambridge University Press.

Keery, John S., Philip B. Holden, and Neil R. Edwards. 2018. "Sensitivity of the Eocene Climate to CO_2 and Orbital Variability." *Climate of the Past* 14 (2): 215–38.

King, Mervyn. 2016. *The End of Alchemy: Money, Banking, and the Future of the Global Economy*. New York: W. W. Norton.

Knutti, Reto, Maria A. A. Rugenstein, and Gabriele C. Hegerl. 2017. "Beyond Equilibrium Climate Sensitivity." *Nature Geoscience* 10:727–44.

Kolstad, Charles D. 1996. "Fundamental Irreversibilities in Stock Externalities." *Journal of Public Economics* 60:221–33.

Krissansen-Totton, Joshua, and David C. Catling. 2017. "Constraining Climate Sensitivity and Continental versus Seafloor Weathering Using an Inverse Geological Carbon Cycle Model." *Nature Communications* 8:15423.

Lewis, Nicholas, and Judith Curry. 2018. "The Impact of Recent Forcing and Ocean Heat Uptake Data on Estimates of Climate Sensitivity." *Journal of Climate* 31 (15): 6051–71.

Lohmann, Ulrike, and David Neubauer. 2018. "The Importance of Mixed-Phase and Ice Clouds for Climate Sensitivity in the Global Aerosol-Climate Model ECHAM6-HAM2." *Atmospheric Chemistry and Physics* 18 (12): 8807–28.

National Academy of Sciences. 2017. *Valuing Climate Damages: Updating Estimation of the Social Cost of Carbon Dioxide.* Washington, DC: National Academies Press.

Nordhaus, William. 2014. "Estimates of the Social Cost of Carbon: Concepts and Results from the DICE-2013R Model and Alternative Approaches." *Journal of the Association of Environmental and Resource Economists* 1 (1/2): 273–312.

Pindyck, Robert S. 2000. "Irreversibilities and the Timing of Environmental Policy." *Resource and Energy Economics* 22:233–59.

———. 2011. "Fat Tails, Thin Tails, and Climate Change Policy." *Review of Environmental Economics and Policy* 5 (2): 258–74.

———. 2013a. "Climate Change Policy: What Do the Models Tell Us?" *Journal of Economic Literature* 51 (3): 860–72.

———. 2013b. "The Climate Policy Dilemma." *Review of Environmental Economics and Policy* 7 (2): 219–37.

———. 2017. "The Use and Misuse of Models for Climate Policy." *Review of Environmental Economics and Policy* 11 (1): 100–114.

———. 2019. "The Social Cost of Carbon Revisited." *Journal of Environmental Economics and Management* 94:140–60.

Pindyck, Robert S., and Daniel L. Rubinfeld. 2018. *Microeconomics.* 9th ed. New York: Pearson.

Roe, Gerard H., and Marcia B. Baker. 2007. "Why Is Climate Sensitivity So Unpredictable?" *Science* 318:629–32.

Skeie, Ragnhild Bieltvedt, Terje Koren Berntsen, Magne Tommy Aldrin, Marit Holden, and Gunnar Myhre. 2018. "Climate Sensitivity Estimates—Sensitivity to Radiative Forcing Time Series and Observational Data." *Earth System Dynamics* 9 (2): 879–94.

Stern, Nicholas. 2015. *Why Are We Waiting? The Logic, Urgency, and Promise of Tackling Climate Change.* Cambridge, MA: MIT Press.

Stock, James H. 2019. "Climate Change, Climate Policy, and Economic Growth." In *NBER Macroeconomics Annual,* ed. Martin S. Eichenbaum, Erik Hurst, and Jonathan A. Parker. Chicago: University of Chicago Press.

Ulph, Alistair, and David Ulph. 1997. "Global Warming, Irreversibility and Learning." *Economic Journal* 107 (442): 636–50.

Weitzman, Martin L. 2009. "On Modeling and Interpreting the Economics of Catastrophic Climate Change." *Review of Economics and Statistics* 91:1–19.

———. 2014. "Fat Tails and the Social Cost of Carbon." *American Economic Review* 104 (5): 544–46.

Weyant, John. 2017. "Some Contributions of Integrated Assessment Models of Global Climate Change." *Review of Environmental Economics and Policy* 11 (1): 115–37.

Global Lessons from Climate Change Legislation and Litigation

Shaikh Eskander, *Grantham Research Institute on Climate Change and the Environment, London School of Economics and Kingston University London,* United Kingdom

Sam Fankhauser, *Grantham Research Institute on Climate Change and the Environment and Centre for Climate Change Economics and Policy (CCCEP), London School of Economics,* United Kingdom

Joana Setzer, *Grantham Research Institute on Climate Change and the Environment and Centre for Climate Change Economics and Policy (CCCEP), London School of Economics,* United Kingdom

Executive Summary

There is no country in the world that does not have at least one law or policy dealing with climate change. The most prolific countries have well over 20, and globally there are 1,800 such laws. Some of them are executive orders or policies issued by governments, others are legislative acts passed by parliament. The judiciary has been involved in 1,500 court cases that concern climate change (more than 1,100 of which were in the United States). We use Climate Change Laws of the World, a publicly accessible database, to analyze patterns and trends in climate change legislation and litigation over the past 30 years. The data reveal that global legislative activity peaked around 2009–14, well before the Paris Agreement. Accounting for effectiveness in implementation and the length of time laws have been in place, the United Kingdom and South Korea are the most comprehensive legislators among G20 countries and Spain within the Organization for Economic Cooperation and Development. Climate change legislation is less of a partisan issue than is commonly assumed: the number of climate laws passed by governments of the left, center, and right is roughly proportional to their time in office. We also find that legislative activity decreases in times of economic difficulty. Where courts have gotten involved, judges outside the United States have ruled in favor of enhanced climate protection in about half of the cases (US judges are more inclined to rule against climate protection).

JEL Codes: K32, Q54, Q58

Keywords: climate change, laws, litigation

Environmental and Energy Policy and the Economy, volume 2, 2021.
© 2021 National Bureau of Economic Research. All rights reserved. Published by The University of Chicago Press for the NBER. https://doi.org/10.1086/711306

I. Introduction

The international climate change architecture commits nations to accelerate their actions on climate change. Under the Paris Agreement, countries are obliged to ratchet up their Nationally Determined Contributions (NDCs) to the Paris process in 2020. According to climate scientists, current emission reduction commitments are likely to result in a global mean temperature rise of around 3°C by 2100, rather than the "well below 2°C" envisaged under Paris (Rogelj et al. 2016).

We observe that national climate action is accelerating. Between 1990 and 1999, only 110 laws and significant policies were passed that directly or indirectly addressed climate change. Between 2010 and 2019 the flow of new laws had grown tenfold to about 1,100 laws and policies. The total stock of climate change laws and policies worldwide now stands at 1,800 and continues to grow.

Our awareness of those initiatives is improving at the same time. In 2013, climate change legislation was tracked in just 33 countries (Townshend et al. 2013). By 2015, the number had risen to 66 countries (Fankhauser, Gennaioli, and Collins 2015a, 2015b). Today coverage is global at the level of nation-states. In the course of the data gathering, understanding also grew about the breadth of actions that are relevant to climate change, which brought additional laws into the count. This was the case especially for adaptation laws, where the delineation with related activities, such as disaster risk management, is necessarily fuzzy.

Climate legislation is an essential part of climate change governance, as successful action against climate change requires a legal basis. Emissions pledges are not credible unless the targets, and the measures enacted to achieve them, are rooted in law. Although climate laws and policies vary greatly in scope and ambition (i.e., at the intensive margin), their growing number (the extensive margin) is an important indicator of countries' ambition on climate change.

In addition to the laws, edicts, and policies passed by executive and legislative bodies, we are observing an increasing participation by the judiciary in the governance of climate change. About 1,500 climate change-related court cases have so far been identified worldwide, three-quarters of which were in the United States.

The relationship between climate legislation and litigation is still unclear (Setzer and Vanhala 2019), but broadly the two appear to serve complementary functions. The judiciary is implementing government policy prescriptions, interpreting climate legislation, and filling enforcement gaps. Although "regulation through litigation" can compensate for deficits in the volume or quality of legislation, the judiciary is also mobilized in countries with progressive climate change legislation. In fact, legal mobilization for climate change—using the courts and legal techniques as an instrument for obtaining wider collective objectives—often occurs in combination with other forms of mobilization, such as legislative activity, but also political pressure and grassroots activism (Setzer and Vanhala 2019).

One of the best tools for tracking global trends in climate change policy, legislation, and litigation is Climate Change Laws of the World (CCLW), a searchable, publicly accessible database created and maintained by the Grantham Research Institute on Climate Change and the Environment at the London School of Economics.[1] The database is a joint initiative with the Sabin Center for Climate Change Law at Columbia Law School. At the end of 2019, it featured 1,800 climate laws in 198 jurisdictions, alongside 355 court cases in 36 jurisdictions.[2] The aim is to provide transparency about the actions of individual countries in addressing global climate change, the ultimate collective action problem.

This paper uses CCLW to analyze patterns and trends in national climate change legislation and litigation over the past 30 years. It provides an overview of what countries are already doing—and what countries that are not yet doing it could potentially do—to implement the objectives of the Paris Agreement. We look at the contribution of governments (the executive), parliaments (the legislature), and courts (the judiciary).

Our interest is in high-level patterns. We do not aspire to provide detailed case studies or carefully identified statistical relationships. There is an emerging literature that is aiming to do this (cited below). We restrict ourselves to a few simple statistics and correlations. The data reveal that global legislative activity peaked before the Paris Agreement in around 2009–14. We find that climate change legislation is in most countries a bipartisan concern and that legislative activity decreases in times of economic difficulty. The United Kingdom and South Korea are the most comprehensive legislators among the G20, and Spain is the most comprehensive legislator within the Organization for Economic Cooperation and Development (OECD). Where courts have gotten involved, judges outside the United States have ruled in favor of enhanced climate protection in about half of the cases.

The next section briefly introduces the CCLW database, including its history, scope, shortcomings, and a few descriptive statistics. Section III discusses some key findings that may be gleaned from the data. Section IV concludes.

II.   The CCLW Database

A.   *Background*

The CCLW database has been compiled over a decade with the help of international partners such as the Inter-Parliamentary Union, the global organization of national parliaments, and the Global Legislators Organization for a Balanced Environment, an international legislators' forum. The impetus for the initiative was a desire to document national climate action following the 2009 Copenhagen summit and debunk the myth that each country was acting alone (Townshend et al. 2011). Over the years, reporting grew from a handful of major emitters to global coverage. Collaboration with the Sabin Center on Climate Change Law at Columbia Law School from 2015 onward (when the database acquired its current name) allowed the extension of the database from climate change legislation to climate change litigation.

Data are collected in real time from official sources such as government websites, parliamentary records, and court documents. There is an internal protocol to ensure new entries conform with CCLW's definition and interpretation of what constitutes climate change legislation and litigation. Most entries contain a link to the actual text of the law or the filing and court decision.

This is the first academic synthesis of the main patterns and trends that the CCLW data reveal. So far, the data have mostly served to assess global progress in adopting climate policies (Dubash et al. 2013; Townshend et al. 2013; Iacobuta et al. 2018), understand the political economy of passing climate laws (Fankhauser et al. 2015a, 2015b), identify good practice in climate change governance (Averchenkova, Fankhauser, and Nachmany 2017; Jordan et al. 2018), and assess the environmental impact of climate legislation (Eskander and Fankhauser 2020). The litigation data have been used to assess trends in climate litigation (Wilensky 2015; Burger et al. 2017; Setzer and Bangalore 2017) and to analyze particular aspects of climate litigation, such as litigation in the financial sector (Solana 2020) and in the Global South (Peel and Lin 2019; Setzer and Benjamin 2020).

B. Climate Change Legislation

The main part of the CCLW database concerns climate change legislation. The legislation database aspires to be a globally comprehensive record of legislation activities in 198 jurisdictions (197 countries and territories, plus the European Union as a bloc). It adopts a broad definition of climate legislation, including legislative acts, executive orders, and policies of equivalent importance. Legislative acts, passed by parliaments, account for about 40% of entries and executive orders and policies, issued by governments, for about 60% (see table 1). For simplicity, we refer to all these interventions as "laws."

Table 1
Descriptive Statistics on Climate Change Legislation

	All Countries (N = 198)	OECD-EU Countries (N = 42)	Other Countries (N = 156)
Total number of laws:			
Total	1,800	605 (33.6% of all laws)	1,195 (66.4%)
Pre-1990	35	24 (68.6%)	11 (31.4%)
1990–1999	110	38 (34.6%)	72 (65.4%)
2000–2009	554	203 (36.6%)	351 (63.4%)
2010–2019	1,101	340 (30.9%)	761 (69.1%)
Laws by topic (1990–2019):			
Framework laws	238	85 (35.7%)	153 (64.3%)
Laws addressing GHG emissions (mitigation laws)	1,620	549 (33.9%)	1,071 (66.1%)
Mitigation laws focused on energy (energy laws)	1,055	395 (37.4%)	660 (62.6%)
Laws addressing climate resilience (adaptation laws)	641	143 (22.3%)	498 (77.7%)
Laws by type (1990–2019):			
Executive orders or policies	1,023	244 (23.9%)	779 (76.1%)
Legislative acts	742	337 (45.4%)	405 (54.6%)
Number of laws by country (1990–2019):			
Mean	8.9	13.8	7.6
Standard deviation	6.3	7.5	5.2
Median	8	12	6
Minimum	1	1	1
Maximum	38	38	28

Note: All data from Climate Change Laws of the World. Some laws deal with multiple issues, hence the higher totals for "laws by topic." GHG = greenhouse gas.

The laws included in CCLW either specifically refer to climate change or promote the sectoral measures required to reduce emissions and increase climate resilience. As such, the database covers the full range of interventions that is relevant to climate change, including:

- overarching policies like carbon pricing schemes (e.g., New Zealand's Climate Change Response [Emissions Trading] Amendment),
- energy sector policies (e.g., Germany's Renewable Energy Sources Act),
- transport interventions (e.g., Brazil's Mandatory Biodiesel Requirements),
- forestry interventions as relate to climate (e.g., the Democratic Republic of Congo's Law on Protection of Nature), and
- adaptation interventions (e.g., Japan's Climate Change Adaptation Act).

A particularly important category is strategic framework laws, which aim to create a unifying institutional structure to reduce greenhouse gas (GHG) emissions or address physical climate risks, or often both. An instructive example is the UK Climate Change Act of 2008, which (1) sets a legally binding long-term mitigation goal (since strengthened to net-zero by 2050), (2) legislates intermediary short-term targets (or carbon budgets), (3) creates an independent advisory body (the Committee on Climate Change), (4) establishes a continual process of adaptation planning, and (5) mandates regular government reporting on progress (Muinzer 2018; Averchenkova, Fankhauser, and Finnegan 2020).[3] Many of these features have been replicated in other framework laws, for example Mexico's General Law on Climate Change (2012),[4] New Zealand's Climate Change Response (Zero Carbon) Amendment Bill (2019),[5] and the climate change acts of several European countries (Nash and Steurer 2019). South Korea's Framework Act on Low-Carbon Growth (2010) stands out because it couches climate action in a wider green growth narrative, combining environmental with industrial policy.[6]

However, the majority of climate laws concern sector-specific interventions, in particular on energy. About 60% of laws contain provisions on energy supply, such as the promotion of renewable energy, and/or energy demand, such as industrial or residential energy efficiency. Interventions on transport and forestry are less frequent. About a third of all laws concern climate resilience and adaptation to climate risks. CCLW now also covers disaster risk management, that is, laws concerned with the impacts of current climate variability, rather than future climate change.

C. Climate Change Litigation

The litigation database within CCLW is different from the legislation database in that it does not aspire to be comprehensive in its geographic coverage or in the number of cases it contains.

CCLW adopts a broad definition of litigation in terms of actors (governmental and nongovernmental), jurisdictional levels (local, regional, national, and international), and the profile of the case (climate as central or peripheral). Included in the database are lawsuits brought before administrative, judicial, and other investigatory bodies that raise issues of law or fact regarding the science of climate change and climate change mitigation and adaptation efforts (Markell and Ruhl 2012; Burger et al. 2017). The case files contain keywords such as climate change, global warming, global change, greenhouse gases (GHGs), and sea level rise. Cases that make only passing reference to the fact of climate change, its causes, or its effects are excluded if they do not address in direct or meaningful fashion the laws, policies, or actions that compel, support, or facilitate climate mitigation or adaptation. Cases that seek incidentally to accomplish (or prevent) climate change policy goals without reference to climate change issues are not included (Burger et al. 2017). Thus, for example, the database does not include cases in which the parties seek to limit air pollution from coal-fired power plants but do not directly raise issues of fact or law pertaining to climate change.

The identification of climate change litigation also involves characterizing the centrality of climate change issues to the case (Peel and Osofsky 2015; Bouwer 2018). Climate change can range from being a central issue in a case to peripheral, that is, litigation that was brought in part over climate change issues but focuses on other grounds (e.g., disputes over the siting of wind farms or about subsidies for renewable energy). Litigation that is not explicitly tied to climate change arguments but is within the context of climate change (e.g., disputes relating to insurance and risk, or intellectual property rights) has been underappreciated by the literature but has important strategic, policy, and governance implications because it could implicitly have impact on accessibility of finance or new technologies to support climate change (Bouwer 2018).

The vast majority of climate change litigation cases (1,154) have been filed in the United States, and these are contained in a separate database. The material difference between US and non-US cases makes cross-country analysis and the comparison of US and non-US trends impracticable. We focus our analysis on the 355 cases that have been filed in 36 non-US jurisdictions (as of the end of 2019). The majority of them are in Australia (96 cases) and the European Union (57 cases). The database also includes 18 cases that have been brought before supranational tribunals such as the UN Human Rights Committee, the Inter-American Commission on Human Rights, and the Inter-American Court on Human Rights. (See table A4 for details.)

More than 80% of the non-US cases have been brought against governments, and typically the plaintiff is either a private company or a nongovernmental organization (NGO). Lawsuits against private defendants are still relatively rare (table 2; see also Wilensky 2015). Most cases are routine and concern the application, interpretation, and enforcement of laws such as planning law or the operation of emissions trading schemes (Markell and Ruhl 2012; Bouwer 2018).

Climate change is at the core of the legal argument in less than 40% of cases (138 out of 355). A smaller number of these lawsuits can be described as strategic cases. The delineation is not firm, but these are high-profile claims brought either against governments, where plaintiffs seek increased mitigation ambition, or against large emitters, where plaintiffs seek compensation for damages caused by, or costs incurred due to, climate change. Their aim is to advance policy outcomes and to drive behavioral shifts by key actors (Peel and Osofsky 2015). Table 3 contains summaries of three landmark cases (*Urgenda Foundation v. State of the Netherlands*, *Leghari v. Federation of Pakistan*, and the *Carbon Majors Inquiry*), which received considerable media attention and have inspired similar cases in other jurisdictions.

D.   Limitations

Although CCLW is arguably the most comprehensive database of its kind, it has some limitations. In terms of legislation data, an important issue is that the database is silent about the quality of different laws. Stringent and comprehensive framework laws like the UK Climate Change Act, which has been praised for its innovative features (Muinzer 2018; Averchenkova et al. 2020), are treated in the same way as unsuccessful laws such as Indonesia's various attempts to combat deforestation.

The delineation of what does and does not constitute a climate change law can be difficult. Although CCLW errs on the side of inclusion, by restricting the collection to certain categories of climate-related laws and

Table 2
Descriptive Statistics on Climate Change Litigation

	All Jurisdictions (Excluding US) ($N = 36$)	OECD-EU (Excluding US) ($N = 21$)	Other Jurisdictions ($N = 15$)	US
Total number of cases:				
Total	355	300 (85%)	55 (15%)	1,154
Pre-1990	0	0	0	2
1990–1999	4	4	0	5
2000–2009	117	109	8	231
2010–2019	234	187	47	916
Number of climate-centric cases:				
Total	138	103 (75%)	35 (25%)	
1990–1999	0	0	0	
2000–2009	28	25	3	
2010–2019	110	78	32	
Number of cases by jurisdiction (1990–2019):				
Mean	9.9	14.3	3.7	
Standard deviation	20.1	25.3	4.7	
Median	2	2	2	
Minimum	1	1	1	
Maximum	96	96	18	
Court cases by type (1990–2019):				
Plaintiff = Public; Defendant = Public	48	32	16	59
Plaintiff = Public; Defendant = Private	17	14	3	27
Plaintiff = Public; Defendant = NGO	10	9	1	8
Plaintiff = Private; Defendant = Public	117	116	1	90
Plaintiff = Private; Defendant = Private	6	6	0	3
Plaintiff = Private; Defendant = NGO	10	10	0	7
Plaintiff = NGO; Defendant = Public	141	107	34	563
Plaintiff = NGO; Defendant = Private	24	19	5	65
Plaintiff = NGO; Defendant = NGO	4	4	0	16

Source: Authors based on Climate Change Laws of the World, Sabin Center data, and McCormick et al. (2018).
Note: Cases by type involves the following three parties: Public (federal, state/local, and tribal government and different departments of the governments), Private (corporations and businesses), and NGO (nonprofit organizations and individuals). There were multiple types of plaintiffs in 10 cases, whereas 12 cases had multiple types of defendants. Data for the United States come from McCormick et al. (2018), who studied 838 cases between 1990 and 2016. The totals under "Court cases by type" therefore differ from the total numbers reported at the top of the table. This list includes cases with international and regional jurisdictions, with EU-jurisdiction cases included in total EU cases. OECD = Organization for Economic Cooperation and Development; EU = European Union; US = United States.

policies, the data set presents an incomplete picture of regulatory efforts relating to climate change (Scotford and Minas 2019). The issue is perhaps most pertinent in the areas of adaptation and land-use change, but similar definitional issues also affect the litigation database.

The legislation database focuses on national climate policy, which means initiatives at the subnational level and by nonstate actors are not covered. State, province, and city-led initiatives are particularly significant in countries with federal structures or where national engagement with climate change has been intermittent, such as Australia, Brazil, Canada, and the United States. In each of these countries, climate policy at subnational level is fairly advanced and often ahead of the national discourse.

Conversely, in EU member states a focus on national climate policy would ignore the important role of the European Union in national climate policy. The European Union has passed 33 climate laws, including legislation to set up an EU-wide emissions trading scheme and establish ambitious targets on renewable energy, which are legally binding for its member states. Fortunately, there is a relatively easy fix to this bias, which is to add all EU laws to the tally of member states (Eskander and Fankhauser 2020).

A potential problem for time series or panel data analysis is that when laws are amended the database only records the latest version, thus omitting earlier activities. Legal provisions are often tightened over time (as, e.g., Switzerland did when revising its CO2 Act in 2013), but there are also cases of reversal (such as the repeal of Canada's Kyoto Implementation Act in 2012 and Australia's Clean Energy Act in 2014). In each case, these events supersede earlier database entries.

The litigation data set has its own limitations. Perhaps the most important one concerns data collection. Although the CCLW data set is the largest one compiled to date, it cannot be deemed representative or comprehensive. Rather, the data set consists of cases from a limited number of countries, dictated by data accessibility and language considerations. The case list heavily relies on partners of the data providers and on media reports, predominantly in English—ultimately meaning we cannot be sure of the full extent of unidentified litigation cases. Moreover, due to different regulation and litigation cultures, the database is highly uneven, with the majority of the cases attributable to a few jurisdictions. Finally, the CCLW data set does not include litigation in the United States, where the majority of cases have been brought and where, due to relative

Table 3
Prominent Strategic Litigation Cases

Case	Year Started	Plaintiff	Defendant	Summary and Status
Urgenda Foundation v. State of the Netherlands	2013	Dutch environmental group, the Urgenda Foundation, and 900 Dutch citizens	State of the Netherlands	The first case to argue successfully for the adoption of stricter emissions reduction targets by a government. In December 2019, the Dutch Supreme Court upheld earlier rulings, which required the Netherlands to reduce its emissions by at least 25% on 1990 levels by 2020. Even before the final decision by the Supreme Court, the case triggered substantial changes in government policy, including the adoption of the Climate Act 2019 and the decision to phase out coal-fired power generation by 2030 (Jodoin, Faucher, and Lofts 2018; Verschuuren 2019). The case motivated a wave of Urgenda-inspired climate change litigation across the world.
Leghari v. Federation of Pakistan	2015	Ashgar Leghari	Federation of Pakistan	An appellate court in Pakistan granted the claims of Ashgar Leghari, a Pakistani farmer, who had sued the national government for failure to implement the National Climate Change Policy of 2012 and the Framework for Implementation of Climate Change Policy (2014–30). The court, citing domestic and international legal principles, determined that "the delay and lethargy of the State in implementing the Framework offend the fundamental rights of the citizens."

54

Case	Year	Defendants	Plaintiffs	Summary
Carbon Majors Inquiry	2015	50 investor-owned Carbon Majors (largest producers of crude oil, natural gas, coal, and cement)	Greenpeace Southeast Asia, Philippine Rural Reconstruction Movement and 12 NGOs, 20 individuals, and 1,288 Filipinos (signatories of a petition)	A group of plaintiffs led by Greenpeace Southeast Asia filed a petition asking the Philippines Commission on Human Rights to investigate "the human rights implications of climate change and ocean acidification and the resulting rights violations in the Philippines," and "whether the investor-owned Carbon Majors have breached their responsibilities to respect the rights of the Filipino people." The commission found that fossil fuel companies have a clear moral responsibility, and the onus falls on individual countries to pass strong legislation and establish legal liability in their courts. The commission further found that existing civil law in the Philippines provided grounds for action, and that it may be possible to hold companies criminally accountable where they have been clearly proved to have engaged in acts of obstruction and willful obfuscation.

Source: Authors based on Climate Change Laws of the World.
Note: NGO = nongovernmental organization.

advantages in procuring information about the cases, the data are closer to being comprehensive.

III.   Insights

A.   *The Peak in Climate Change Legislation Predates the Paris Agreement*

Practically all climate change laws have been passed over the last 30 years (fig. 1). In 1990, there were only 35 laws with relevance to climate change worldwide (table 1). Because there was little awareness of the climate issue at that time, most of these laws had related objectives such as energy efficiency (e.g., Costa Rica's Energy Law of 1990). Other early laws had wider environmental objectives that were later applied to climate change. For example, the US Clean Air Act of 1963 is concerned with air pollution, but after a 2007 ruling by the Supreme Court (*Massachusetts v. Environmental Protection Agency*), the Obama administration used it as the legal basis to regulate GHG emissions.

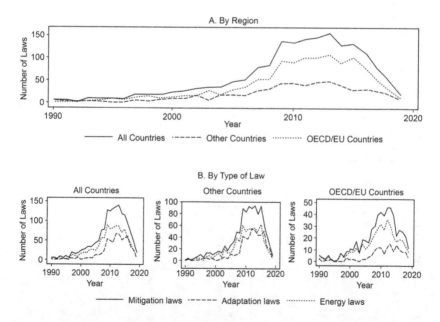

Fig. 1.   Climate change legislation over time. *A*, By region. *B*, By type of law. OECD = Organization for Economic Cooperation and Development; EU = European Union.
Source: Authors based on Climate Change Laws of the World.

By the mid-1990s, the number of climate laws began to rise. Prominent early examples are Sweden's Carbon Tax Act of 1991 and Japan's Act on Promotion of Global Warming Counter Measures of 1998. Lawmaking reached a peak in the period 2009–14, when more than 120 new laws were passed each year. During this heyday, significant framework laws were passed, for example in the United Kingdom (2008), South Korea (2010), and Mexico (2012). The European Union's 2020 Climate and Energy Package with its 20-20-20 targets (for emissions, renewable energy, and energy efficiency) was also passed in this period. In the United States, a law of similar standing, the American Clean Energy and Securities Act of 2009, known as the Waxman-Markey Bill after its sponsors, was approved by the House of Representatives but not tabled in the Senate. After 2014, legislative activity began to tail off.

The 2009–14 peak was supported by increased activity in developing countries, sometimes with the support of development agencies. Many of these interventions concerned adaptation, which was a bigger legislative focus than in the industrialized world. Most of them were policy documents, such as Ethiopia's Climate-Resilient Green Growth Strategy of 2011. Legislative acts passed by parliament are much rarer (table 1), although there are notable exceptions, such as Kenya's Climate Change Act of 2016.

Climate change litigation cases peaked at around the same time, although the rise was more sudden, with very few cases before the mid-2000s (fig. 2). Litigation was spearheaded in industrialized countries (EU and OECD member states, including the United States), with a much slower ramp-up of cases elsewhere.

It is difficult to discern an impact of external factors, such as the international climate negotiations, on national climate legislation or litigation. Fankhauser et al. (2015b) found a statistically significant difference in legislative activity between Annex 1 (industrialized) and non-Annex 1 (developing) countries in the aftermath of the Kyoto Protocol, which imposed binding obligations on the former. However, the effect was temporary and relatively small.

The impact of the Paris Agreement appears equally limited. The peak in legislative activity clearly predates the agreement, which was signed in December 2015. Only about 230 climate-relevant laws were passed in the subsequent 4 years, which is less than half the annual rate than during the peak years.

The more significant impact of the Paris Agreement was perhaps on the ambition of new laws (the intensive margin) rather than their number (the

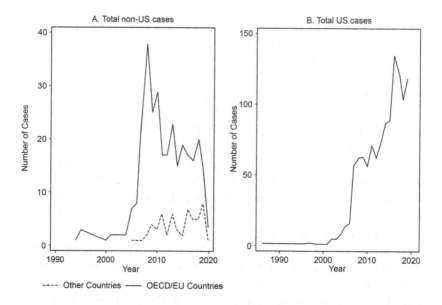

Fig. 2. Climate change litigation over time. *A,* Total non-US cases. *B,* Total US cases. OECD = Organization for Economic Cooperation and Development; EU = European Union; US = United States.

Source: Authors based on Climate Change Laws of the World and Sabin Center data.

extensive margin). Several countries, including Sweden (2017), France (2019), New Zealand (2019), and the United Kingdom (2019), have passed acts to put into law an economy-wide net-zero emissions target (i.e., a balance between emissions and their removal from the atmosphere) in line with the Paris objectives. However, analysis has shown that very few of the emissions pledges contained in countries' NDCs are matched by legislated national emissions targets (Nachmany and Mangan 2018). The legislative implementation of the Paris Agreement is still far from complete.

B.   Spain, the United Kingdom, and South Korea Are the Most Comprehensive Legislators

Every country in the world now has at least one climate law, as defined by CCLW, and in some jurisdictions the number is well over 20 (fig. 3*A*). The median country has passed eight climate change laws and policies (table 1).

   The number of climate laws a country has passed tells us something about the interest of its lawmakers in climate change. However, it is

A. Climate Legislation (Number of laws at the end of 2019)

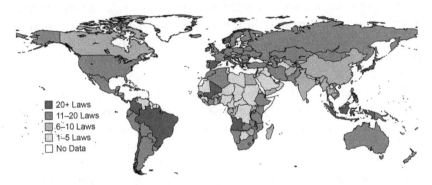

B. Climate Litigation (Number of cases at the end of 2019)

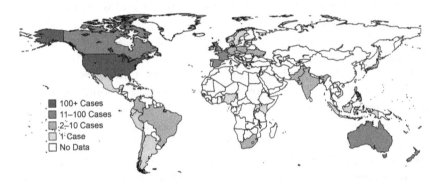

Fig. 3. Climate legislation and litigation by country. *A*, Climate legislation (Number of laws at the of 2019). *B*, Climate litigation (Number of cases at the end of 2019).
Source: Authors based on Climate Change Laws of the World.

not a perfect indicator of climate action. Simply counting the number of laws ignores the considerable heterogeneity that exists in countries' legislative approaches to climate change (Averchenkova et al. 2017). What is covered in one overarching piece of legislation in one country may require several separate interventions in another. China, for example, has only eight climate change laws, but this includes powerful provisions incorporated in the 12th and 13th Five Year Plan. In comparison, Brazil has 28 recorded climate change laws, including 8 interventions trying to halt deforestation. In Europe, Sweden has 11 climate change laws, compared with 20 laws in the United Kingdom. Yet both countries are seen as leaders in the fight against climate change.

Bearing this caveat in mind, we calculate three statistics that we believe are informative about countries' determination to act on climate change. The first indicator is the number of laws that were on the statute book (or more accurately, in the CCLW database) by the end of 2019. The second indicator accounts for government effectiveness. The presumption is that laws passed by effective governments are more likely to be implemented, and therefore have a higher real-world impact, than those passed by ineffectual governments. Our effectiveness indicator is the Rule of Law variable from the Worldwide Governance Indicators by Kaufman, Kraay, and Mastruzzi (2010). The variable captures "perceptions of the extent to which agents have confidence in and abide by the rules of society, and in particular the quality of contract enforcement, property rights, the police, and the court" (Kaufman et al. 2010).[7]

The third indicator factors in the date when a law was passed, by calculating the number of law-years in a country. For example, the UK Climate Change Act, which was passed in 2008, has a weight of 12. The presumption is that laws that were passed early on have had a longer and therefore bigger impact on climate policy. Law-years are again weighted by the level of government effectiveness to account for differences in implementation.

Table 4 reports the top and bottom five performers among three (overlapping) sets of countries—the G20 group of leading economies, the member states of the OECD, and the member states of the European Union—during the period of interest. The full set of results can be found in table A1.

The three indicators lead to very consistent results, with rank correlations of .88 or more between them. However, for individual countries there can be interesting deviations, related to the effectiveness with which laws are implemented. European countries like Spain, Italy, and the United Kingdom are among the most prolific legislators, with more than 20 laws each (not counting EU-level laws, which also apply to member states). Spain and the United Kingdom, and to a lesser extent Italy, also score well in the other two indicators, as European countries tend to have relatively effective governments and many of their climate laws are several years old. However, government effectiveness makes a difference in Brazil and Indonesia. Both countries are in the top five G20 countries in terms of number of laws, but controlling for government effectiveness and law-years, the best G20 performers are the United Kingdom and South Korea.

Table 4
Legislative Activity by Countries

Ranking	Laws ISO Code	Laws Number	Quality-Adjusted Laws ISO Code	Quality-Adjusted Laws Number	Lifetime Quality-Adjusted Laws ISO Code	Lifetime Quality-Adjusted Laws Number
	A. G20 Countries					
1	BRA	28	GBR	16.85	GBR	209.68
2	ITA	24	AUS	15.41	KOR	204.77
3	IDN	22	KOR	15.25	ITA	184.01
4	KOR	22	DEU	15.03	DEU	163.00
5	GBR	20	JPN	15.01	AUS	138.48
15	CAN	10	IND	5.14	ZAF	58.17
16	IND	10	RUS	4.09	RUS	40.94
17	MEX	10	MEX	3.97	MEX	28.81
18	CHN	8	CHN	3.25	CHN	26.08
19	SAU	3	SAU	1.61	SAU	13.45
	B. OECD Countries					
1	ESP	38	ESP	27.20	ESP	234.21
2	CHL	26	CHL	19.65	GBR	209.68
3	ITA	24	GBR	16.85	KOR	204.77
4	KOR	22	AUS	15.41	NOR	186.10
5	GBR	20	KOR	15.25	ITA	184.01
31	CZE	9	ISL	5.93	ISL	57.91
32	ISL	7	SVN	4.92	SVN	43.58
33	SVN	7	MEX	3.97	MEX	28.81
34	EST	3	EST	2.23	EST	17.81
35	LTU	2	LTU	1.34	LTU	10.34
	C. EU Countries					
1	ESP	38	ESP	27.20	ESP	234.21
2	ITA	24	GBR	16.85	GBR	209.68
3	GBR	20	DEU	15.03	ITA	184.01
4	DEU	18	IRL	14.95	DEU	163.00
5	IRL	18	ITA	14.57	DNK	139.93
24	SVN	7	SVN	4.92	SVN	43.58
25	EST	3	EST	2.23	EST	17.81
26	LTU	2	LTU	1.34	LVA	11.42
27	LVA	2	LVA	1.31	LTU	10.34
28	CYP	1	CYP	.71	CYP	4.92

Note: Data on climate laws and policies come from Climate Change Laws of the World. See table A1 for the full list of countries and detailed statistics. Quality-adjusted laws are derived by multiplying each law by the Rule of Law score of Kaufman et al. (2010) in the year it was passed. Lifetime quality-adjusted laws are calculated as the number of years a law has been in force, multiplied by the Rule of Law score in each year. All calculations are done over the period 1990–2019. OECD = Organization for Economic Cooperation and Development; EU = European Union.

C.   Climate Legislation Is Less of a Partisan Issue
Than Commonly Assumed

A striking feature of the climate change debate, particularly in anglo-phone countries like Australia, Canada, and the United States, is the strong party-political divide. There is evidence that left-of-center gov-ernments are generally more inclined to legislate on the environment (Neumayer 2003), but the issue appears particularly pronounced for cli-mate change, where we observe a notable undercurrent of climate skep-ticism on the political right (McCright and Dunlap 2011a, 2011b; Painter and Ashe 2012). However, the effect of party politics on environmental policy is complex (Carter et al. 2018), and it has also been suggested that right-wing climate skepticism may primarily be an Anglo-Saxon phe-nomenon (Fankhauser et al. 2015a). There may also be a gender dimen-sion (Mavisakalyan and Tarverdi 2019).

To shed more light on this debate, we look at climate change legislation in the democratic countries of the sample, defined as countries with a de-mocracy score of 6 or more in the Polity IV data set (a standard measure of democratic quality).[8] For each of these countries, we calculate the fraction of climate change laws that was passed by administrations of a particular political orientation (right, left, or center), divided by the share of years they have been in power. Algebraically, the indicator for partisanship P has the form

$$P_i = \frac{\frac{L_i}{L_{tot}}}{\frac{Y_i}{Y_{tot}}},$$

$$(1)$$

where L denotes number of laws passed, Y denotes years in power, and subscript i denotes political orientation, $i = \{left, right, center\}$. Data on party-political orientation were taken from the World Bank's Database of Political Institutions (DPI).[9]

The indicator has a straightforward interpretation: a score greater than 1 suggests that governments of political persuasion i are dispropor-tionately inclined to pass climate change legislation. Their share of cli-mate laws is greater than their relative time in power. A score less than 1 suggests a comparative reluctance to legislate on climate change.

Figure 4 shows the distribution of scores across the 99 democratic coun-tries we considered, split by legislative acts (passed by parliament) and executive orders (issued by governments). For the country-level results of

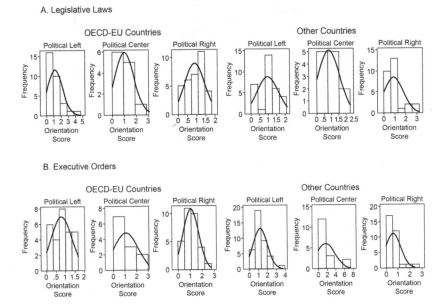

Fig. 4. Climate laws and political orientation. *A*, Legislative laws. *B*, Executive orders. Note: Countries with a democracy score of 6 or more in the Polity IV data set only. Data on political orientation are taken from the World Bank Database of Political Institutions (DPI). Orientation scores greater than 1 suggest political parties of that orientation are disproportionately inclined to pass climate laws, relative to their time in power. Median (mean) left-wing scores for all, Organization for Economic Cooperation and Development–European Union (OECD-EU), and other countries are 1.0 (1.141), 0.909 (1.118), and 1.012 (1.160), whereas center-government scores are 1.0 (1.234), 1.0 (0.961), and 1.0 (1.431), and right-wing scores are 0.961 (0.891), 1.111 (0.923), and 0.8 (0.813).

combined (parliamentary and executive) activity, see table A2. We would expect the distribution for the right-wing index to be to the left of 1 (i.e., most countries score less than 1) and those for left and center parties to be to the right of 1. However, this is not what we find. For most distributions we cannot reject the hypothesis that their mean is equal to 1 (table 5). In industrialized countries (OECD and EU members), and for all countries in the case of legislative acts, there is no statistical evidence that the number of climate laws passed by governments of the left, center, and right is not proportional to their time in office. Only in the case of executive orders issued by governments outside the OECD/European Union does the political right appear to be less inclined to act on climate change.

Table 5
Statistical Tests of Political Orientation

Null Hypothesis	Alternative Hypothesis	Legislative Acts			Executive Orders		
		All Countries	OECD-EU Countries	Other Countries	All Countries	OECD-EU Countries	Other Countries
One-sample *t*-test:							
Left-wing score = 1	< 1	Not rejected	Not rejected	Not rejected	Not rejected	Rejected	Not rejected
	≠ 1	Not rejected	Not rejected	Not rejected	Not rejected	Rejected	Rejected
	> 1	Not rejected	Not rejected	Not rejected	Not rejected	Not rejected	Rejected
Center score = 1	< 1	Not rejected	Not rejected	Not rejected	Not rejected	Not rejected	Not rejected
	≠ 1	Not rejected	Not rejected	Not rejected	Not rejected	Not rejected	Not rejected
	> 1	Not rejected	Not rejected	Not rejected	Not rejected	Not rejected	Not rejected
Right-wing score = 1	< 1	Not rejected	Not rejected	Not rejected	Rejected	Not rejected	Rejected
	≠ 1	Not rejected	Not rejected	Not rejected	Rejected	Not rejected	Rejected
	> 1	Not rejected	Not rejected	Not rejected	Rejected	Not rejected	Not rejected
Two-sample Wilcoxon rank-sum (Mann-Whitney) test:							
Left-wing score: OECD-EU countries = Other countries	≠	Not rejected			Rejected		
Center score: OECD-EU countries = Other countries	≠	Not rejected			Not rejected		
Right-wing score: OECD-EU countries = Other countries	≠	Not rejected			Rejected		

Note: Data on climate laws and policies come from Climate Change Laws of the World. Data on political orientation come from the World Bank's Database of Political Institutions. All calculations are done over the period 1990–2017. OECD = Organization for Economic Co-operation and Development; EU = European Union.

Although we do not control for confounding factors, this suggests that the task of passing climate change legislation is less of a partisan issue than the public debate in countries like Australia, Canada, and the United States would make us believe.

Of course, indicators like equation (1) mask important political dynamics, and the left-right divide does not always mirror a divide on environmental matters (Carter 2018; Carter et al. 2018). The United Kingdom, for example, has a low right-wing party score of 0.6 (table A2), but climate policy has mostly transcended party lines. The opposition Conservatives supported many of the laws put forward by Labour governments, most notably the Climate Change Act of 2008. The US score of 1.3 reflects the fact that the legislative and executive are often controlled by different parties. President Obama's flagship Clean Power Plan, for example, was an executive order passed in 2015, when Congress was in Republican hands.

D.   Climate Legislation Slows during Difficult Economic Times

Climate change requires persistent policy intervention over decades and as such it should cut across the business cycle. Nevertheless, there is a question about countries' determination to pursue climate policy in difficult economic times.

There are two sides to the argument. On the one hand, concern for the environment may have less political traction during a recession, when issues like growth and employment take center stage. Kahn and Kotchen (2010) found that interest in the environment tends to wane in difficult economic times. On the other hand, green investment—or a "green deal"—can be an effective fiscal stimulus, as argued by Barbier (2010) and Zenghelis (2012). In the aftermath of the 2008 financial crisis, governments in Europe and elsewhere saw climate investment as a promising way to kick-start an ailing economy (Bowen and Stern 2010). The same call is now being made with respect to the COVID-19 recovery (Hepburn et al. 2020).

CCLW can help to shed some light on the link between climate legislation and the business cycle (see Doda 2014 for a related application). We use Hodrick-Prescott decomposition to calculate the cyclical component of gross domestic product (GDP) and identify the periods during 1990–2017 when national economies were performing above trend

(HP > 0) and below trend (HP < 0).[10] Using the same structure as equation (1), we then calculate the share of climate laws passed while the economy is underperforming, divided by the fraction of years when this was the case.

Countries where legislative activity slowed down in difficult economic times will have a score of less than 1, whereas countries that sought to implement green deal-style policies may have a score greater than 1. Figure 5 displays the distribution of scores across countries (the full results are reproduced in table A3). The scores are skewed slightly to the left, suggesting a majority of countries legislate less in difficult economic times. This is confirmed by statistical tests (table 6).

We conclude that the business cycle has had a material impact on the pace of climate change legislation, notwithstanding the fact that the peak in climate legislation coincided with the aftermath of the 2008 financial crisis (fig. 1). This raises questions about the likelihood of ratcheting up NDCs

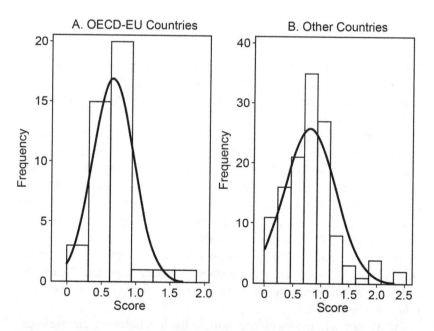

Fig. 5. Climate laws and economic crises. *A*, OECD-EU countries. *B*, Other countries. OECD = Organization for Economic Co-operation and Development; EU = European Union. Source: Author's own calculations, using World Bank gross domestic product data and Hodrick-Prescott decomposition. Countries with scores less than 1 are less inclined to pass climate laws in difficult economic times.

Table 6
Statistical Tests of Business Cycle Effects

Null Hypothesis	Alternative Hypothesis	Decision		
		All Countries	OECD-EU Countries	Other Countries
One-sample *t*-test:				
Economic crisis = 1	< 1	Rejected	Rejected	Rejected
	≠ 1	Rejected	Rejected	Rejected
	> 1	Not rejected	Not rejected	Not rejected
Two-sample Wilcoxon rank-sum (Mann-Whitney) test: OECD-EU countries = Other countries	≠	Rejected		

Note: Data on climate laws and policies come from Climate Change Laws of the World database. Data on business cycles are calculated from real gross domestic product data from the World Development Indicators database. All calculations are done over the period 1990–2017 for 169 countries. OECD = Organization for Economic Co-operation and Development; EU = European Union.

in accordance with the Paris Agreement, as the next round of NDC reviews will likely occur during a global recession caused by COVID-19.

E.   Non-US Judges Tend to Rule in Favor of Climate Action

The role of the judiciary in climate change governance does not just depend on the number of cases brought but also on their outcomes. We are therefore interested in the extent to which judges rule against or in favor of tighter climate action. CCLW contains this information for most cases where a ruling has been issued.

The way judges rule is particularly material in the case of strategic court cases (such as those in table 3), which play an important supporting role in ensuring the national implementation of international emission-reduction commitments and the alignment of national laws with the Paris Agreements (Peel and Osofsky 2015; Setzer and Vanhala 2019). However, we are interested in the broader role of courts beyond just high-profile cases.

To inform this issue, court rulings have been classified as either strengthening climate action or weakening climate action. The distinction is similar to another classification found in the literature, which splits court cases into "pro" and "anti" regulatory suits, depending on the aims of the plaintiffs (Hilson 2012; Markell and Ruhl 2012). "Pro" (also known as "favorable") cases are brought with the objective of increasing regulation or liability associated with climate change; and "anti" (also known as "con" or "hindering") cases aim to decrease regulation or liability (Wilensky 2015). However, here we are interested in the ruling of the judge rather than the objective of the plaintiff.

In the United States, an earlier analysis of cases brought between 1990 and 2016 found that outcomes favored anti-regulatory litigants compared with pro-regulatory litigants by a ratio of 1.4 to 1 (McCormick et al. 2018). We reexamined 534 of these cases and found that judges ruled in favor of more climate regulation in 225 (42%) of them (table 7). Examined by topic, pro-regulation litigants have tended to win renewable energy and energy efficiency cases but frequently lost coal-fired power plant cases (McCormick et al. 2018). This win ratio seems to have been enough to shape some policy outcomes. According to Osofsky (2012), climate litigation has brought about credible steps to increase the share of renewable energy in the US electricity mix.

Table 7
Pro-Climate Rulings by the Judiciary

	Non-US Cases			
Time Period	All Non-US (N = 36)	OECD-EU (N = 21)	Non-OECD-EU (N = 15)	US Cases
Total cases with a ruling	355	300	55	534
Cases with a pro-climate ruling	187 (53%)	153 (51%)	34 (62%)	225 (42%)
Pro-climate cases over time:				
1990–1999	0	0	0	
2000–2009	68	62	6	
2010–2019	119	91	28	

Source: Authors based on Climate Change Laws of the World and McCormick et al. (2018). For results by country, see table A4. OECD = Organization for Economic Co-operation and Development; EU = European Union; US = United States.
Note: Outside the United States, a court ruling has been issued in 355 cases between 1990 and 2019. These are contained in Climate Change Laws of the World. For the United States, we reexamined 534 court rulings during 1990–2016 from McCormick et al. (2018); here a ruling is pro-climate if judges supported a "pro-regulation" plaintiff or ruled against an "anti-regulation" plaintiff.

Outside the United States, judges appear more inclined to support climate action. There are 355 non-US court cases where a judgment has been reached and the climate change outcome has been assessed. Among these, the ruling has been supportive of climate change action in 187 cases, or about half of the time (table 7). The number is slightly lower than in Setzer and Byrnes (2019), who found that judges favored pro-regulatory litigants over anti-regulatory litigants by a ratio of 1.6 to 1. In Australia, the country with the highest number of cases outside the United States, these court rulings have apparently been instrumental in forcing administrative decision makers to consider climate change impacts in the approval of certain large-scale projects (Peel 2011; Preston 2011; Hughes 2019).

IV. Conclusions

This paper uses CCLW, a publicly accessible, searchable database hosted by the Grantham Research Institute on Climate Change at the London School of Economics, to identify trends in climate change legislation and litigation over the past 30 years.

CCLW documents the explosion of national climate change legislation over this period, although global action on climate change still falls short of what the Paris Agreement requires. By the end of 2019, the database contained 1,800 climate change laws and policies of similar status worldwide, compared with 35 laws in 1990 and 145 laws in 1999. Only about 40% of these laws are legislative acts passed by parliaments. The remainder are executive orders, decrees, or significant policies issued by governments.

The judiciary got involved in 1,500 court cases in which climate change was a concern, three-quarters of which were in the United States. In about half of the non-US cases for which there is a ruling, the judges strengthened or upheld climate change concerns. Earlier (pre-2017) evidence for the United States suggests that the odds of a pro-climate outcome are lower in the United States.

There is no country in the world that does not have at least 1 law or policy dealing with climate change, and the most prolific countries have well over 20 such laws. Accounting for government effectiveness and the length of time a law has been in effect, Spain, the United Kingdom, and South Korea are the most comprehensive legislators on climate change.

Global legislative activity peaked in the period 2009–14, when jurisdictions like the European Union, Mexico, South Korea, and the United

Kingdom passed their flagship framework laws on climate change. Although unable to ascertain causality, the fact that climate legislation peaked before the 2015 Paris Agreement suggests that a push in national climate legislation could have facilitated the Paris Agreement, rather than the other way round.

The Paris Agreement has probably influenced national climate legislation more with respect to the ambition of climate laws rather than their number. Following Paris, several countries—most notably France, New Zealand, Sweden, and the United Kingdom—have adopted binding net-zero emissions targets that are consistent with the Paris objectives. However, most of the emissions pledges contained in NDCs have yet to be translated into legislated targets.

Without going into careful statistical identification, the data reveal some interesting and perhaps surprising patterns. We find that climate change legislation is much less of a partisan issue worldwide than the debate in countries like Australia, Canada, and the United States would suggest. In industrialized countries (OECD plus EU members), the number of climate laws passed by governments of the left, center, and right is proportional to their time in office. Only in democracies outside this group is the political right less inclined to legislate on climate change.

We further find that legislative activity fluctuates with the business cycle and slows down in times of economic difficulty. This is despite the fact that the peak in climate change legislation coincided with the aftermath of the 2008 global financial crisis. It suggests that the pace of climate action may decline in the aftermath of the coronavirus pandemic.

CCLW has so far mainly been aimed at policy audiences, where it has helped to build trust among international policy makers and support legislators in drafting their own climate laws. It is only now starting to be utilized in academic research. Initial applications have used the data to assess global progress in adopting climate policies, understand the political economy of passing climate laws, identify good practice in climate change governance, assess the environmental impact of climate legislation, and identify general trends in climate litigation. It is hoped that this paper will stimulate other scholars to use the data in their own research.

Appendix

Table A1
Legislative Activity by Countries

| | | | | | Number of Climate Laws | | |
| | | | | | | Quality-Adjusted Number | Lifetime Quality-Adjusted Number |
ISO Code	Country Name	G20	OECD	EU	Number	Quality-Adjusted Number	Lifetime Quality-Adjusted Number
AFG	Afghanistan	0	0	0	9	1.47	12.03
AGO	Angola	0	0	0	21	5.55	31.98
ALB	Albania	0	0	0	3	1.17	10.36
ARE	United Arab Emirates	0	0	0	6	3.78	20.88
ARG	Argentina	1	0	0	17	7.09	72.17
ARM	Armenia	0	0	0	8	3.33	47.92
ATG	Antigua and Barbuda	0	0	0	5	3.23	21.16
AUS	Australia	1	1	0	18	15.41	138.48
AUT	Austria	0	1	1	9	7.87	99.38
AZE	Azerbaijan	0	0	0	4	1.39	13.97
BDI	Burundi	0	0	0	4	1.08	8.16
BEL	Belgium	0	1	1	11	8.53	105.21
BEN	Benin	0	0	0	3	1.17	9.34
BFA	Burkina Faso	0	0	0	12	4.82	35.74
BGD	Bangladesh	0	0	0	10	3.30	31.55
BGR	Bulgaria	0	0	1	11	5.24	66.73
BHR	Bahrain	0	0	0	2	1.18	15.25
BHS	The Bahamas	0	0	0	4	2.67	25.22
BIH	Bosnia and Herzegovina	0	0	0	1	.46	1.27
BLR	Belarus	0	0	0	15	4.30	57.70
BLZ	Belize	0	0	0	3	1.19	10.81
BOL	Bolivia	0	0	0	16	5.00	53.87
BRA	Brazil	1	0	0	28	12.86	117.33
BRB	Barbados	0	0	0	4	2.91	30.56
BRN	Brunei Darussalam	0	0	0	4	2.45	15.90
BTN	Bhutan	0	0	0	8	4.46	45.17
BWA	Botswana	0	0	0	5	3.11	34.96
CAF	Central African Republic	0	0	0	2	.43	4.95
CAN	Canada	1	1	0	10	8.52	91.32
CHE	Switzerland	0	1	0	9	7.86	102.59
CHL	Chile	0	1	0	26	19.65	172.26
CHN	China	1	0	0	8	3.25	26.08
CIV	Côte d'Ivoire	0	0	0	14	4.62	26.82
CMR	Cameroon	0	0	0	5	1.41	13.33

					Number of Climate Laws		
ISO Code	Country Name	G20	OECD	EU	Number	Quality-Adjusted Number	Lifetime Quality-Adjusted Number
COG	Congo	0	0	0	7	1.78	21.10
COK	Cook Islands	0	0	0	4	1.25	11.79
COL	Colombia	0	0	0	23	9.88	62.92
COM	Comoros	0	0	0	1	.32	1.80
CPV	Cabo Verde	0	0	0	7	4.23	40.21
CRI	Costa Rica	0	0	0	24	14.40	116.34
CUB	Cuba	0	0	0	9	3.36	46.91
CYP	Cyprus	0	0	1	1	.71	4.92
CZE	Czech Republic	0	1	1	9	6.09	78.76
DEU	Germany	1	1	1	18	15.03	163.00
DJI	Djibouti	0	0	0	8	2.65	28.08
DMA	Dominica	0	0	0	5	3.10	26.58
DNK	Denmark	0	1	1	12	10.70	139.93
DOM	Dominican Republic	0	0	0	10	3.82	43.95
DZA	Algeria	0	0	0	13	4.63	54.79
ECU	Ecuador	0	0	0	13	3.88	28.00
EGY	Egypt	0	0	0	6	2.42	20.15
ERI	Eritrea	0	0	0	2	.48	9.13
ESP	Spain	0	1	1	38	27.20	234.21
EST	Estonia	0	1	1	3	2.23	17.81
ETH	Ethiopia	0	0	0	13	4.54	64.95
FIN	Finland	0	1	1	12	10.76	95.86
FJI	Fiji	0	0	0	5	2.22	22.73
FRA	France	1	1	1	15	11.84	77.17
FSM	Micronesia	0	0	0	4	1.96	14.37
GAB	Gabon	0	0	0	7	2.81	25.73
GBR	United Kingdom	1	1	1	20	16.85	209.68
GEO	Georgia	0	0	0	2	1.13	3.88
GHA	Ghana	0	0	0	9	4.41	60.59
GIN	Guinea	0	0	0	3	.76	9.60
GMB	Gambia	0	0	0	6	2.38	25.48
GNB	Guinea-Bissau	0	0	0	2	.48	4.08
GNQ	Equatorial Guinea	0	0	0	1	.21	1.11
GRC	Greece	0	1	1	14	8.75	101.63
GRD	Grenada	0	0	0	6	3.17	33.68
GTM	Guatemala	0	0	0	8	2.34	22.26
GUY	Guyana	0	0	0	3	1.22	10.11
HND	Honduras	0	0	0	9	2.86	32.53
HRV	Croatia	0	0	1	15	8.18	66.52
HTI	Haiti	0	0	0	2	.44	3.40
HUN	Hungary	0	1	1	11	7.24	76.95

					Number of Climate Laws		
ISO Code	Country Name	G20	OECD	EU	Number	Quality-Adjusted Number	Lifetime Quality-Adjusted Number
IDN	Indonesia	1	0	0	22	8.51	75.77
IND	India	1	0	0	10	5.14	64.64
IRL	Ireland	0	1	1	18	14.95	125.94
IRN	Iran	0	0	0	10	3.26	45.52
IRQ	Iraq	0	0	0	1	.16	1.99
ISL	Iceland	0	1	0	7	5.93	57.91
ISR	Israel	0	1	0	17	11.68	156.05
ITA	Italy	1	1	1	24	14.57	184.01
JAM	Jamaica	0	0	0	4	1.73	19.09
JOR	Jordan	0	0	0	3	1.72	18.04
JPN	Japan	1	1	0	19	15.01	118.29
KAZ	Kazakhstan	0	0	0	11	3.57	55.53
KEN	Kenya	0	0	0	14	5.11	32.87
KGZ	Kyrgyzstan	0	0	0	7	1.97	21.48
KHM	Cambodia	0	0	0	6	1.65	17.46
KIR	Kiribati	0	0	0	11	5.93	57.65
KNA	Saint Kitts and Nevis	0	0	0	4	2.44	18.88
KOR	South Korea	1	1	0	22	15.25	204.77
LAO	Lao PDR	0	0	0	5	1.55	13.83
LBN	Lebanon	0	0	0	4	1.35	7.28
LBR	Liberia	0	0	0	8	2.12	21.85
LBY	Libya	0	0	0	2	.54	5.16
LCA	Saint Lucia	0	0	0	5	3.24	32.02
LIE	Liechtenstein	0	0	0	6	4.78	51.09
LKA	Sri Lanka	0	0	0	8	4.04	46.33
LSO	Lesotho	0	0	0	5	2.30	24.59
LTU	Lithuania	0	1	1	2	1.34	10.34
LUX	Luxembourg	0	1	1	12	10.27	73.37
LVA	Latvia	0	0	1	2	1.31	11.42
MAR	Morocco	0	0	0	14	6.55	48.20
MCO	Monaco	0	0	0	2	1.38	8.14
MDA	Moldova	0	0	0	6	2.57	27.53
MDG	Madagascar	0	0	0	10	3.52	26.35
MDV	Maldives	0	0	0	7	3.06	35.33
MEX	Mexico	1	1	0	10	3.97	28.81
MHL	Marshall Islands	0	0	0	5	2.41	13.25
MKD	FYR Macedonia	0	0	0	6	2.73	23.57
MLI	Mali	0	0	0	25	9.44	74.51
MLT	Malta	0	0	1	8	6.10	48.38
MMR	Myanmar	0	0	0	7	1.64	10.35
MNE	Montenegro	0	0	0	4	1.96	16.73
MNG	Mongolia	0	0	0	12	5.57	59.91

						Number of Climate Laws	
ISO Code	Country Name	G20	OECD	EU	Number	Quality-Adjusted Number	Lifetime Quality-Adjusted Number
MOZ	Mozambique	0	0	0	11	4.08	41.16
MRT	Mauritania	0	0	0	3	1.06	14.08
MUS	Mauritius	0	0	0	6	4.02	29.45
MWI	Malawi	0	0	0	11	4.98	50.79
MYS	Malaysia	0	0	0	6	3.56	43.27
NAM	Namibia	0	0	0	11	6.03	56.27
NER	Niger	0	0	0	4	1.50	27.67
NGA	Nigeria	0	0	0	5	1.47	10.28
NIC	Nicaragua	0	0	0	11	3.95	48.24
NIU	Niue	0	0	0	8	2.75	24.30
NLD	Netherlands	0	1	1	16	13.82	131.05
NOR	Norway	0	1	0	17	15.22	186.10
NPL	Nepal	0	0	0	5	1.67	22.70
NRU	Nauru	0	0	0	4	1.77	18.61
NZL	New Zealand	0	1	0	10	8.75	101.82
OMN	Oman	0	0	0	4	2.36	19.61
PAK	Pakistan	0	0	0	11	3.78	28.66
PAN	Panama	0	0	0	10	4.83	49.56
PER	Peru	0	0	0	16	6.22	56.19
PHL	Philippines	0	0	0	16	6.73	88.86
PLW	Palau	0	0	0	8	5.08	57.22
PNG	Papua New Guinea	0	0	0	10	3.37	25.05
POL	Poland	0	1	1	12	7.49	79.69
PRK	North Korea	0	0	0	4	.95	12.06
PRT	Portugal	0	1	1	15	10.78	101.29
PRY	Paraguay	0	0	0	12	3.98	45.47
QAT	Qatar	0	0	0	2	1.24	18.83
RUS	Russia	1	0	0	12	4.09	40.94
RWA	Rwanda	0	0	0	8	3.30	32.94
SAU	Saudi Arabia	1	0	0	3	1.61	13.45
SDN	Sudan	0	0	0	1	.23	3.14
SEN	Senegal	0	0	0	17	7.59	80.31
SGP	Singapore	0	0	0	9	7.42	84.86
SLB	Solomon Islands	0	0	0	6	2.38	18.94
SLE	Sierra Leone	0	0	0	8	2.54	21.96
SLV	El Salvador	0	0	0	8	2.93	30.66
SMR	San Marino	0	0	0	3	2.06	18.32
SRB	Serbia	0	0	0	5	2.21	15.15
SSD	South Sudan	0	0	0	2	.26	1.54
STP	São Tomé and Principe	0	0	0	2	.69	5.58
SUR	Suriname	0	0	0	3	1.39	10.98

					Number of Climate Laws		
ISO Code	Country Name	G20	OECD	EU	Number	Quality-Adjusted Number	Lifetime Quality-Adjusted Number
SVK	Slovakia	0	1	1	17	10.30	103.58
SVN	Slovenia	0	1	1	7	4.92	43.58
SWE	Sweden	0	1	1	11	9.80	108.61
SWZ	Swaziland	0	0	0	4	1.58	19.89
SYC	Seychelles	0	0	0	7	3.64	26.11
SYR	Syrian Arab Republic	0	0	0	4	1.20	9.77
TCD	Chad	0	0	0	3	.72	3.88
TGO	Togo	0	0	0	14	4.68	42.32
THA	Thailand	0	0	0	10	4.71	50.84
TJK	Tajikistan	0	0	0	7	1.72	26.44
TKM	Turkmenistan	0	0	0	1	.22	1.65
TON	Tonga	0	0	0	6	3.04	28.81
TTO	Trinidad and Tobago	0	0	0	6	2.92	37.79
TUN	Tunisia	0	0	0	4	1.99	19.58
TUR	Turkey	1	1	0	14	7.13	67.31
TUV	Tuvalu	0	0	0	8	5.35	56.71
TWN	Taiwan	0	0	0	5	3.48	27.78
TZA	Tanzania	0	0	0	14	5.80	48.16
UGA	Uganda	0	0	0	6	2.56	30.54
UKR	Ukraine	0	0	0	13	4.18	63.17
URY	Uruguay	0	0	0	17	10.71	96.72
USA	United States of America	1	1	0	11	9.03	102.86
UZB	Uzbekistan	0	0	0	6	1.50	16.99
VCT	Saint Vincent and the Grenadines	0	0	0	3	1.97	14.80
VEN	Venezuela	0	0	0	4	.69	7.76
VNM	Vietnam	0	0	0	15	6.09	58.11
VUT	Vanuatu	0	0	0	7	3.96	34.29
WSM	Samoa	0	0	0	9	5.85	56.28
YEM	Yemen	0	0	0	6	1.56	20.45
ZAF	South Africa	1	0	0	12	6.23	58.17
ZMB	Zambia	0	0	0	15	6.42	52.84
ZWE	Zimbabwe	0	0	0	9	1.68	14.45

Note: Data on climate laws and policies come from Climate Change Laws of the World. Quality-adjusted laws are derived by multiplying each law by the Rule of Law score (Kaufman et al. 2010) in the year it was passed. Lifetime quality-adjusted laws are calculated as the number of years a law has been in force, multiplied by the Rule of Law score in each year. All calculations are done over the period 1990–2019.

Table A2
Climate Laws and Political Orientation

ISO Code	Left-Wing Score	Center Score	Right-Wing Score	ISO Code	Left-Wing Score	Center Score	Right-Wing Score
ALB	1.244		.718	KGZ			1.000
ARG	1.400	0	.800	KOR		.742	1.193
AUS	1.394		.659	LBN		0	1.067
AUT	1.185		.444	LKA	1.455	0	
BEL	1.852		.884	LSO	1.000		
BFA	0	7.500	0	LUX		1.000	
BGR	0		1.111	LVA		0	1.636
BHS		1.615	.467	MDA	.902	1.533	0
BLZ			1.000	MDV			1.000
BOL	1.422	.250	.700	MEX		1.167	.778
BRA	1.077	4.308	0	MKD	1.000		
BRB	.500		1.500	MLI		1.000	
BWA			1.000	MLT	1.750		.795
CAN	.830		1.197	MWI			1.000
CHL	.971	1.071		NAM	1.000		
COL		0	3.250	NGA	1.800		.900
COM		1.000		NIC	1.012		.971
CPV	1.333	.750		NLD	.444		1.263
CRI	1.663		.117	NOR	.878		1.140
CYP	4.800		0	NPL	1.000		
CZE	1.250		.500	NZL	2.450		.194
DEU	.667		1.111	PAK	1.333		0
DNK	.583		1.313	PAN			1.000
DOM	1.400	1.318	0	PER	2.036	.622	.170
ECU	1.000			PHL	0	1.045	
ESP	.686		1.314	POL	.348	1.533	1.643
FIN	.333	1.021	1.867	PRT	1.149		.828
FRA	.909		1.091	PRY	.467		1.116
GBR	1.508		.560	ROU	2.500	0	0
GHA	1.215		.617	RUS		1.000	
GNB	1.000			SEN	0		1.917
GRC	1.205		.701	SLE	1.000		
GRD	1.867		.519	SLV	2.188		.525
GTM	3.000		.600	SVK	1.000		
GUY	1.000			SVN	.863	1.533	0
HND			1.000	SWE	.599		1.620
HRV	.600	2.880	.568	TTO	1.436		.622
HUN	.898		1.157	TUN	.758	2.778	
IND	.982		1.037	UKR	.833	1.042	
IRL		.737	1.556	URY	2.027		.110
ISL		0	1.438	USA	.795		1.273
ISR	1.235		.961	VUT	1.048		.917
ITA	.971	.809	1.165	ZAF	1.217		0
JAM	.609		2.800	ZMB	1.000		
JPN	0		1.111				

Note: Data on climate laws and policies come from Climate Change Laws of the World. Data on political orientation come from the World Bank's Database of Political Institutions. All calculations are done over the period 1990–2017.

Table A3
Climate Laws and Business Cycle

ISO Code	Score	ISO Code	Score	ISO Code	Score	ISO Code	Score
BIH	0	ISL	.533	PHL	.750	MYS	.933
COM	0	JPN	.538	SGP	.750	SWZ	.933
GNB	0	SLV	.538	NOR	.760	VEN	.933
KGZ	0	TUR	.538	BHR	.778	ZAF	.955
KWT	0	LUX	.545	ERI	.778	MNG	.972
LBR	0	MOZ	.545	LBN	.778	BWA	.988
LBY	0	MAR	.574	MEX	.778	AZE	1.000
LTU	0	SVK	.581	KAZ	.783	IRN	1.000
SSD	0	BLZ	.583	MDV	.800	NER	1.000
TKM	0	EST	.583	SVN	.800	SLE	1.000
TLS	0	MRT	.583	ZWE	.800	TJK	1.000
TUN	0	PAK	.599	FJI	.800	FRA	1.018
CZE	.207	THA	.600	NGA	.800	LAO	1.018
MLI	.240	AGO	.614	NPL	.800	NAM	1.018
VNM	.249	ARE	.622	NZL	.808	MKD	1.050
ESP	.267	ECU	.622	BRN	.824	OMN	1.077
YEM	.275	FIN	.622	LVA	.824	RWA	1.077
GAB	.286	GIN	.622	NLD	.824	SLB	1.077
RUS	.292	SUR	.622	ROU	.824	UKR	1.089
TTO	.311	KOR	.636	URY	.824	GTM	1.094
USA	.318	AFG	.655	IND	.830	CMR	1.120
CIV	.333	BOL	.656	DNK	.848	COG	1.143
BLR	.339	MLT	.656	MMR	.848	CPV	1.143
PNG	.346	TUV	.656	MWI	.848	ARM	1.167
BFA	.359	TZA	.663	SAU	.848	BEN	1.167
KEN	.359	GRC	.667	IRL	.857	BHS	1.167
HUN	.364	GHA	.667	ATG	.862	LKA	1.167
AUS	.380	GRD	.667	COD	.862	BGD	1.200
IDN	.381	HRV	.688	NIC	.862	ALB	1.244
LSO	.400	ITA	.696	ETH	.862	TCD	1.244
TGO	.424	DOM	.700	PRT	.862	BEL	1.292
UZB	.424	UGA	.718	BDI	.875	MUS	1.292
CHL	.449	BRA	.718	BTN	.875	BRB	1.400
DZA	.462	AUT	.732	EGY	.875	GUY	1.436
ISR	.471	CHE	.732	POL	.875	VUT	1.436
COL	.500	MDG	.737	PRY	.897	SDN	1.750
CRI	.500	QAT	.737	HND	.915	CYP	1.867
GBR	.500	PAN	.747	CAF	.933	JAM	1.867
ARG	.509	PER	.747	CHN	.933	JOR	1.867
SWE	.509	ZMB	.747	GMB	.933	GEO	2.000
DEU	.519	BGR	.749	KHM	.933	GNQ	2.000
CAN	.519	SEN	.749	MDA	.933	IRQ	2.333
						HTI	2.545

Note: Data on climate laws and policies come from Climate Change Laws of the World. Data on business cycles are calculated from real gross domestic product data from the World Development Indicators database. All calculations are done over the period 1990–2017.

Table A4
Number of Climate Litigation Cases by Jurisdiction

ISO Code	Total Number	Cases with a Pro-environment Decision	ISO Code	Total Number	Cases with a Pro-environment Decision
ARG	1	0	IRL	3	2
AUS	96	56	JPN	3	0
AUT	1	1	KEN	1	1
BEL	1	0	LUX	1	0
BRA	6	4	MEX	1	1
CAN	20	7	NGA	1	1
CHE	2	1	NLD	2	1
CHL	2	0	NOR	1	0
COL	2	2	NZL	17	6
CZE	1	0	PAK	4	2
DEU	5	2	PER	1	0
ECU	1	1	PHL	2	1
ESP	13	5	POL	2	0
EUU	57	37	SWE	1	0
FRA	11	6	UGA	1	0
GBR	60	28	UKR	2	1
IDN	1	8	USA	1,154	n/a
IND	10	0	ZAF	4	2
INT	18	11			

Note: This list includes the European Union (EUU) and International (INT) cases. n/a = not applicable. Refer to table A1 for definitions of the other ISO codes.

Endnotes

Author email addresses: Eskander (S.M.Eskander@lse.ac.uk), Fankhauser (s.fankhauser@lse.ac.uk), Setzer (j.setzer@lse.ac.uk). We acknowledge financial support from the Grantham Foundation for the Protection of the Environment, and from the UK Economic and Social Research Council (ESRC) through its support of the Centre for Climate Change Economics and Policy (CCCEP). We are grateful to Caterina Gennaioli, Matthew Kotchen, and Michal Nachmany for their insights and feedback. For acknowledgments, sources of research support, and disclosure of the authors' material financial relationships, if any, please see https://www.nber.org/books-and-chapters/environmental-and-energy-policy-and-economy-volume-2/global-lessons-climate-change-legislation-and-litigation.

1. Climate Change Laws of the World can be accessed at https://climate-laws.org. There are other databases, which focus on particular policy processes, sectors, or subsets of countries. The Climate Policy Database project (http://climatepolicydatabase.org) gathers information on which countries are implementing good-practice policies or policies to reduce carbon emissions. The International Energy Agency (IEA) Policies and Measures Database (https://www.iea.org/policies) provides access to information on past, existing, or planned government policies and measures to reduce GHG emissions, improve energy efficiency, and support the development and deployment of renewables and other clean energy technologies. ClimateWatch (https://www.climatewatchdata.org) tracks progress with NDCs to the Paris Agreement.

2. Information on climate change litigation in the United States is contained in a separate database maintained by the Sabin Center. The data can be accessed at http://climatecasechart.com/us-climate-change-litigation/. The database is maintained in collaboration with the law firm Arnold & Porter, to which the Sabin Center has close links.

3. Full text and summary available at https://climate-laws.org/cclow/geographies/united-kingdom/laws/climate-change-act-34405aa9-396e-4a78-a662-20cad9696365.

4. Full text and summary available at https://climate-laws.org/cclow/geographies/mexico/laws/general-law-on-climate-change. For challenges in implementing the law, see Averchenkova and Guzman Luna (2018).

5. Full text and summary available at https://climate-laws.org/cclow/geographies/new-zealand/laws/climate-change-response-act-2002-as-amended-by-the-climate-change-response-zero-carbon-amendment-act.

6. Full text and summary available at https://climate-laws.org/cclow/geographies/south-korea/laws/framework-act-on-low-carbon-green-growth-regulated-by-enforcement-decree-of-the-framework-act-on-low-carbon-green-growth.

7. The Worldwide Governance Indicators are collected by the World Bank and available on https://info.worldbank.org/governance/wgi/. The indicators reflect the views of a large number of enterprises, citizens, and experts on different aspects of governance, including inter alia the Rule of Law. The original scale was converted into a [0,1] range as follows: $g_i = (g_i^{orig} - g^{min})/(g^{max} - g^{min})$.

8. Polity IV is an annual, cross-national time series that assesses democratic and autocratic patterns of authority and regime changes in all independent countries. The data are available on https://www.systemicpeace.org/inscrdata.html.

9. DPI contains data on institutional and electoral factors, such as checks and balances, tenure and stability of the government, party affiliations, and ideology, among others. The data are available on https://datacatalog.worldbank.org/dataset/wps2283-database-political-institutions.

10. The Hodrick-Prescott filter (after Hodrick and Prescott 1997) is a common decomposition method used in macroeconomics. It is calculated in statistical packages like Stata (using the command "tsfilter hp").

References

Averchenkova, A., S. Fankhauser, and J. Finnegan. 2020. "The Impact of Strategic Climate Legislation: Evidence from Expert Interviews on the UK Climate Change Act." *Climate Policy*. https://doi.org/10.1080/14693062.2020.1819190.

Averchenkova, A., S. Fankhauser, and M. Nachmany, eds. 2017. *Trends in Climate Change Legislation*. Cheltenham: Edward Elgar.

Averchenkova, A., and S. Guzman Luna. 2018. "Mexico's General Law on Climate Change: Key Achievements and Challenges Ahead." Policy brief, Grantham Research Institute on Climate Change and the Environment and Centre for Climate Change Economics and Policy, London School of Economics and Political Science. http://www.lse.ac.uk/GranthamInstitute/wp-content/uploads/2018/11/Policy_brief_Mexico%E2%80%99s-General-Law-on-Climate-Change-Successes-and-challenges_8pp_AverchenkovaGuzman-2.pdf.

Barbier, E. B. 2010. *A Global Green New Deal: Rethinking the Economic Recovery*. Cambridge: Cambridge University Press.

Bouwer, K. 2018. "The Unsexy Future of Climate Change Litigation." *Journal of Environmental Law* 30 (3): 483–506. https://doi.org/10.1093/jel/eqy017.

Bowen, A., and N. Stern. 2010. "Environmental Policy and the Economic Downturn." *Oxford Review of Economic Policy* 26 (2): 137–63.

Burger, M., J. Gundlach, A. Kreilhuber, L. Ognibene, A. Kariuki, and A. Gachie. 2017. *The Status of Climate Change Litigation. A Global Review.* New York: United Nations Environment Programme. http://columbiaclimatelaw.com/files /2017/05/Burger-Gundlach-2017-05-UN-Envt-CC-Litigation.pdf.

Carter, N. 2018. *The Politics of the Environment: Ideas, Activism, Policy.* Cambridge: Cambridge University Press.

Carter, N., R. Ladrech, C. Little, and V. Tsagkroni. 2018. "Political Parties and Climate Policy: A New Approach to Measuring Parties' Climate Policy Preferences." *Party Politics* 24 (6): 731–42.

Doda, B. 2014. "Evidence on Business Cycles and CO_2 Emissions." *Journal of Macroeconomics* 40:214–27.

Dubash, N. K., M. Hagemann, N. Höhne, and P. Upadhyaya. 2013. "Developments in National Climate Change Mitigation Legislation and Strategy." *Climate Policy* 13 (6): 649–64.

Eskander, S., and S. Fankhauser. 2020. "Reduction in Greenhouse Gas Emissions by National Climate Laws and Policies." *Nature Climate Change* 10 (8): 750–756.

Fankhauser, S., C. Gennaioli, and M. Collins. 2015a. "The Political Economy of Passing Climate Change Legislation: Evidence from a Survey." *Global Environmental Change* 35:52–61.

———. 2015b. "Do International Factors Influence the Passage of Climate Change Legislation?" *Climate Policy* 16 (3): 318–31.

Hepburn, C., B. O'Callaghan, N. Stern, J. Stiglitz, and D. Zenghelis. 2020. "Will COVID-19 Fiscal Recovery Packages Accelerate or Retard Progress on Climate Change?" *Oxford Review of Economic Policy* 36:3–17.

Hilson, C. J. 2012. "UK Climate Change Litigation: Between Hard and Soft Framing." In *Criminological and Legal Consequences of Climate Change*, ed. S. Farrall, T. Ahmed, and D. French. Oxford: Hart.

Hodrick, R. J., and E. C. Prescott. 1997. "Postwar US Business Cycles: An Empirical Investigation." *Journal of Money, Credit, and Banking* 29 (1): 1–16.

Hughes, L. 2019. "The Rocky Hill Decision: A Watershed for Climate Change Action?" *Journal of Energy and Natural Resources Law.* https://doi.org/10 .1080/02646811.2019.1600272.

Iacobuta, G., N. K. Dubash, P. Upadhyaya, M. Deribe, and N. Höhne. 2018. "National Climate Change Mitigation Legislation, Strategy and Targets: A Global Update." *Climate Policy* 18 (9): 1114–32.

Jodoin, S., R. Faucher, and K. Lofts. 2018. "Look Before You Jump: Assessing the Potential Influence of the Human Rights Bandwagon on Domestic Climate Policy." In *Routledge Handbook of Human Rights and Climate Governance*, ed. S. Duyck, S. Jodoin, and A. Johl, 167–82. New York: Routledge.

Jordan, A., D. Huitema, H. Van Asselt, and J. Forster, eds. 2018. *Governing Climate Change: Polycentricity in Action?* Cambridge: Cambridge University Press.

Kahn, M., and M. Kotchen. 2010. "Environmental Concern and the Business Cycle: The Chilling Effect of Recession." Working Paper no. 16241, NBER, Cambridge, MA.

Kaufman, D., A. Kraay, and M. Mastruzzi. 2010. "The Worldwide Governance Indicators: Methodology and Analytical Issues." Policy Research Working Paper no. 5430, World Bank, Washington, DC. http://papers.ssrn.com /sol3/papers.cfm?abstract_id=1682130.

Markell, D. L., and J. B. Ruhl. 2012. "An Empirical Assessment of Climate Change in the Courts: A New Jurisprudence or Business as Usual?" *Florida Law Review* 64 (1): 15–86.

Mavisakalyan, A., and Y. Tarverdi. 2019. "Gender and Climate Change: Do Female Parliamentarians Make Difference?" *European Journal of Political Economy* 56:151–64.

McCormick, S., R. L. Glicksman, S. J. Simmens, L. Paddock, D. Kim, and B. Whited. 2018. "Strategies in and Outcomes of Climate Change Litigation in the United States." *Nature Climate Change* 8:829–33.

McCright, A., and R. Dunlap. 2011a. "The Politicization of Climate Change and Polarization in the American Public's Views of Global Warming, 2001–2010." *Sociological Quarterly* 52 (2): 155–94.

———. 2011b. "Cool Dudes: The Denial of Climate Change among Conservative White Males in the United States." *Global Environmental Change* 21 (4): 1163–72.

Muinzer, T. L. 2018. *Climate and Energy Governance for the UK Low Carbon Transition: The Climate Change Act 2008.* Cham: Palgrave Pivot.

Nachmany, M., and E. Mangan. 2018. "Aligning National and International Climate Targets." Policy brief, Grantham Research Institute on Climate Change and the Environment, London School of Economics. http://www.lse.ac.uk/GranthamInstitute/publication/targets/.

Nash, S., and R. Steurer. 2019. "Taking Stock of Climate Change Acts in Europe: Living Policy Processes or Symbolic Gestures?" *Climate Policy* 19 (8): 1052–65.

Neumayer, E. 2003. "Are Left-Wing Party Strength and Corporatism Good for the Environment? Evidence from Panel Analysis of Air Pollution in OECD Countries." *Ecological Economics* 45 (2): 203–20.

Osofsky, H. M. 2012. "Litigation's Role in the Path of U.S. Federal Climate Change Regulation: Implications of AEP v. Connecticut." *Valparaiso University Law Review* 46:447–57. https://scholarship.law.umn.edu/faculty_articles/187.

Painter, J., and T. Ashe. 2012. "Cross-National Comparison of the Presence of Climate Scepticism in the Print Media in Six Countries, 2007–10." *Environmental Research Letters* 7 (4): 044005.

Peel, J. 2011. "Issues in Climate Change Litigation." *Carbon and Climate Law Review* 5 (1): 15–24. https://doi.org/10.21552/CCLR/2011/1/162.

Peel, J., and J. Lin. 2019. "Transnational Climate Litigation: The Contribution of the Global South." *American Journal of International Law* 113 (4): 679–726.

Peel, J., and H. M. Osofsky. 2015. *Climate Change Litigation Regulatory Pathways to Cleaner Energy.* Cambridge, MA: Cambridge University Press.

Preston, B. J. 2011. "Climate Change Litigation (Part 1)." *Carbon and Climate Law Review* 5 (1): 3–14.

Rogelj, J., M. Den Elzen, N. Höhne, T. Fransen, H. Fekete, H. Winkler, R. Schaeffer, F. Sha, K. Riahi, and M. Meinshausen. 2016. "Paris Agreement Climate Proposals Need a Boost to Keep Warming Well Below 2°C." *Nature* 534 (7609): 631–39.

Scotford, E., and S. Minas. 2019. "Probing the Hidden Depths of Climate Law: Analysing National Climate Change Legislation." *Review of European, Comparative and International Environmental Law* 28 (1): 67–81.

Setzer, J., and M. Bangalore. 2017. "Regulating Climate Change in the Courts." In *Trends in Climate Change Legislation*, ed. A. Averchenkova, S. Fankhauser, and M. Nachmany, 175–92. London: Edward Elgar.

Setzer, J., and L. Benjamin. 2020. "Climate Litigation in the Global South: Constraints and Innovations." *Transnational Environmental Law* 9 (1): 77–101.

Setzer, J., and R. Byrnes. 2019. "Global Trends in Climate Change Litigation: 2019 Snapshot." Policy report, Grantham Research Institute on Climate Change and the Environment, London School of Economics. http://www.lse.ac.uk /GranthamInstitute/wp-content/uploads/2019/07/GRI_Global-trends-in -climate-change-litigation-2019-snapshot.pdf.

Setzer, J., and L. C. Vanhala. 2019. "Climate Change Litigation: A Review of Research on Courts and Litigants in Climate Governance." *Wiley Interdisciplinary Reviews: Climate Change* 10 (3): e580.

Solana, J. 2020. "Climate Litigation in Financial Markets: A Typology." *Transnational Environmental Law* 9 (1): 103–135.

Townshend, T., S. Fankhauser, R. Aybar, M. Collins, T. Landesman, M. Nachmany, and C. Pavese. 2013. "How National Legislation Can Help to Solve Climate Change." *Nature Climate Change* 3 (May): 430–32.

Townshend, T., S. Fankhauser, A. Matthews, C. Feger, J. Liu, and T. Narciso. 2011. "Legislating Climate Change at the National Level." *Environment* 53 (5): 5–16.

Verschuuren, J. 2019. "The State of the Netherlands v Urgenda Foundation: The Hague Court of Appeal Upholds Judgment Requiring the Netherlands to Further Reduce Its Greenhouse Gas Emissions." *Review of European, Comparative and International Environmental Law* 28 (1): 94–98.

Wilensky, M. 2015. "Climate Change in the Courts: An Assessment of Non-U.S. Climate Litigation." *Duke Environmental Law and Policy Forum* 26 (1): 131–79.

Zenghelis, D. 2012. "A Strategy for Restoring Confidence and Economic Growth through Green Investment and Innovation." Policy brief, Grantham Research Institute on Climate Change and the Environment, London School of Economics. http://www.lse.ac.uk/GranthamInstitute/publication /a-strategy-for-restoring-confidence-and-economic-growth-through-green -investment-and-innovation/.

Revenue at Risk in Coal-Reliant Counties

Adele C. Morris, *The Brookings Institution,* United States of America

Noah Kaufman, *Columbia University,* United States of America

Siddhi Doshi, *The Brookings Institution,* United States of America

Executive Summary

This paper examines the implications of a carbon-constrained future on coal-reliant county governments in the United States. We review modeling projections of coal production and argue that some local governments face important revenue risks. Complex systems of revenue and intergovernmental transfers and insufficiently detailed budget data make it difficult to parse out how exposed jurisdictions are to the coal industry. A look at three illustrative counties shows that coal-related revenue may fund a third or more of their budgets. When extrapolated outside the sample, our regression analysis of 27 coal-reliant counties suggests that the demise of coal could lower these counties' revenue by about 20%. This does not account for the potential downward spiral of other revenues and economic activity as the collapse of the dominant industry erodes the tax base. Coal-dependent communities have issued outstanding bonds that will mature in a period in which climate policy is likely. Our review of illustrative bonds indicates that municipalities have not appropriately characterized their coal-related risks. Climate policies can be combined with investments in coal-dependent communities to support their financial health. We discuss how a small fraction of revenue from a federal carbon price could fund assistance to coal-dependent communities and workers.

JEL Codes: H2, H7, H71, H74, H83, Q32, Q4, Q48, Q5, Q52, Q54, Q58, R11

Keywords: coal, local public finance, carbon tax, climate policy, severance tax, industrial collapse, fiscal risk, municipal bonds

I. Introduction

Some governments across the United States rely heavily on revenues that derive directly or indirectly from fossil fuel production. Those most reliant on coal face a particularly risky fiscal future. Coal production in the United States has already declined significantly over the past decade, and if federal climate policy is implemented, coal production is likely to decline even more precipitously. In that scenario, coal-dependent jurisdictions will experience a steep fall in economic activity, shrinking revenue, falling property values, and a dislocated workforce. Policy makers may be able to head off some of this disproportionate burden with the right mix of offsetting policies, but much research remains to ascertain the most effective approaches.

We begin with a review of the history of US coal production and projections with and without new policies, including evidence on where in the United States climate policy will have the greatest effect on coal production. Then we analyze revenue and budget data for select county governments across the United States to understand their dependence on coal and how their fiscal conditions are likely to deteriorate in a carbon-constrained future. We find that coal-related revenue may fund a third or more of their budgets. Regression analysis of 27 coal-reliant counties outside the same suggests they could lose on average about 20% of their revenue with the demise of the industry. To learn from other contexts, we consider previous instances in which geographically concentrated industries have collapsed and explore the extent to which policy responses buffered the effect.[1]

Coal-dependent communities have issued a variety of outstanding bonds, and the risk of collapse of the coal industry threatens their ability to repay them. Our review of illustrative bonds indicates that municipalities have not appropriately characterized their coal-related risks. Ratings reports are only now beginning to document the risks associated with the exposure of some local governments to the coal industry.

Climate policies can be combined with investments in coal-dependent communities to support their financial health. A logical source of funding for such investments would be the revenues from a price on carbon dioxide emissions, which could be part of a cost-effective strategy for addressing the risks of climate change. We discuss how a small fraction of revenue from a federal carbon price in the United States could fund billions of dollars in annual investments in the economic development of coal-dependent communities and direct assistance to coal industry workers.

II. Quantifying the Fiscal Exposure to Coal

To understand the coal industry's profound effects on economic conditions in coal-producing jurisdictions, it helps to reflect on how dramatically

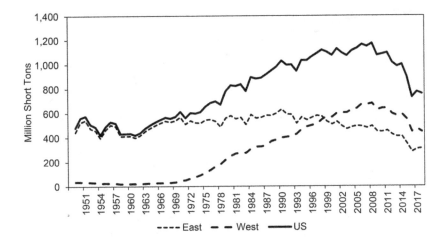

Fig. 1. Tons of Coal Output per Year, by United States Region (1949–2018)
Source: US Energy Information Administration.

production has shifted in recent years and how climate policy could hasten the decline of the industry. As shown in figure 1, US coal consumption nearly tripled between the early 1960s and 2000s, with growth disproportionately in the Powder River Basin in Wyoming and Montana. The abundant resource led to fiscal systems that depended on it, and from a distributional standpoint it made sense to pass the incidence to out-of-state coal buyers. But between 2007 and 2017, the tide turned, and total coal production in the United States declined by 32%.

As shown in figure 2, coal remains the second-largest fuel for electricity generation in the country, trailing only natural gas, and generates more than one-quarter of all US electricity (EIA 2019a). The United States has not had a federal climate policy, but much like a carbon price would, the declining price of natural gas over the past decade has made coal-fired power plants less competitive relative to natural gas-fired power plants (Cullen and Mansur 2017). This has been the primary driver of the decline in coal use (Coglianese, Gerarden, and Stock 2020). To a lesser extent, other factors also drove coal's decline, including declining costs of renewable power, slower-than-expected increases in US electricity demand (caused by the Great Recession and improved efficiency), weak exports, and air quality regulations (Houser, Bordoff, and Marsters 2017; Kolstad 2017). Coal-fired power plant retirements peaked in 2015 when the Mercury and Air Toxics Standards rule went into effect (EIA 2018), but retirements in 2018 were not far behind. As shown in figure 3, industrial uses of coal have not offset its decline in the US power sector.

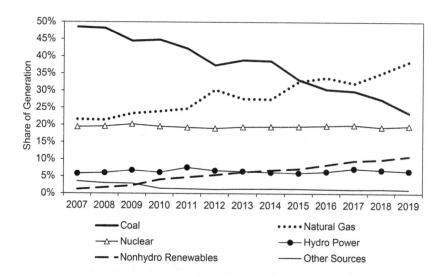

Fig. 2. Composition of US Electricity Generation by Energy Source
Source: US Energy Information Administration, *Short-Term Energy Outlook*, April 2020.

Employment declines for coal workers have largely mirrored coal production levels, but mining productivity improvements have amplified the trend. At coal's employment peak in the 1920s, 860,000 Americans worked in the industry. In the second half of the twentieth century,

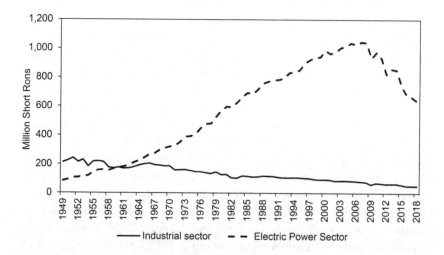

Fig. 3. US Coal Consumption by Sector
Source: US Energy Information Administration. Note: Two series have been merged to achieve continuity of data.

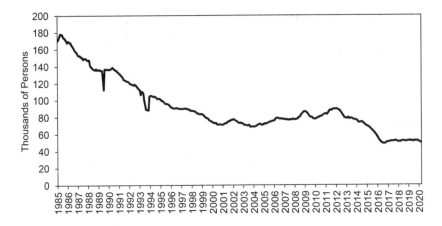

Fig. 4. US Coal Mining Employment

Source: US Bureau of Labor Statistics.

improvements in technology began to cut into the coal industry's labor demand, and by 2003, only 70,000 US coal workers remained. Labor productivity in US coal mining (i.e., tons of coal production per hour of work by miners) has not increased since the early 2000s (Kolstad 2017), suggesting the recent decline in employment has been caused primarily by the decline in production levels. As shown in figure 4, as of March 2020, coal mining employed only about 50,000 people.

The most concentrated job losses have been in Appalachia. Employment in the coal mining industry declined by more than 50% in West Virginia, Ohio, and Kentucky between 2011 and 2016. State-level effects mask even more severe effects at local levels. In Mingo County, West Virginia, coal mining employed more than 1,400 people at the end of 2011. By the end of 2016, that number had fallen below 500. Countywide, employment fell from 8,513 to 4,878 over this period (Houser et al. 2017), suggesting important labor market spillovers from mining to the broader economy.

A. The Future of US Coal Production

The decline of the US coal industry thus far begs the question of its future. A wide range of future outcomes are possible. Even if natural gas prices do not fall further and no new policies are adopted, projections suggest that coal consumption and production will continue to decline over the next decade, perhaps to 15%–25% below 2018 levels (Larsen et al. 2018; EIA 2019b). The long-run effects of the coronavirus pandemic and its economic consequences are uncertain, but in the short run, coal demand is down significantly. The US Energy Information Administration (EIA) forecasts that 2020 US coal production will total 537 million short tons (MMst) in 2020, down 22% from 2019. Lower production reflects declining demand for coal in the electric power sector, lower demand for US exports, and a number of coal mines that have been idled for extended periods as a result of COVID-19.[2] To the extent that the sinking global economy also reduces steel demand, a decline in the production of metallurgical coal is also in the picture.

If policy makers adopt measures to control greenhouse gas emissions, estimates suggest future declines in coal are likely to be much larger and permanent. This is the even more fraught scenario facing coal-reliant local governments. An extensive literature explores the potential effects of different climate policy options in the United States. The EIA uses the National Energy Modeling System (NEMS) to project policy outcomes relative to a no-new-policy reference case. In its 2018 *Annual Energy Outlook*, the EIA examined the implications of putting a price on emissions of CO_2 from the power sector only. This "side case" imposes a price of $25 per metric ton of CO_2 in 2020, rising at 5% over inflation each year thereafter. Under this side case, the EIA projects a rapid decline in total US coal production such that by 2030 total US coal production will be 78% below 2018 levels (see fig. 5).

The EIA projects that the sharpest reduction in coal mining would occur in Wyoming's Powder River Basin, currently the source of nearly 40% of US coal. In the EIA's carbon price side case, Powder River Basin

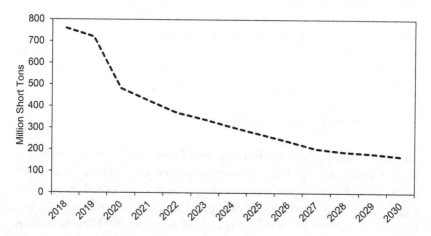

Fig. 5.   US Coal Production under EIA $25+ per ton scenario
Source: US Energy Information Administration.

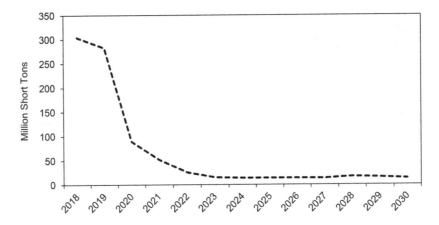

Fig. 6.   Powder River Basin Coal Production under EIA $25+ per ton scenario
Source: US Energy Information Administration.

coal production declines by 95% between 2016 and 2030 (fig. 6). One explanation is that Powder River Basin coal is overwhelmingly subbituminous coal from surface mines that is burned at power plants in the United States. The EIA projects that coal produced elsewhere in the western United States would experience a similarly dramatic and rapid decline.

The EIA projections for the $25 per ton carbon price scenario also show a collapse in coal production from the midwestern and southeastern United States, although not quite as rapid as in the western region. As shown in figure 7, coal production from northern Appalachia (accounting for 16% of current US production and comprised of Pennsylvania, Ohio, Maryland, and northern West Virginia) declines by nearly 80% between 2016 and 2030, whereas production from central and southern Appalachia and the Eastern Interior region (accounting for a quarter of US production and comprised of southern West Virginia, Kentucky, Illinois, Indiana, Mississippi, Alabama, Virginia, and Tennessee) falls by roughly half over that period.

One should interpret the results from any single energy model with caution given the large uncertainties in future technologies, economic activity, and behavior of consumers and producers. We focus here on projections from the NEMS model because of its prominence and its publicly available and regionally disaggregated results.

Other modeling teams have analyzed policies like the EIA side case. They also project that climate change policy would cause large and rapid declines in the US coal industry, though not necessarily as rapid as projected by the EIA. For example, as part of the Stanford Energy Model

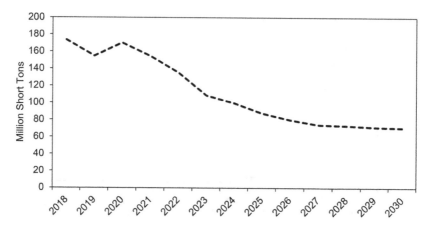

Fig. 7. Appalachia Region Coal Production under EIA $25+ per ton scenario
Source: US Energy Information Administration.

Forum project 32 (EMF 32), 11 modeling teams analyzed the effects of an economy-wide US CO_2 tax starting at $25 per metric ton in 2020 and increasing at 5% over inflation per year (McFarland et al. 2018). Figure 8 displays the results, which show that on average, national coal consumption would fall relative to current levels by about 60% by 2030 as compared with a decline of nearly 80% over a similar time period in the EIA's power-sector-only $25 per ton scenario.

Few of the EMF 32 modelers estimated the policy's effects on US coal production by region. One exception is the NewERA model, from NERA Economic Consulting.[3] NERA's results are similar on a nationwide basis to those of the EIA (see fig. 9), although the authors find the decline is more equally distributed across the east and west regions of the country.

Some may hope that with appropriate research and development, coal could be saved by deploying carbon capture and storage (CCS) technologies, which strip CO_2 from waste gases and sequester them permanently underground. At one point, this may have been plausible. In the late 2000s when Congress last seriously debated comprehensive climate change policy, the American Clean Energy and Security Act[4] included numerous provisions intended to preserve coal use with CCS technologies. However, the decline since then in coal's economics relative to natural gas and renewables suggests CCS cannot save the coal industry.

Modeling bears this out. By the time the carbon price is high enough to warrant CCS, coal is already largely displaced, and CCS comes in with natural gas. Only one of the eleven models participating in EMF 32 showed any significant deployment of coal-fired electricity with CCS

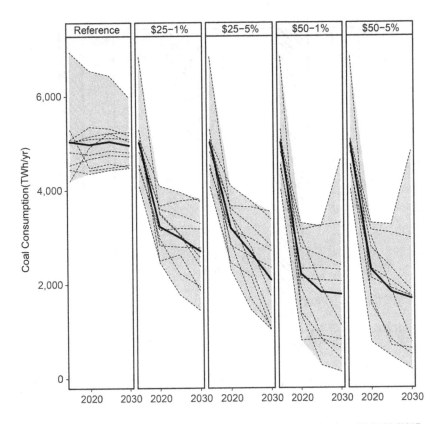

Fig. 8. US Coal Consumption under Four Carbon Tax Trajectories from EMF 32 (2015–2030)

Note: Gray bands represent the range of model results. Dashed lines show the individual model results, and the solid lines show the average value. The column titles report the initial carbon tax rates per metric ton of CO_2 (e.g., $25) in 2020 and the rate of real increase in the tax each year thereafter (e.g., 1%).

between 2020 and 2040, even in the highest carbon tax scenario (Environment and Climate Change Canada's multisector, multiregion [EC-MSMR] Computable General Equilibrium model; McFarland et al. 2018). Another recent study of a federal US carbon tax that rises to $115 per metric ton by 2030 shows that such a policy could result in significant deployments of natural gas with CCS (about 15% of US generation by 2030) but no significant deployment of coal with CCS (Kaufman et al. 2019, 17).

To be sure, strong national climate policy in the United States is not certain. Experts have long recommended strong policy action to reduce emissions, and for years, policy makers have largely ignored their advice. Nevertheless, with growing support by the public and policy makers,

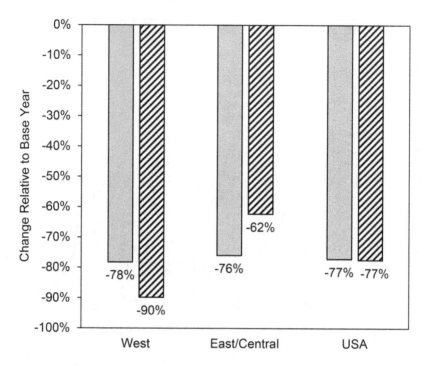

Fig. 9.   Change in Coal Production, \$25+ CO_2 Price Scenarios
Source: NEMS data are from the EIA's side case from its *Annual Energy Outlook 2018*. NewERA data are from authors of the EMF 32 exercise.

meaningful climate policy in the United States may be on the horizon, and those dependent on coal have new risks to manage.

B.   Revenue from Coal Production

How might the projected declines in coal production translate into revenue declines for state and local governments? Ideally, we would project coal production in both no-policy and climate policy scenarios, estimate the respective revenue streams that coal generates, and compare the two outcomes. This is harder than it sounds.

For one thing, the way state and local governments collect and spend coal revenue varies widely, and the types of revenue instruments, tax rates, and intergovernmental transfers differ across states and substate governments (Headwater Economics 2017). For example, in some places and for some taxes, coal revenue goes directly to county governments and local school districts. In other cases, it flows to counties or school systems via coal-funded state trust funds, and some states use coal revenue to pay directly for public services that would otherwise fall to counties, such as construction and maintenance of county roads. This means that the translation between coal production and fiscal flows to local governments is complicated.

Even tracking revenues just from sources directly tied to coal is challenging.[5] Typically, state mineral severance taxes are a percentage of gross or net value at the point of production, but some states apply it to the volume of production.[6] Severance tax rates and bases vary widely across and within states, by type of mineral or well or by volume of production.[7] Severance taxes can apply to production on both private and public land. Owing to variations in both production quantities and commodity prices, revenue from severance taxes can be volatile. It can also amplify the fiscal effects of a downturn in the coal industry. For example, in West Virginia, severance taxes raised $483 million in 2011, or 12% of general revenue. In 2016, severance taxes fell to $262 million, or 6% of general revenue.

States also receive royalties, lease bonuses, and rents from mineral production on state lands, and the federal government gives states a cut of the royalties from production on federal lands in their jurisdictions. Royalties are a payment for extracted resources, determined by a percentage of the resources' production value.[8] A lease bonus is a payment to the landowner upon the signing of the mineral lease. Royalty rates to state governments are typically set in law, but lease auctions often determine the bonus payments. Lessees may also be subject to annual administrative fees and rent payments, which are usually a small share of their overall payments to the state. Royalty receipts vary significantly, owing in part to variation in the patterns of land ownership across states, even ones that are major fossil energy producers. For example, more than 61% of the land in Alaska is administered by federal government agencies, whereas the federal government administers less than 2% of Texas land (Vincent, Hanson, and Argueta 2017). As documented by Fitzgerald (2014), western states have retained relatively more state-owned land and are more likely to have active leasing programs.

The typical federal royalty rate is 12.5% of the gross value of production (US Government Accountability Office 2017). According to Tax Foundation calculations, state governments receive about 17.5% of the royalties the federal government collects (Malm 2013).

Finally, in some cases states set local tax rates and bases, collect taxes, and/or distribute the revenues. So even when the volume of dollars flowing is clear, who controls the spigots may not be. Given the wide variation in the channels of fiscal exposure of substate governments to coal, we focus on the finances of a few illustrative jurisdictions and learn what we can through their particulars. We chose three illustrative counties in three different states: Campbell County in Wyoming, Boone County in West Virginia, and Mercer County in North Dakota.

C. Finances of Illustrative Coal-Reliant Counties

The US Department of Agriculture's (USDA) Economic Research Service defines a county as "mining dependent" if 8% or more of its employment is engaged in the mining industry (US Department of Agriculture 2019). Applying that threshold to 2015 employment data (the most recent year available), 27 counties across 10 states in the United States are coal mining dependent. Figure 10 shows the top 12 counties, each with more than 13% of their 2015 labor force tied to coal mining.

Figure 10 shows that Boone County, West Virginia, and Campbell County, Wyoming, have the highest labor shares in coal mining. To choose a third county in another state, we skip over tiny Oliver County, North Dakota (population 1,898) to its larger neighbor, Mercer County

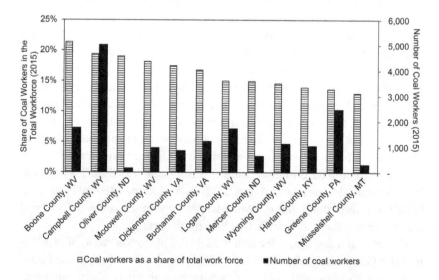

Fig. 10.   Top 12 US Counties by Coal Employment Share
Source: US Bureau of Labor Statistics.

(population 8,267).[9] These are three of the most coal mining dependent counties in the United States, so they represent the most coal-exposed economies. Further research is necessary to consider the fiscal implications of climate policy in coal-reliant counties that are also dependent on natural gas and oil production. Our focus is strictly on coal because modeling suggests that coal would be the fossil fuel most rapidly and dramatically wrung out of the economy under climate policies, but we do not intend to suggest that dependence on the other fuels is unimportant, particularly over the longer run.

Although we primarily discuss revenues to the county governments themselves, each county also contains a collection of municipalities, school systems, and special districts, such as for libraries and fire departments. Each of these has its own exposure to the coal industry via state funds, property tax revenues, and the like.

Boone County, West Virginia

Boone County (population 22,000) lies in southern West Virginia and forms part of the Central Appalachian coal basin. Along with other southern West Virginia counties, it has long been a center of coal extraction (US Department of the Interior 2016). The county revenue directly from coal is primarily from property and severance taxes. Because coal production has already fallen dramatically in Boone County, its challenges illustrate the trouble that may face other coal-reliant jurisdictions. Property taxes fund both county governments and school systems in West Virginia. Proceeds from coal severance taxes flow to local governments primarily via transfers from the state; percentage points of the 5% severance tax go to the state government.[10] The state distributes 75% of the remaining 0.35 percentage points to coal-producing counties and 25% to other counties and municipalities (West Virginia Treasurer's Office 2015, 11).

Coal-producing counties in West Virginia can recapture some of the state's share when they face budget shortfalls, a policy known as a reallocation tax. This revenue funds the county commission, jails, community programs, public transit, the health department, and trash collection activities. The most recent data that distinguish coal-related revenue from other revenue are from 2015. The numbers suggest that about a third of Boone County's revenues directly depended on coal in the form of property taxes on coal mines and severance taxes. In 2015, 21% of Boone County's labor force and 17% of its total personal income were tied to coal.[11] Coal property (including both the mineral deposit and industrial equipment) amounted to 57% of Boone County's total property valuation.[12] Property taxes on all property generated about half of Boone County's general fund budget,[13] which means that property taxes just on coal brought in around 30% of the county's general fund. Property taxes on coal also funded about $14.2 million of the $60.3 million school budget (24%).[14]

In total, coal-related property taxes generated approximately $21 million for Boone County's schools, the county government, and specific services.[15] In addition, Boone County received more than $1.6 million from severance taxes and an additional $800,000 from the reallocation tax.[16] In 2012, 31 mines in the county produced 16.4 MMst of coal. Just 5 years later in 2017, only 11 mines remained, producing only 5.0 MMst, a 70% decline.[17] This resulted in a 50% decline in property tax revenue for the county government and a 38% decline in its total revenue.[18] Coal prices were fairly flat over the period, so the relationship is mostly a function of the volumes of coal produced.

Revenue declines have driven painful spending cuts. In 2015, Boone County closed three of its 10 elementary schools (Jenkins 2015). Bankruptcies of coal companies left the county with $8 million in uncollected property tax revenue in 2015 (Kent 2016), and West Virginia passed an emergency bill for school funding in 2016 to provide for a $9 million shortfall due to one such bankruptcy (WSAZ News 2016). To make up for these shortfalls, Boone County cut back services such as its solid waste program. To attract more investment and employment by coal companies, West Virginia passed two bills in 2019 giving tax breaks to the coal industry. House Bill 3142 reduces for 2 years the severance tax rate from 5% to 3% on coal that is used in power plants.[19] House Bill 3144 creates a 35% investment tax credit that would offset up to 80% of a coal company's severance tax liability.[20]

Campbell County, Wyoming

Campbell County (population 46,170) lies in northeast Wyoming in the Powder River Basin.[21] It is home to the largest coal mine in the world, and mining is its largest sector, employing about 20% of the county's labor force (Campbell County Board of County Commissioners 2017). In Wyoming, coal generates government revenues through four main instruments: property taxes, federal mineral royalties, coal lease bonuses, and severance taxes. The generation and flow of these revenues to local governments is complex.[22] Some coal-related revenue goes directly to local governments. Coal-related revenues to the state travel via various trust funds to a myriad of substate jurisdictions. Some are targeted to specific local expenditure categories, and some amounts are contingent on whether a certain revenue threshold is exceeded. If one wanted to design a fiscal system to obscure local governments' full dependence on coal production, it would be hard to improve on the current approach in Wyoming.

The composition of 2018 revenues to the Campbell County government appears in figure 11 (Campbell County 2018a, 25). The property tax generates more than half of the county's tax revenue. It includes the county tax on assessed property values and an ad valorem tax on the value of minerals extracted in the county, including coal, natural gas, and oil. The next-largest revenue sources are the sales and use tax and intergovernmental transfers.

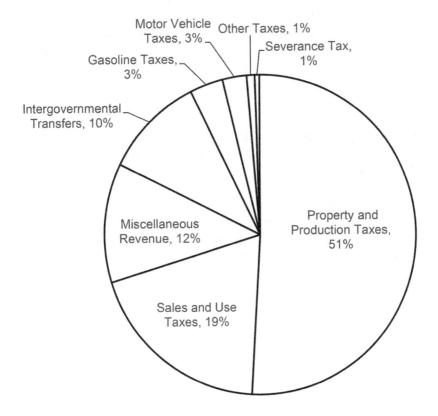

Fig. 11. Campbell County Revenue Sources, Fiscal Year 2018
Source: Campbell County Audit, FY Ending June 2018.

The coal-specific share of the wedges in figure 11 is difficult to parse out but includes the coal share of the property and production tax, the coal-related share of sales and use tax proceeds, and some of the transfers from the state and federal governments. According to the county's 2018 audit statement, mineral production taxes comprise about 81% of the property and production tax, but how much was from coal is not specified (Campbell County 2018a, 51).

A 2017 special report by the Campbell County Board of Commissioners sheds some light on this. Of the $5.3 billion in total county assessed property valuation (which includes the value of minerals produced) in the 2016–17 fiscal year, 89% was oil and gas production and coal mining and their associated production and transportation facilities (Campbell County Board of Commissioners 2017, 10). More narrowly, 79% was from mineral production, and coal was 75% of that, meaning in that year, about 59% of the county's overall property and production valuation was directly associated with coal mining (Campbell County Board of Commissioners 2017, 37). In that same year, 29% of the county's total sales and use tax revenue came from mining, but the share from coal per se is not reported. Likewise, it is unclear what shares of intergovernmental transfers flow from state coal-related revenues.

Coal revenues are falling. In 2018, including revenues to the county government, the school system, and other special districts within the county, the property and production tax in Campbell County raised more than $266 million. This was a sharp decline from 2016, when those collections were more than $317 million (Wyoming Department of Revenue 2018, 17–23).

County officials recognize the challenge of a declining coal-related tax base. The county's fiscal year 2017–18 report addresses the issue directly: assessed valuation for the 2015–16 fiscal year (derived from 2014 calendar year production and property) was $6.2 billion. The assessed valuation for the 2016–17 fiscal year declined to $5.3 billion and then to $4.2 billion for the 2017–18 fiscal year. Proactive decisions by this board, and previous boards, helped to make this transition as painless as possible because of substantial investments in savings and reserves, a relatively new age of facilities and plants, and an early retirement incentive that lowered employment expenses. It is important for Campbell County to effectively plan for a future with significantly less coal production and the ad valorem taxes that it pays (Campbell County 2018b, 3–4).

To prepare for a future with lower coal production, the county established reserve and maintenance funds for capital replacement, vehicle fleet management, buildings, and recreation facilities. Nonetheless, concerns are rising that coal production in Wyoming is declining faster than the area can absorb (Richards 2019). Wind power development in the Midwest is dampening demand for coal in key markets, and natural gas prices remain low. Layoffs at Powder River Basin coal mines follow the pandemic-driven declines in power demand.

Like Boone County, Campbell County has experienced the costs of coal-related bankruptcies, and more could be on the horizon. The 2015 bankruptcy of coal producer Alpha Natural Resources left Campbell County with more than $20 million in unpaid taxes. Campbell County litigated and collected most of the money, but its legal expenses were significant. Subsequently, local leaders have called for changes in laws and tax collection structures in Wyoming to place the interests of taxing entities above investors and creditors (Campbell County 2018; McKim 2018).

Mercer County, North Dakota

Mercer County is in central North Dakota. Along with its neighbors, McLean County and Oliver County, Mercer County is home to the largest mines in North Dakota. These counties primarily produce lignite coal, nearly 80% of which is used to generate electricity. In 2015, the mining sector employed about 15% of Mercer County's labor force.[23]

Compared with Wyoming and West Virginia, the North Dakota government is less dependent on the coal industry (North Dakota Tax Commissioner 2018, 3). However, coal-producing counties like Mercer are highly dependent on coal and would face major shortfalls if the industry collapses. Three main county revenue streams derive from coal-related revenue at the state level that the state then transfers to counties and other substate jurisdictions. The most important is the coal severance tax. The state deposits 30% of the revenue from the severance tax into a permanent trust fund that distributes construction loans to school districts, cities, and counties affected by coal development (North Dakota Tax Commissioner 2018, 16). The remaining 70% is distributed to counties. The state also imposes a coal conversion tax on operators of facilities that produce electricity from coal or convert coal to gaseous fuels or other products.[24] Third, North Dakota distributes half of its share of federal mineral royalties to counties in proportion of their mineral production and the other half to school districts (North Dakota Tax Commissioner 2018, 16).

The North Dakota state government provides documentation of its payments to substate jurisdictions, so we can quantify the flows to

Mercer County. According to the North Dakota state tax website, in 2018, Mercer County government received $1.3 million in coal severance tax distributions, $0.84 million in coal conversion taxes, and $0.37 million in mineral royalty distributions (North Dakota State Treasurer n.d.). We do not know how much of the mineral royalty distribution is related specifically to coal.

The most recent Mercer County audit report is from 2016, so we can put the coal revenue in context for that year. According to the audit statement for the year ending December 31, 2016, the Mercer County general fund received $1.71 million from coal severance taxes, $1.25 million from coal conversion taxes, and $0.76 million from mineral royalty revenue (Mercer County, North Dakota 2016). Overall county general revenues were $7.5 million, making the three sources about half of all county revenues. The exposure is compounded because school districts and other special districts within Mercer County also receive coal-dependent revenue.

III.   Analysis of Revenue's Relationship with Coal Production

The three counties illustrate the variety of coal-related fiscal flows in specific areas. Next we endeavor to generalize the relationship between county-level revenue and coal production across a broader set of coal-intensive counties. We first calculate county-level revenue from the US Census Bureau's Annual Survey of State and Local Government Finances for the years 2012 through 2017. Revenue includes taxes, intergovernmental transfers, utility and alcohol tax revenue, and social insurance revenue. In some regressions, labeled "county government revenue," we include only revenue that goes directly to the county government. In others, labeled "total revenue," we also include revenue to special (e.g., sewer) and school districts in the county. We exclude revenue to townships in all cases. We adjust all revenue figures to 2018 dollars using the Consumer Price Index for Urban Consumers.

We aggregate the EIA's mine-level coal production data, which include both surface and underground coal mines, to compute county-level coal production for each year from 2012 to 2017. We lag the coal production variable by 1 year to reflect the typical delay between coal production levels and the subsequent revenue collections. We include in our regression state-level fixed effects to control for the different revenue structures across states and other time-invariant state characteristics. We also include year effects to account for broad trends in coal markets and the macroeconomy.

Table 1
Summary Statistics for 27 Coal-Reliant Counties

All 27 Coal-Intensive Counties 2012–2017	Mean	Standard Deviation	Minimum	Maximum
All revenue (2018 $1,000)	95,225	117,124	7,071	524,884
County revenue (2018 $1,000)	30,232	33,230	1,840	147,035
Coal production in short tons, lagged 1 year (1,000)	22,895	67,457	654	389,022
Share of coal employment in labor force	.133	.038	.084	.214

We include all 27 counties that had (as of 2015) at least 8% of their labor force in coal mining, mirroring the definition of a mining-dependent jurisdiction used by the USDA. The summary statistics appear in table 1.

Mean total revenue is roughly triple mean county revenue, demonstrating that revenue to school and special districts is a large share of overall local fiscal flows.

The regression equation is:

$$\text{Revenue}_{it} = c + \beta(\text{coal production})_{it-1} + S_i + Y_t + \varepsilon_{it}$$

Revenue_{it} is the total real revenue to county i in year t. The variable c is the constant. The variables S_i are the state indicators for each county. The Y_t are the year indicators, and the variables ε_{it} are the error terms that reflect random variation in revenue. The estimated coefficient β is the relationship between lagged coal production and revenue to the county. We specify the relationship as linear rather than log because many of the revenue sources tied to coal, such as severance taxes and royalties, are linear functions of production levels. Of course, by the time the revenue gets to counties the relationship is not that simple, but in principle linear should be a better fit than log.

The results from the regressions appear in table 2. The two columns show the results for all 27 counties. Column 1 includes the expansive measure of revenue (e.g., including school district revenue), and column 2 includes only revenue that goes directly to the county government.

In both regressions, the estimated coefficient on coal production is positive and significantly different from zero.[25] The magnitude of the coefficient is more than double for total revenue as it is for the more limited county revenue. This suggests that coal features significantly in the revenue streams for schools and other special districts.

Table 2
Panel Regressions of Government Revenue on Lagged Coal Production (*t*-Statistics in Parentheses)

	(1)	(2)
	Total Revenue, All 27 Coal-Dependent Counties	County Government Revenue, All 27 Coal-Dependent Counties
County-level coal production, lagged by 1 year	.812**	.351**
	(2.96)	(2.97)
Constant	65,634,720***	8,476,680
	(3.53)	(1.06)
Observations	140	140
R^2	.941	.864

**p < .01.
***p < .001.

The regression coefficient of 0.812 on the coal production variable indicates that a decrease in coal production of 1,000 short tons will decrease expected total revenue by $812. In 2018, the national average sale price for coal was $36 per short ton.[26] At that price, a decrease of 1,000 short tons is a decrease of $36,000 in coal sales, holding everything else constant. The average decrease in coal production for the mining-intensive counties from 2012 to 2017 was 3.5 MMst per county. Applying the estimated coefficient, this would have produced an average decrease in total revenue of $2.8 million per county from 2012 to 2017. Given that mean total revenue is more than $95 million, this is not that worrisome. On the other hand, this relationship (if it holds outside the sample) would imply that if all coal production were eliminated in a county with mean coal production of about 22.9 MMst, as shown in table 1, expected total revenue would decrease by about $18.6 million, or about 20% of mean total revenue.

In the context of the total collapse of the industry locally, one might expect revenue to decline nonlinearly as noncoal revenues (such as property and sales taxes) and economic conditions spiral downward. As explored in the next section, experiences from other contexts illustrate how the rapid demise of a dominant industry can create negatively reinforcing deterioration in local fiscal conditions, including tax capacity, creditworthiness, and public service provision.

IV. Experience from Other Contexts

The previous section illustrated how certain counties in the United States are directly dependent on the coal industry for revenue. Indirect dependencies are important as well but are more difficult to quantify. But we do know from experience, when a major industrial employer collapses, service sector economic activity could also collapse, leading to lower revenues from sales taxes and amplifying the fiscal stress. In addition, as residents migrate out of the area in search of jobs, they may leave behind unsaleable vacant homes, further depressing property values and tax revenue. The social safety net in the United States has arguably shown its weaknesses in such circumstances, and in the next section we consider the policy implications of the risks for coal country.

Instructive examples of these downward spirals abound through history, both in the United States and abroad. In many cases the collapse begins in a resource industry, such as silver, whaling, fisheries, old-growth forestry, and kelp. Often, exacerbating factors include technological change and shifts in comparative advantage across different locations. For example, coal-producing areas of the United Kingdom, steel towns in Pennsylvania, and Detroit, with an economy dominated by the automobile industry, all endured the decline of their major industry, and they all experienced a collapse in fiscal conditions, resulting in prolonged periods of attempts at revitalization and dependence on external financial support. Although each decline arose from different factors in very different geographies, the fiscal effects have strong parallels.

A search for successful precedents for the kind of economic transition that will be necessary in coalfield areas comes up wanting. Although policy makers have targeted federal assistance to a number of abrupt economic transitions, the most successful examples are quite different than the challenges facing coal country. For example, the Servicemen's Readjustment Act of 1944,[27] aka the GI Bill, offered an extraordinary opportunity for soldiers returning from World War II to get an education, buy a home, start a business, and build a new future. The program was a major political and economic success and arguably set the course for strong postwar economic growth. However, the opportunities available to healthy twentysomethings who can move anywhere to work or study are not the same as those facing small rural towns and older families that have had the whole economic rug pulled out from under them.

One might look to the federal Trade Adjustment Assistance (TAA) program, which provides assistance for those negatively affected by freer trade. The results of TAA assistance are mixed. Some data suggest that program participants who leave the labor force for extended training (particularly older workers) can lose ground relative to otherwise similar nonparticipants. This research suggests that job training programs must be carefully designed and delivered to ensure they truly benefit their participants.

Another possible model arises in the way the US Department of Defense (DoD) assists local economic transitions when it closes military bases, makes major adjustments in workforce levels, or ends large defense contracts. In most instances, communities have the advantage of advance notice of the major DoD changes and can plan ahead to minimize the economic dislocation. Also, unlike with most abandoned mines, in many cases the DoD leaves behind buildings, airports, and other infrastructure that communities can convert to commercial purposes. Nonetheless, technical and financial support for local economic diversification planning appears to be a useful coordinating role for the federal program.

V.   Municipal Bonds

Local governments are not the only ones with risks tied to coal. To the extent that they have issued bonds or taken on other debt, those creditors could share in their jeopardy. Municipal bond market participants have only begun to acknowledge the unique risks facing jurisdictions that rely on coal production. In part this may be because municipal bonds are generally considered safe assets. According to analysis by the ratings agency Moody's, recent default rates in this market were approximately 0.18%, a rate that is significantly lower than that of corporate bonds (Muni Facts 2019).

Governments that issue bonds are legally required to disclose risks that could affect their ability to pay back investors, both when the bonds are issued and throughout their lifetimes. In primary offerings, the bond issuers must produce an "official statement," a document informing investors about the issuer and the project. Bonds from coal-reliant jurisdictions make up a small share of overall subfederal US debt. In 2018, the issuances for top coal-producing state governments comprised only about 10% of the national total of $388 billion. The share of bonds issued by regions in coal-dependent communities within these states is even smaller. Table 3 lists some of the active bonds issued in two of the three coal-dependent counties discussed in Section II.C.[28] The Boone County government had no active issuances.[29]

Table 3
Bond Issues in Select Coal-Reliant Counties

No.	CUSIP Number	Issuer	Type of Bond	Maturity Date	Purpose	Principal Amount ($000)	Ratings (Moody's)
1	13433Q AA0-AQ5	Campbell County, WY	Hospital Revenue Bonds	2012–2034	Campbell County Memorial Hospital	$47,395	
2	134331DH7	Campbell County, WY	Industrial Development Revenue Bonds	November 1, 2037	Solid waste disposal facility for waste coal	$445,480	
3	134333AD5	Campbell County, WY	Pollution Control Revenue Bond	October 1, 2024	Pollution control facilities	$12,200	Baa2
4	134340AA6	Campbell County, WY	Solid Waste Facilities Revenue Bonds	July 15, 2039	Solid waste disposal facilities	$150,000	Baa1
5	587849 AA8-AG5	Mercer County, ND	General Obligation Bonds	2017–2036	County courthouse and jail expansion	$3,500	Baa2
6	587850DN5/DP0	Mercer County, ND	Pollution Control Revenue Bond	2028–2038	Refund of outstanding principal	$100,000	Aaa
7	587850DM7	Mercer County, ND	Pollution Control Revenue Bond	September 1, 2022	Refund of outstanding principal	$20,790	A2

Source: Electronic Municipal Market Access (EMMA), MSRB https://emma.msrb.org/.

Most bonds fund construction of facilities such as hospitals and solid waste disposal facilities, for which repayment would ostensibly come from the income and fees associated with the facility. Principal amounts range from $3.5 million to $445 million. The bond terms range over 20–30 years, maturing between 2022 and 2039. In the climate policy projection in figure 5, US Coal Production under EIA $25+ per ton scenario, US coal production in 2030 falls by about 78% below 2018 levels. Thus, many of the bond interest payments and the principal payment could be due during a period of precipitous decline in the coal industry.

The official statements for the bonds in table 3 document their amounts, maturity provisions, trustees, underwriters, and other details. The statements vary widely in their discussion of bondholders' risks. There is no standard format for the statements, and it takes careful reading to dig out any important details disclosing material risks. Some statements allude vaguely to exposure to government policy and economic conditions, whereas others make no mention of risks of any kind. Only two describe the potential for policies that regulate CO_2 to have "a significant impact" on the relevant facilities. None discuss the important connections between climate policy, coal production, and the economic and fiscal conditions of local communities.

For example, the statement for the first bond in the table, which funds a hospital construction project, highlights bondholders' risks such as changes in Medicare and Medicaid policies. With regard to other risks, it reads as follows (PiperJaffray 2009, 12):

Future economic and other conditions, including demand for healthcare services, the ability of the District to provide the services required by residents, public confidence in the District, economic developments in the service area, competition, rates, costs, third-party reimbursement and governmental regulations may adversely affect revenues and, consequently, payment of principal of and interest on the Series 2009 Bonds.

So it notes the relevance of "economic developments in the service area" but does not explain what that might mean. The statement lacks any recognition of the prospects or local effects of greenhouse gas regulation, which in 2009 was a lively debate in Congress. Indeed, an appendix describes the local coal-based economy in positive terms (PiperJaffray 2009, Appendix D-1):

Campbell County, known as the energy capital of the nation, is located in the heart of the resource rich Powder River Basin. Over 30% of the nation's coal is produced in area surface mines. Over 25% of Campbell County jobs are mineral-based, directly attributed to coal mining, oil and gas extractions, and supporting operations.

The statement also lists mining and energy companies as the top 10 tax-payers in the county.

Let us consider the other bonds in the table. The second bond finances costs related to a facility that handles waste coal (Citi 2007). The third bond finances costs of pollution control facilities at a power plant (Lasalle Capital Markets 2004). Neither of the official statements discusses bond-holders' risks.

The fourth bond funds solid waste disposal and sewage treatment fa-cilities at Dry Fork Station, a coal-fired power plant. The risk factors the issuance discloses are reasonably comprehensive and, although not quan-titative, characterize the broad array of environment-related factors that could affect the net revenue from the power plant. The documented risks include the large amount of long-term debt the power company is incur-ring, along with potential delays or termination of the project owing to opposition from environmental groups and/or regulatory measures. The statement also notes that the company may rely on technology that be-comes less competitive, and it describes how laws and regulations related to climate change may "adversely affect our operations and future finan-cial performance." It even mentions the cap-and-trade legislation passed by the House of Representatives in June 2009 and potential environmental regulation in states that purchase power from the project. However, the document does not address risks to the economy of the surrounding com-munity (Goldman Sachs 2009). If the coal economy collapses and demand for power declines along with it, we have no information about what that would mean for bondholders' risks.

The fifth bond in the table, a general obligation bond issued by Mercer County, North Dakota, includes just one sentence describing risks (Piper-Jaffray 2016, 80): "Mercer County is exposed to various risks of loss relat-ing to torts; theft of, damage to, and destruction of assets; errors and omissions; injuries to employees; and natural disasters." It lists the major employers, which include energy and mining companies, and the Reve-nue Obligations page notes that "debt is supported by coal severance and conversion tax receipts." Most of the ledgers reporting tax receipts do not break down tax revenues related to coal and other sources, but one that does shows that of about $7 million in general revenues for Mer-cer County, about $3.3 million came from the coal severance and conver-sion taxes (PiperJaffray 2009, Appendix A-16). This extreme dependence on coal production seems an obvious material risk, yet the statement in-cludes no discussion of it.

The statement for the sixth bond, another pollution control issuance for energy operations, reads much like the fourth bond, including a discussion of climate and water quality regulations. It also highlights risks associated with natural gas prices and Federal Energy Regulatory Commission policy. However, like the fourth bond, the document does not address risks associated with the economy of the surrounding community (Goldman Sachs 2004).

The seventh bond lists factors affecting the business operations of the company (Edward D. Jones 2001, 3):

Future Economic Conditions. The Company's operations and financial performance may be adversely affected by a number of factors including, but not limited to, the Company's ongoing involvement in diversification efforts, the timing and scope of deregulation and open competition, growth of electric revenues, impact of the investment performance of the utility's pension plan, changes in the economy, governmental and regulatory action, weather conditions, fuel and purchased power costs, environmental issues, resin prices, and other factors discussed from time to time in reports the corporation files with the Securities and Exchange Commission.

It is interesting that resin prices rise to the significance of specific mention, whereas the potentially calamitous effects of climate policy on coal production do not.

In principle, investors can turn to ratings agencies for guidance. Ratings agencies have assessed most of the bonds in table 3, ranging from Baa to Aaa, with most bonds falling somewhere in between. In some instances, ratings reports are not much better than official statements in describing the risks, and sometimes they are worse. For example, Fitch gave the seventh bond in the table an A+ rating in 2015, highlighting only the upside potential of energy development and indicating no risk associated with climate or other environmental policies.

That said, some ratings are shifting and ratings agencies are paying new attention to coal-dependent regions. Two of the seven bonds in the table received systematic downgrades from ratings agencies, with exposure to coal cited as a factor in the ratings agencies' reviews. None have received an upgrade. For example, in 2018 Moody's downgraded the fifth bond in table 3 to Baa1 "based on the county's narrowed financial position following consecutive years of declines in liquidity driven by negative expenditure variances. The rating also reflects the county's moderate tax base with consecutive years of tax base growth, but with some concentration in coal mining and power generation, strong demographics, low fixed costs and debt burden with moderate pension burden." Still, even Moody's downgraded rating places the security as "investment grade" with only "moderate credit risks."[30]

According to a 2019 report from S&P Global Ratings, "For nearly a decade, U.S. coal production has been on the decline. Global efforts to stem emissions of carbon dioxide from fossil fuels and the availability of cheap alternative renewable energy sources will limit future growth of coal production. In S&P Global Ratings' opinion, reliance on coal-related revenue and economic activity, absent diversification, may result in long-term credit deterioration for some U.S. government entities. . . . Severance tax volatility, eroding property tax assessments, and economic decline are the major credit factors affecting coal-reliant regions" (2019, 1).

VI. Conclusions and Implications for Policy

Coal industry jobs in the United States have declined for decades due to labor-saving automation. In recent years, coal demand and production have begun to fall as well, owing primarily to lower-cost alternatives. Economic modeling shows this decline will dramatically steepen under a price on carbon or regulatory program. Although obstacles remain, momentum for federal climate change policy is growing in the United States and threatening the fiscal future of coal-reliant areas.

Several policy implications arise. First, diversifying a rural economy that is deeply integrated with a particular industry is a difficult task, but it is central to long-run sustainability—as is a more diverse revenue base. Attracting new nonfossil business investment may bring new residents and demands on public services. Unless the tax system includes nonmineral revenue instruments like property and sales taxes, an inflow of residents can be a net negative on district budgets. Some jurisdictions may be able to attract new businesses by offering favorable business environments and by investing in local infrastructure that makes the area a more desirable place to live. The town of Greenville, South Carolina, is one example. Once the "textile center of the world," a combination of incentives and attractive amenities helped Greenville transform into a popular destination for new businesses (Torres and Saraiva 2018).

Second, economic revitalization will require large investments and thus significant external support for already struggling coal-dependent communities and workers. A federal carbon tax could provide tens to hundreds of billions of dollars per year in new federal government revenues, a small fraction of which could be devoted to coal communities and workers. For example, the US Congressional Budget Office estimates that a greenhouse gas tax starting at $25 per ton of CO_2 equivalent, rising at 2% over inflation each year, could raise more than $1 trillion over 10 years.[31] Polling suggests that American households would be willing to spend carbon tax revenues on assisting displaced workers in the coal industry by enough to compensate each miner nearly $146,000 (Kotchen, Turk, and Leiserowitz 2017). External support does not necessarily need to be funded with carbon pricing. For example, in 2019 some Democratic presidential candidates pledged generous support for displaced fossil fuel workers, including wage supplements, health care, housing, relocation assistance, and job training.

The question arises how and how much money should be spent to best ameliorate the burdens in coal country. Relatively straightforward options include temporarily backfilling lost state and local coal-related revenue, supplementing miners' pension and health benefits, replenishing funds for black lung disease benefits, and paying to reclaim areas mined by bankrupt companies. Other options, such as workforce and community development and water quality remediation, may be important to a successful transition, but the optimal approaches may vary widely across different locations. Health needs also vary locally. As discussed in Metcalf and Wang (2019), some coal-reliant areas are pummeled by opioid addiction. To the extent feasible, it could make sense to bolster health benefits and economic development with additional substance abuse assistance.

Further research is needed to elaborate these and other approaches as well as to estimate appropriate funding levels. A brief review suggests spending in some categories would range in the tens of billions of dollars cumulatively over the coming decades—still quite small relative to potential carbon pricing revenue. For example, the Black Lung Benefits Act[32] provides monthly payments and medical benefits to coal miners disabled by lung disease from their job. Currently underfinanced by an excise tax on coal, the Black Lung Liability Trust Fund's cumulative outstanding shortfall could exceed $15 billion by 2050 (US Government Accountability Office 2018).

Mine reclamation is another potential line item that could also create local jobs. By law, mine operators must restore the land (federal or private) to a condition no worse than that supporting the uses the land could support before mining. However, some firms have not appropriately planned for their cleanup liabilities, both because they have insufficiently bonded and because some states have allowed them to "self-bond," that is to underwrite the reclamation guarantees with the assets of the firm rather than through third-party contracts. According to the US Department of the Interior, total unfunded costs for reclamation of about \$10.7 billion could fall to states and tribes (Congressional Research Service 2020). This number could grow substantially with more coal mining bankruptcies.

Delays in reclamation can produce greater and longer-lasting ecological damage. Ongoing drainage from coal mines can contaminate drinking water and soil, causing long-term health damages, disrupting aquatic organisms, and corroding infrastructure. If residents cannot even drink their local water, attracting new investment could be nearly impossible. About 28% of coal-rich Central Appalachian water streams are impaired by mine drainage.[33] In West Virginia, the cost of correcting acidic mine drainage-related problems with currently available technology is estimated at \$5–\$15 billion.[34] Rapidly addressing water quality can minimize damages and lower overall cleanup costs (Kefeni et al. 2017).

Some may argue that if states have to absorb underfunded cleanup costs, it is the natural consequence of allowing industries to capture their regulators, and federal taxpayers should not bail them out. However, lifting the reclamation burden from coal states (perhaps with the proviso of no further self-bonding) and otherwise ameliorating the disproportionate burdens of climate policy on coal-reliant areas may be critical elements of a deal that enables the adoption of federal climate policy.

Endnotes

Author email addresses: Morris (AMorris@brookings.edu), Kaufman (nk2792@columbia.edu), Doshi (sdoshi@brookings.edu). The authors would like to thank the editors of *EEPE* for their helpful feedback and suggestions. The authors would also like to acknowledge the contributions of Ali Zaidi, Edwin Saliba, Hao Wang, Jason Bordoff, Mathew Robinson, Artealia Gilliard, Ron Minsk, Genna Morton, Stephanie Damassa, and Anna Gossett. This work was made possible by support from the Center on Global Energy Policy (CGEP) and the Laura and John Arnold Foundation. More information about CGEP is available at https://energypolicy.columbia.edu/about/partners. The views expressed in this report should not be construed as reflecting the views of the Columbia SIPA CGEP, the Brookings Institution, or any other entity. The words "we" and "our" refer to the authors' own opinions. For acknowledgments, sources of research support, and disclosure of the authors' material financial relationships, if any, please see https://www.nber.org/books-and-chapters/environmental-and-energy-policy-and-economy-volume-2/revenue-risk-coal-reliant-counties.

1. This paper draws heavily from Morris, Kaufman, and Doshi (2019).

2. As reported by the EIA *Short-Term Energy Outlook*: https://www.eia.gov/outlooks/steo/report/index.php.

3. Details about the model can be found here: https://www.nera.com/practice-areas/energy/newera-model.html#tab-1.

4. American Clean Energy and Security Act of 2009, H.R. 2454, 111th Congress (2009–2010).

5. An analysis of state and local revenue sources and uses from oil and gas production appears in Newell and Raimi (2018).

6. A compendium of state severance tax policies for natural gas appears here: http://www.ncsl.org/research/energy/taxing-natural-gas-production.aspx. Weber, Wang, and Chomas (2016) also has an appendix that documents state severance tax policies.

7. The variation of severance tax policies by state appears here: http://www.ncsl.org/research/energy/oil-and-gas-severance-taxes.aspx#severance.

8. "Natural Resources Revenue Data," US Department of Interior, accessed June 2019, https://revenuedata.doi.gov/.

9. Population estimate as of July 1, 2018. Demographics of Mercer County appear here: https://www.census.gov/quickfacts/fact/table/mercercountynorthdakota,US/PST045218.

10. As described by the West Virginia State Tax Department, p. 1: https://tax.wv.gov/Documents/Reports/SeveranceTaxes.TaxData.FiscalYears.2015-2020.pdf.

11. Data for 2015 from the US Census Bureau, US Bureau of Labor Statistics, and US Bureau of Economic Employment.

12. The total assessed valuation for Boone County for 2015 is $1.47 billion as per Boone County Government (2015, 2). The total valuation for coal industrial and mineral property is $840 million, as calculated from Kent (2016, 13–14). This implies that coal forms about 57% of total Boone County valuation. This is in line with the findings of O'Leary (2011, 6), that coal forms about 60% of the total property tax revenue for Boone County.

13. Calculated by authors from West Virginia State Auditor (2016). Property taxes generate about $6.3 million of the county's $12.5 million budget.

14. We calculated this by applying the schools total levy rate for class 3 and 4 property (1.69%) from Boone County Government (2015, 1) to the assessed valuation of coal as described in endnote 12 above.

15. We calculated this by applying the total levy rate for class 3 and 4 property (2.53%) from Boone County Government (2015, 1) to the assessed valuation of coal as described in endnote 12 above.

16. We calculated annual revenues by combining amounts derived from quarterly severance and reallocation tax distribution documents published by the West Virginia State Treasurer: https://www.wvtreasury.com/Banking-Services/Revenue-Distributions/CoalSeverance-Tax/Coal-Severance-Tax-Archive.

17. Data from the 2018 and 2012 Annual Coal Report published by the EIA.

18. Kent (2016) found that revenues from coal severance tax to West Virginia counties declined from a total of $30.5 million in 2011 to $16.1 million in 2015. Boone County severance tax revenue declined from $5 million in 2011 to $1.6 million in 2015.

19. Relating to reducing the severance tax on thermal or steam coal. House Bill 3142. Regular Session (2019).

20. North Central Appalachian Coal Severance Tax Rebate Act. House Bill 3144. Regular Session (2019).

21. Population estimate as of July 1, 2018. Demographics of Campbell County appear here: https://www.census.gov/quickfacts/campbellcountywyoming.

22. Flowcharts of various revenue streams appear in the Wyoming Legislative Service Office's 2019 Budget Fiscal Data Book.

23. Data from US Bureau of Labor Statistics and US Mine Safety and Health Administration.

24. The land on which the plant is located is still subject to property tax.

25. We also perform the analysis with data from only the top 20 most coal mining dependent counties, which all have more than 10% of the labor force in coal mining. For the regressions on total revenue, we find that the estimated coefficient on coal production is statistically significant and a little larger for the full set of 27 counties (0.74) than it is for the top 20 most coal-intensive counties (0.54). For county revenue, the estimated coefficients are nearly the same.

26. https://www.eia.gov/energyexplained/coal/prices-and-outlook.php.

27. Servicemen's Readjustment Act of 1944, 38 U.S.C. § 3701.

28. As found on the EMMA website operated by MSRB, as of April 2020.

29. West Virginia has issued infrastructure general obligation bonds secured in part by severance tax collections. Entities, such as towns within Boone County, have issued bonds; they tend to be much smaller than the bonds in table 1. A compendium appears here: http://mbc.wv.gov/AnnualReports/AnnualReport2018.pdf.

30. The Moody's rating scale and definitions can be found at: https://www.moodys.com/sites/products/productattachments/ap075378_1_1408_ki.pdf.

31. Detailed revenue estimates can be found here: https://www.cbo.gov/budget-options/2018/54821.

32. Black Lung Benefits Act of 1972, 30 U.S.C. §901.

33. According to the West Virginia Department of Environmental Protection, Division of Water and Waste Management: http://www.appalmad.org/wp-content/uploads/2010/11/IR_Report_Only_EPA.pdf.

34. As estimated by the US Geological Survey: https://www.usgs.gov/special-topic/water-science-school/science/mining-and-water-quality?qt-science_center_objects=0#qt-science_center_objects.

References

Boone County Government. 2015. *Boone County Assessments & Levies 2015–2016.* https://www.wvsao.gov/LocalGovernment/.

Campbell County. 2018a. *Financial and Compliance Report for the Fiscal Year Ending June 30, 2018.* https://www.ccgov.net/ArchiveCenter/ViewFile/Item/477.

———. 2018b. *Fiscal Year 2017–2018 Annual Report.* https://www.ccgov.net/ArchiveCenter/ViewFile/Item/478.

Campbell County Board of County Commissioners. 2017. *A Campbell County Profile: Socioeconomics.* https://www.wyo-wcca.org/files/4015/0462/2986/Socioeconomic_profile_-_Campbell_County_March_2017.pdf.

Citi. 2007. *Official Statement: Campbell County, Wyoming Tax-Exempt Industrial Development Revenue Bonds (Two Elk Partners Project) Series 2007.* https://emma.msrb.org/MS265732-MS241040-MD470550.pdf.

Coglianese, J., Todd D. Gerarden, and James H. Stock. 2020. "The Effects of Fuel Prices, Regulations, and Other Factors on U.S. Coal Production, 2008–2016." *Energy Journal* 41 (1): 55–81.

Congressional Research Service. 2020. *The Abandoned Mine Reclamation Fund: Issues and Legislation in the 116th Congress.* https://crsreports.congress.gov/product/pdf/IF/IF11352.

Cullen, Joseph A., and Erin T. Mansur. 2017. "Inferring Carbon Abatement Costs in Electricity Markets: A Revealed Preference Approach Using the Shale Revolution." *American Economic Journal: Economic Policy* 9 (3): 106–33.

Edward D. Jones. 2001. *Official Statement: Pollution Control Refunding Revenue Bonds (Otter Tail Corporation Project) Series 2001.* https://emma.msrb.org/MS183463-MS158771-MD306963.pdf.

EIA (Energy Information Administration). 2018. *Annual Energy Outlook 2018.* https://www.eia.gov/outlooks/aeo/pdf/AEO2018.pdf.

———. 2019a. *FAQ: What Is U.S. Electricity Generation by Energy Source?* https://www.eia.gov/tools/faqs/faq.php?id=427&t=3.

———. 2019b. *In 2018, U.S. Coal Production Declined as Exports and Appalachian Region Prices Rose.* Today in Energy. https://www.eia.gov/todayinenergy/detail.php?id=38132.

Fitzgerald, Timothy. 2014. "Importance of Mineral Rights and Royalty Interests for Rural Residents and Landowners." *Choices*, 4th Quarter. http://www.choicesmagazine.org/choices-magazine/theme-articles/is-the-natural-gas-revolution-all-its-fracked-up-to-be-for-local-economies/importance-of-mineral-rights-and-royalty-interests-for-rural-residents-and-landowners.

Goldman Sachs. 2004. *Official Statement: Mercer County, North Dakota Pollution Control Refunding Revenue Bonds, 2004 Series A and B*. https://emma.msrb .org/MS226122-MS201430-MD391208.pdf.

Goldman Sachs. 2009. *Official Statement: Basin Electric Power Cooperative*. https:// emma.msrb.org/EP291992-EP8484-EP630668.pdf.

Headwater Economics. 2017. *Coal Extraction Revenue and Spending: A Comparison among Western States*. https://headwaterseconomics.org/energy/coal/coal-fiscal-policies.

Houser, Trevor, Jason Bordoff, and Peter Marsters. 2017. "Can Coal Make a Comeback?" *Center on Global Energy Policy*, Columbia SIPA. https://energypolicy .columbia.edu/sites/default/files/Center%20on%20Global%20Energy%20 Policy%20Can%20Coal%20Make%20a%20Comeback%20April%202017 .pdf.

Jenkins, Jeff. 2015. "Boone County Looks to Close One-Third of Its Elementary Schools." *MetroNews: The Voice of West Virginia*, November 2. http:// wvmetronews.com/2015/11/02/boone-county-looks-to-close-one-third-of -its-elementary-schools/.

Kaufman, Noah, John Larsen, Peter Marsters, Hannah Kolus, and Shashank Mohan. 2019. "An Assessment of the Energy Innovation and Carbon Dividend Act." *Center on Global Energy Policy*, Columbia SIPA. https:// energypolicy.columbia.edu/sites/default/files/file-uploads/EICDA_CGEP -Report.pdf.

Kefeni, Kebede K., Titus A. M. Msagati, and Bheki B. Mamba. 2017. "Acid Mine Drainage: Prevention, Treatment Options, and Resource Recovery: A Review." *Journal of Cleaner Production* 151:475–93.

Kent, Calvin. 2016. *The Cruel Coal Facts: The Impact on West Virginia Counties from the Collapse of the Coal Economy*. Huntington, WV: National Association of Counties.

Kolstad, Charles D. 2017. "What Is Killing the US Coal Industry?" Policy brief. *Stanford Institute for Economic Policy Research*. https://siepr.stanford.edu/re search/publications/what-killing-us-coal-industry.

Kotchen, Matthew J., Zachary M. Turk, and Anthony A. Leiserowitz. 2017. "Public Willingness to Pay for a US Carbon Tax and Preferences for Spending the Revenue." *Environmental Research Letters* 12 (2017): 094012. https://doi .org/10.1088/1748-9326/aa822a.

Larsen, John, Kate Larsen, Whitney Herndon, Peter Marsters, Hannah Pitt, and Shashank Mohan. 2018. "Taking Stock 2018." *Rhodium Group*. https://rhg .com/research/taking-stock-2018/.

Lasalle Capital Markets. 2004. *Campbell County, Wyoming Pollution Control Refunding Revenue Bonds (Black Hills Power. Inc. Project) Series 2004*. https://emma .msrb.org/MS228118-MS203426-MD395197.pdf.

Malm, Elizabeth. 2013. "Federal Mineral Royalty Disbursements to States and the Effects of Sequestration." *Tax Foundation*. https://taxfoundation.org /federal-mineral-royalty-disbursements-states-and-effects-sequestration/.

McFarland, James R., Allen A. Fawcett, Adele C. Morris, John M. Reilly, and Peter J. Wilcoxen. 2018. "Overview of the EMF 32 Study on U.S. Carbon Tax Scenarios." *Climate Change Economics* 9 (1): 1840002. https://doi.org/10.1142 /S201000781840002X.

McKim, Cooper. 2018. "How the Alpha Bankruptcy Could Lead to Change in the Law." *Wyoming Public Media*, June 29. https://www.wyomingpublic media.org/post/how-alpha-bankruptcy-could-lead-change-law.

Mercer County, North Dakota. 2016. Audit Report. https://www.nd.gov/audi tor/sites/www/files/documents/Reports/Local%20Gov/mercer-county-2016 .pdf.

Metcalf, Gilbert E., and Qitong Wang. 2019. "Abandoned by Coal, Swallowed by Opioids?" Working Paper no. 26551, National Bureau of Economic Research, Cambridge, MA.

Morris, Adele, Noah Kaufman, and Siddhi Doshi. 2019. "The Risk of Fiscal Collapse in Coal-Reliant Communities." *Center on Global Energy Policy, Columbia University*. https://energypolicy.columbia.edu/research/report/risk-fiscal -collapse-coal-reliant-communities.

Muni Facts. 2019. Pamphlet. *Municipal Securities Rulemaking Board*. http:// www.msrb.org/msrb1/pdfs/MSRB-Muni-Facts.pdf.

Newell, Richard G., and Daniel Raimi. 2018. "US State and Local Oil and Gas Revenue Sources and Uses." *Energy Policy* 112:12–18.

North Dakota State Treasurer. n.d. Website. North Dakota State Government. http://www.nd.gov/treasurer/revenue-distribution/.

North Dakota Tax Commissioner. 2018. *State and Local Taxes: An Overview and Comparative Guide*. Ryan Rauschenberger. https://www.nd.gov/tax/data /upfiles/media/2018-red-book-web.pdf?20190630151441.

O'Leary, Sean. 2011. "Property Taxes: A West Virginia Primer." Charleston, WV: West Virginia Center on Budget and Policy.

PiperJaffray. 2009. *Official Statement: Campbell County Hospital District Hospital Revenue Bonds Series 2009*. https://emma.msrb.org/EP686950.pdf.

PiperJaffray. 2016. *Official Statement: General Obligation Correction Center Bonds, Series 2016 Mercer County, North Dakota*. https://emma.msrb.org/EP923706 -EP717043-EP1118876.pdf.

Richards, Heather. 2019. "Wyoming Coal Is Likely Declining Faster Than Expected." *Star Tribune*, April 8. https://trib.com/business/energy/wyoming -coal-is-likely-declining-faster-than-expected/article_be851caa-22df-558a-b7f5 -51b24f077282.html.

S&P Global Ratings. 2019. *Environmental, Social, and Governance: Long-Term Credit Challenges Facing U.S. State and Local Governments in Coal-Producing Regions*. https://www.spglobal.com/ratings/en/research/articles/190925 -environmental-social-and-governance-long-term-credit-challenges-facing -u-s-state-and-local-governments-in-coal-11137772.

Torres, Craig, and Catarina Saraiva. 2018. "The New Startup South." *Bloomberg Businessweek*, June 21. https://www.bloomberg.com/news/features/2018 -06-21/the-textile-town-becoming-the-silicon-valley-of-the-south.

US Department of Agriculture. 2019. "Descriptions and Maps: County Economic Types, 2015 Edition." *Economic Research Service*. https://www.ers.usda.gov/data -products/county-typology-codes/descriptions-and-maps.aspx#mining.

US Department of the Interior. 2016. *Boone, Logan, and Mingo Counties, West Virginia*. Webpage. Case Studies, Natural Resources Revenue Data. https://www .doi.gov/sites/doi.gov/files/uploads/06102016_useiti_county_case_study _updates-_boone_county.pdf.

US Government Accountability Office. 2017. "Oil, Gas, and Coal Royalties: Raising Federal Rates Could Decrease Production on Federal Lands but Increase Federal Revenue." GAO-17-540. https://www.gao.gov/products/GAO-17 -540.

———. 2018. "Black Lung Benefits Program." GAO-18-351. https://www.gao .gov/products/GAO-18-351.

Vincent, Carol Hardy, Laura A. Hanson, and Carla N. Argueta. 2017. "Federal
    Land Ownership: Overview and Data." *Congressional Research Service* R42346.
    https://fas.org/sgp/crs/misc/R42346.pdf.
Weber, Jeremy G., Yongsheng Wang, and Maxwell Chomas. 2016. "A Quantitative
    Description of State-Level Taxation of Oil and Gas Production in the Continental
    U.S." Munich Personal RePEc Archive 71733 (June). https://mpra.ub
    .unimuenchen.de/71733/.
West Virginia State Auditor—Local Government Services Division. 2016. Boone
    County Budget Review Sheet. James A. Gore. https://www.wvsao.gov/local
    government/.
West Virginia Treasurer's Office. 2015. *State of the Treasury Report*. John D. Per-
    due. https://www.wvtreasury.com/Portals/wvtreasury/content/About
    %20the%20Office/Financial%20Reports/SotTR/SotTR%202015s.pdf.
WSAZ News. 2016. "W.Va. House Passes Boone County Schools Funding Bill."
    June 14. https://www.wsaz.com/content/news/WVa-Senate-passes-bill
    -to-help-fund-Boone-County-Schools-382856441.html.
Wyoming Department of Revenue. 2018. *2018 Annual Report*. http://revenue
    .wyo.gov/dor-annual-reports
Wyoming Legislative Service Office. 2018. "2019 Budget Fiscal Data Book."
    Wyoming, December. https://wyoleg.gov/budget/2019databook.pdf.

Cobenefits and Regulatory Impact Analysis: Theory and Evidence from Federal Air Quality Regulations

Joseph Aldy, *Harvard University and NBER,* United States of America

Matthew J. Kotchen, *Yale University and NBER,* United States of America

Mary Evans, *Claremont McKenna College,* United States of America

Meredith Fowlie, *University of California, Berkeley, and NBER,* United States of America

Arik Levinson, *Georgetown University and NBER,* United States of America

Karen Palmer, *Resources for the Future,* United States of America

Executive Summary

This article considers the treatment of cobenefits in benefit-cost analysis of federal air quality regulations. Using a comprehensive data set on all major Clean Air Act rules issued by the Environmental Protection Agency over the period 1997–2019, we show that (1) cobenefits make up a significant share of the monetized benefits; (2) among the categories of cobenefits, those associated with reductions in fine particulate matter are the most significant; and (3) cobenefits have been pivotal to the quantified net benefit calculation in nearly half of cases. Motivated by these trends, we develop a simple conceptual framework that illustrates a critical point: cobenefits are simply a semantic category of benefits that should be included in benefit-cost analyses. We also address common concerns about whether the inclusion of cobenefits is problematic because of alternative regulatory approaches that may be more cost-effective and the possibility for double counting.

JEL Codes: D61, Q53, Q58

Keywords: benefit-cost analysis, regulatory impact analysis, Clean Air Act, cobenefits, air quality, regulatory rebound, double counting

I. Introduction

Benefit-cost analysis (BCA) is a useful and widely employed tool for informing and evaluating public policy decision making. Its primary objective is to assess whether a particular policy or policy proposal promotes

Environmental and Energy Policy and the Economy, volume 2, 2021.

economic efficiency compared with a baseline scenario. At the most general and comprehensive level, BCA is a systematic aggregator of all anticipated or realized impacts, positive and negative, to all relevant parties, and at all relevant points in time. The benefit-cost criterion is simply a test of whether the benefits exceed the costs: if the net benefits are positive, then the policy promotes economic efficiency compared with the baseline status quo.

The use of BCA by agencies of the US federal government has a long bipartisan history. President Reagan established a requirement for regulatory actions such that "the potential benefits to society for the regulation outweigh the potential costs to society" (EO 12291). As part of this objective, the Reagan administration also required agencies to produce a regulatory impact analysis (RIA)—in effect, a BCA in most cases—of major rules.[1] President Clinton continued the requirement for BCA but modified the standard so that agencies "shall assess both the costs and the benefits of the intended regulation and, recognizing that some costs and benefits are difficult to quantify, propose or adopt a regulation only upon a reasoned determination that the benefits of the intended regulation justify its costs" (EO 12866). Every administration since has employed this same approach to guide its review of federal regulations, including most recently the Trump administration, which added new provisions seeking to manage overall regulatory costs (EO 13771; OMB 2017).

BCA has played a particularly important role in support of federal regulations aimed at protecting human health and environmental quality. Those analyses applied to regulations focused on improving air quality often yield the greatest quantified costs and benefits of all regulations across government agencies. For example, in a review of all new federal regulations during the 10-year period from FY 2007 to FY 2016, the Office of Management and Budget (OMB 2019) finds that Environmental Protection Agency (EPA) rules account for 80%–84% of all monetized benefits and 63%–71% of all monetized costs.[2] Moreover, rules coming out of the EPA's Office of Air and Radiation in particular are found to have especially high net benefits.

The anticipated impacts of many federal policies are broad, with some benefits and costs directly linked to the policy's intended focus and other benefits and costs arising only indirectly. Nevertheless, BCAs conducted in line with best practices seek to count all significant benefits and costs, whether they arise as a direct result of the policy's intended objectives or as a result of an ancillary change attributed to the policy. Historically, BCAs conducted by the EPA have treated ancillary benefits and costs in ways consistent with economic theory and regulatory guidance—on an equal footing with benefits more directly linked to the policy. Recently, however, the EPA has made decisions and solicited feedback that indicate a potential shift in—or at least questioning of—its treatment of ancillary benefits and costs, here referred to generally as "cobenefits" and "cocosts."[3]

It is within that context that the present article considers the treatment of cobenefits in BCAs, with a particular focus on air quality regulations, where the issues are front and center. Specifically, the article has two primary objectives:

1. to provide a descriptive overview of the role cobenefits have played in BCAs of federal air quality regulations, using detailed data from all available RIAs, 1997–2019; and

2. to develop a simple theoretical framework to clarify how cobenefits are simply another category of benefits that should be included in BCAs and elucidate some of the unique challenges that arise for measuring them well.

The next section provides background on cobenefits in the context of energy and environmental policy and recent policy actions. Section III describes our data collection, reports a range of descriptive statistics and trends over time, and discusses a few specific cases to illustrate salient issues. Section IV develops a theoretical framework that introduces major concepts and definitions, and it explicitly addresses some concerns raised about cobenefits. Section V concludes with a summary of our findings and observations about the political economy of why cobenefits have become increasingly important and a growing topic of concern.

II.   Background and Recent Actions

A.   Cobenefits and Cocosts

Cobenefits (or cocosts) arise when compliance with a regulation leads to benefits (or costs) that are not directly tied to a regulation's intended target. Although we focus on air quality regulations, the notions of cobenefits and cocosts are not unique to this setting. Consider, for example, the Emergency Highway Energy Conservation Act of 1974, which established a speed limit of 55 miles per hour. The purpose was to "conserve fuel during periods of current and imminent fuel shortages," and thus the direct benefits of the act included fuel savings. However, a cobenefit of the act was reduced road fatalities (Friedman, Hedeker, and Richter 2009). Another example is the Americans with Disabilities Act, which mandated that sidewalks have curb cuts to benefit individuals in wheelchairs, but the curb cuts also helped pedestrians pushing strollers, pulling heavy carts, or wheeling luggage, and those are considered cobenefits (Blackwell 2017).

There are many examples in the environmental economics literature where cobenefits and cocosts have played a role. Sigman (1996) shows that regulations of hazardous waste disposal lead to increases in air pollution emissions. Kotchen et al. (2006) conduct an ex post BCA of a hydroelectric project's effect on river flows, yet the analysis accounts for the cobenefits of reduced emissions because of displaced electricity generation from fossil fuels. In another example, Hansman, Hjort, and León (2018) show that a regulation designed to limit overfishing exacerbates air pollution from fishmeal processing plants.

A growing literature also explores the local air pollution implications of policies targeting greenhouse gas (GHG) emissions and climate change. Lutter and Shogren (2002) illustrate how regulating carbon dioxide (CO_2) emissions under a cap-and-trade program improves local air quality, primarily through reductions of particulate matter (PM). Burtraw et al. (2003) show cobenefits of taxing CO_2 emissions in the form of reduced nitrous oxide (NO_x) emissions and lower compliance costs with other NO_x and sulfur dioxide (SO_2) regulations. More generally and recently, Karlsson, Alfredsson, and Westling (2020), reviewing 239 peer-reviewed studies that assess the cobenefits of climate mitigation policies, find that most studies focus on air pollution-related benefits, where the cobenefits alone often outweigh compliance costs. Other cobenefits that emerge from their review include enhancements to biodiversity, energy security, and water quality.

Overall, the range of studies in the academic literature recognizes that the ancillary pollutant effects could either worsen or improve as a consequence of regulating the targeted pollutant. Moreover, these examples illustrate the appropriateness and importance of accounting for both cobenefits and cocosts.

B.   Regulatory Guidelines

Federal agencies have formally recognized the potential importance of cobenefits and cocosts to their rulemakings. They have therefore developed guidance for systematically accounting for these indirect effects in evaluations of regulatory proposals. OMB, which is responsible for reviewing major regulations before they are finalized, directs all agencies to account for cobenefits and cocosts in its guidance for agency RIAs. It states that when evaluating the benefits and costs of regulations, agencies should "identify the expected undesirable side-effects and ancillary benefits of the proposed regulatory action and the alternatives. These should be added to the direct benefits and costs as appropriate" (OMB 2003, 2–3). This general guidance makes clear that the scope of regulatory analysis extends beyond determining whether the regulation achieves the statute's primary goal. That is, cobenefits and cocosts should be included in the analysis.

The EPA's *Guidelines for Preparing Economic Analyses*, with specific provisions for conducting BCAs, likewise calls for explicit accounting of cobenefits and cocosts: "An economic analysis of regulatory or policy options should present all identifiable costs and benefits that are incremental to the regulation or policy under consideration. These should include directly intended effects and associated costs, as well as ancillary (or co-) benefits and costs" (EPA 2014, 11–12).[4]

C. Cobenefits and the Clean Air Act

Air quality regulations have a long history of delivering multiple types of social benefits, including cobenefits. Some of these were accounted for in the design stages of the Clean Air Act (CAA); others were not fully understood until after CAA regulations were introduced. Here we review several examples.

To reduce air pollution from cars and light trucks, the EPA has often regulated both vehicles and the fuels they use (Aldy 2018). This system-based approach has delivered multiple emissions benefits. In 1973, the EPA promulgated a regulation requiring gasoline stations to market unleaded gasoline (EPA 1973). This regulation was motivated by the fact that lead in the fuel harmed catalytic converters, a new technology mandated by other CAA regulations intended to reduce tailpipe emissions of carbon monoxide. The EPA subsequently established a National Ambient Air Quality Standard (NAAQS) for lead in 1976 (EPA 1976). Removing lead from gasoline therefore delivered on two air quality objectives in the 1970s and 1980s: reducing ambient concentrations of carbon monoxide and of lead (Nichols 1997).

The 1990 CAA Amendments authorized the first cap-and-trade program for power plant SO_2 emissions. The primary goal was to reduce the risks posed by acid rain, including the acidification of forests and waterbodies (Schmalensee and Stavins 2013). Most of the monetized benefits, however, have resulted from reducing human exposure to fine PM that contributes to premature mortality. In this case, the sizable health benefits caused by the reduction in SO_2—an important precursor to PM formation—were not fully appreciated or anticipated at the time the regulation was implemented. Advances in epidemiology after the 1990 CAA Amendments provided increasingly strong evidence on the public health risk of fine PM.

Another prominent example is from 2015, when the EPA promulgated the Clean Power Plan to reduce CO_2 emissions in the power sector (EPA 2015). Cobenefits played an important role in this rulemaking because it was anticipated that, in the process of reducing CO_2, power plants would also significantly reduce SO_2 and NO_x, with subsequent reductions in fine PM and ozone because of chemical precursor relationships. As a result, the agency projected billions of dollars of monetized benefits per year from mitigating climate change and billions of dollars of monetized benefits per year from reductions in premature mortality due to reduced exposure to ambient PM and ozone.

Sometimes Congress has specifically amended legislation to expand the target objectives of existing rules, effectively converting cobenefits into targeted benefits. This has happened when rules targeted at fossil fuel consumption were expanded to mitigate climate change. For example, the 1975 Energy Policy and Conservation Act created the corporate average fuel economy standards and introduced fuel economy labels for new vehicles in response to the 1973–74 oil shock. The goal was to reduce fuel consumption.[5] The Energy Independence and Security Act of 2007 added the goal of reducing GHG emissions, setting more ambitious fuel efficiency standards and directing the Department of Transportation (DOT) to revise fuel economy labels to include information about GHG emissions.[6]

A similar expansion occurred with respect to biofuels in transportation. The Energy Policy Act of 2005 created renewable fuel standards with annual goals for biofuel consumption, with the goal of reducing US oil consumption.[7] The Energy Independence and Security Act of 2007 revised this program, recognizing GHG cobenefits by setting more ambitious biofuel volume goals and mandating multiple low-carbon biofuel categories so that the policy could simultaneously reduce oil consumption and CO_2 emissions.[8]

D. Recent Actions Related to the Inclusion of Cobenefits and Cocosts

Despite the important role that cobenefits (and cocosts) have played in shaping outcomes under past CAA regulations, and the well-established regulatory guidance about including them, the EPA has undertaken recent actions with the potential to diminish the value of cobenefits or to question their inclusion in economic analyses.

EPA Science Transparency Proposed Rule, 2018. The EPA (2018b) issued the proposed rule in the name of improving transparency and replicability of the science underlying its assessment of regulatory benefits and costs. This proposal does not explicitly address cobenefits. Instead, it raises obstacles to including monetized value of PM improvements that form the basis for many of the cobenefits in recent EPA rulemakings. In particular, the proposed rule would limit the EPA's use of proprietary or confidential health data of the type commonly used to evaluate the consequences of PM exposure. In many cases, these studies are done with the understanding that individual information will be kept confidential and thus not made publicly available.

EPA Affordable Clean Energy Final Rule, 2019. The EPA (2019b) issued the Affordable Clean Energy rule (ACE), a replacement for the 2015 Clean Power Plan, which set CO_2 emissions standards for existing power plants. In its summarization of the benefits and costs of ACE, the EPA presented two tables. One followed the standard practice, reporting the costs, climate benefits, ancillary health benefits, and overall net benefits. The second summary table contained the same information but with the ancillary benefits excluded. That exclusion runs contrary to OMB guidance, EPA guidance, and standard practice. The presentation of results in this way is significant because it substantially reduces the overall net benefits and signals a shift within the EPA away from counting all benefits on an equal footing.

EPA Increasing Consistency and Transparency in Considering Benefits and Costs in the Clean Air Act Rulemaking Process Proposed Rule, 2020. The EPA (2018a) solicited public feedback on the conduct of BCAs, including the following: "What improvements would result from a general rule that specifies how the Agency will factor the outcomes or key elements of the benefit-cost analysis into future decision making? For example, *to what extent should EPA develop a general rule on how the Agency will weigh the benefits from reductions in pollutants that were not directly regulated (often called 'co-benefits' or 'ancillary benefits')* . . . ?" (EPA 2018a, 27527, emphasis added). In 2020, the EPA (2020b) proposed a new rule focused on BCAs of CAA regulations. Under the proposal, future

EPA CAA regulations would include two summaries of the RIA: one characterizing all benefits and costs, as has been standard practice, and the other including only "a listing of the benefit categories arising from the environmental improvement that is targeted by the relevant statutory provision, or provisions[,] and would report the monetized value to society of these benefits" (EPA 2020b, 35622).

EPA MATS Appropriate and Necessary Determination, 2020. The EPA (2020c) finalized a new rule reversing its previous finding on the legal basis of the Mercury and Air Toxics Standards (MATS), a regulation designed to reduce the emissions of mercury and other hazardous air pollutants (HAPs) from power plants. Whereas the EPA concluded in 2011 and 2016 that it was "appropriate and necessary" to regulate mercury and other HAPs under authority of the CAA, it reversed this decision in 2020. The reversal rests entirely on omitting from consideration the cobenefits of reducing fine PM, which accounted for the vast majority of monetized benefits in the original 2011 RIA (Aldy et al. 2019, 2020). The EPA's new rationale is that only the target pollutant benefits should count when making the legal determination.

EPA Oil and Natural Gas Sector: Emission Standards for New, Reconstructed, and Modified Sources Review, 2019. The EPA's new approach to the ancillary impacts of regulation does not, however, appear to be consistently applied across rulemakings. The proposed amendments to the New Source Performance Standards (NSPS) for the oil and gas sector reflect an inconsistent regulatory treatment of cobenefits. In the case of this proposed rule, the EPA (2019a) argues that regulating volatile organic compounds (VOCs) results in a cobenefit: lower methane emissions. As a result, the agency's proposal opts against setting methane-specific standards because they "are entirely redundant of the existing NSPS for VOCs" (EPA 2019a, 50254).

EPA/DOT Tailpipe CO_2/Fuel Economy Final Rule, 2020. The EPA's new approach that discounts the ancillary effects of regulations is also not represented in the revision to the EPA tailpipe CO_2 emission standards and National Highway Traffic Safety Administration (NHTSA) fuel economy rules. Issued in 2020, this joint rule targets fuel economy and GHG emissions from automobiles. But the EPA analysis accounted for expected cobenefits and cocosts arising from changes in traffic fatalities and traffic congestion (EPA and NHTSA 2020). These ancillary changes were included in the calculations of the total net benefits of the rule, not weighted differently from the primary objectives of the EPA's authority for the regulations under Title II of the CAA.

Those recent EPA rulemakings trouble us, for two reasons. First, as noted, they appear to be inconsistent. Sometimes cobenefits and cocosts are excluded from BCA analyses or listed separately, as in the case of ACE or MATS. But other recent rulemakings include cobenefits and cocosts, as in the NSPS for oil and gas and the joint EPA-NHTSA fuel economy rules. And second, treating cobenefits and cocosts differently from targeted benefits and costs departs from standard EPA practice. To document the extent of that departure, in the next section we review the EPA's treatment of cobenefits in its RIAs for major CAA rules since 1997.

III. Trends and Patterns across CAA RIAs

We now examine long-term trends and patterns in the role of cobenefits in EPA analysis of CAA rules and regulations. We begin with an overview of our data collection and preparation, before turning to the results of our analysis. The complete database that we created, along with additional details to those described later, are available in the online supplementary information to this article.[9]

A. Constructing the Sample

We focus on the category of major rules, because these consistently have well-developed assessments of the economic impacts of the regulations in question. We reviewed the OMB annual reports to Congress on the benefits and costs of regulations to identify all major CAA rules issued by the EPA over the period 1997–2019. We provide further details in the appendix, along with full citations to all rules and RIAs compiled in our data set. Over this 23-year period, the EPA issued 58 major regulations identified in the OMB annual reports, and figure 1 shows the number of rules issued in each year. In some cases, especially for rules promulgated in the 1990s, the EPA conducted cost-effectiveness analysis rather than a BCA. This means that those RIAs focus on estimating the regulatory expenditures per ton of emissions reduced, rather than on estimating the monetized value of air quality benefits. After excluding these cases, we compiled a sample of 48 air quality rules for which the EPA published a prospective BCA that explicitly monetized at least some of the rule's benefits in its RIA.[10]

B. Distinguishing between "Targeted Benefits" and "Cobenefits"

To determine the "targeted benefits" of a rule and distinguish these from the "cobenefits," we reviewed the RIAs and the promulgated regulations.

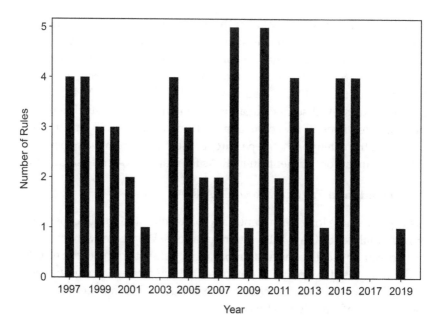

Fig. 1. Major Clean Air Act regulations promulgated by Environmental Protection Agency, 1997–2019. Annual counts were produced by the authors based on a review of Office of Management and Budget reports to Congress.

Each EPA rule describes the relevant statutory authority or authorities that motivate the regulatory action, which can often identify the pollutant or pollutants targeted under the law. The rule and the RIA also describe the specific emissions standards by pollutant, and the identification of each pollutant that must be monitored under the rule is one way to identify those that are targeted. There are, however, a variety of cases in which the targeted benefit is identified in the statutory authority, yet the specific emission standards set in the rule apply to emission precursors for that pollutant. An example is ozone as a targeted pollutant, with emissions standards that apply to the precursors of NO_x and VOCs.

In some cases, the identification of the targeted benefits appears quite straightforward. For example, during our sample period, the EPA issued National Ambient Air Quality Standards for lead, ozone, $PM_{2.5}$ (particulate matter less than 2.5 μm in diameter), and SO_2. These regulations set the maximum permissible ambient air quality concentrations for these specific air pollutants—and thus the targeted benefits of the lead standard, for example, are those benefits clearly associated with the reduction in lead pollution.

In other cases, the identification of the targeted benefits is more complicated. To illustrate some of the challenges involved and to describe our procedure, we walk through a particular example: the 1998 "NO_x SIP Call" rule (regulation identifier number [RIN] 2060-AH10).[11] The rule was motivated by the need to address the cross-state transport of ozone pollution and the adverse public health consequences of high ambient ozone concentrations (Napolitano et al. 2007). Indeed, it built on and expanded the then-existing Ozone Transport Commission NO_x trading program for Mid-Atlantic and Northeast states (Linn 2008). To achieve reductions in ozone, the rule focused on NO_x, a precursor to atmospheric ozone. The monetized benefits of the rule arise from reductions of ozone, $PM_{2.5}$, and water pollution through nitrogen deposition.

The question in this case is whether to treat the targeted pollutant as ozone or NO_x: the choice has important consequences for the categorization of benefits. We treat ozone as the targeted pollutant because of the rule's clear intent and classify the benefits associated with fine PM and water pollution—which result from the NO_x emissions but are distinct from ozone pollution—as cobenefits.

More generally, we apply the following classification procedures for identifying the monetized targeted benefits from the monetized cobenefits. First, we review the rule as published in the *Federal Register* to identify specific statutory authorizations. Second, we review the rule and the RIA for information on specific pollutant emission standards. Third, we review the rule and the RIA to assess how regulating a precursor pollutant may connect to the targeted pollutant under the statutory authority. Finally, we account for (but do not automatically follow) the EPA's specific description of some benefits as cobenefits.

Two further conventions that we employ are worth mentioning to clarify how we made classifications. The first is that all benefits directly associated with a targeted pollutant are considered targeted benefits. For example, ozone benefits of the NO_x SIP Call rule include those associated with ozone effects on worker productivity, commodity crop production, and commercial forest production, all of which go beyond the public health focus of the primary NAAQS. The second convention is that when targeted pollutants are themselves precursors to other pollutants for which reductions lead to monetized benefits, these "downstream" benefits are considered cobenefits. This scenario is most common when the target pollutant is SO_2, which is a precursor for fine PM and often generates significant cobenefits.

Finally, we recognize that, for some rules, the classification procedures we employ require a degree of subjectivity. We have nevertheless sought to define categories in ways that respond to emerging concerns about the role of cobenefits in EPA RIAs. Although a central part of our theoretical contribution later in the article is that such categorizations should not matter in BCAs, having some empirical foundation on which to anchor the discussion is important. We provide additional information in our data appendix (https://doi.org/10.7910/DVN/J2HWDA), including a link to our database so that other scholars, analysts, and stakeholders can replicate, modify, and expand on this analysis.

C.   Selecting Benefits and Costs Estimates

Few of the RIAs in our sample produce present values for the streams of costs and benefits over time. Notable exceptions are the joint EPA-NHTSA rules that address CO_2 emissions and fuel efficiency in vehicles. These RIAs produce annual streams of benefits and costs out to 2050.

As we will show later, EPA RIAs have consistently accounted for all the targeted and ancillary benefits and costs of regulations. But on other issues, RIAs have been considerably less consistent. The most common practice is to generate a "snapshot" estimate for the annual costs and benefits in a future year during "full implementation" of the rule. In many but not all of these cases, the benefits are not discounted to produce a present value in the year the regulation is promulgated. They are the value of benefits and costs in some future year expressed in some base year dollar equivalent. In a subset of these cases, the premature mortality benefits associated with PM—some of which occur with a period of latency—are discounted back to the snapshot year at either a 3% or a 7% discount rate. In addition, reducing CO_2 emissions and methane (CH_4) emissions that occur in a snapshot year generate benefits, which are spread out over hundreds of years, that are monetized using the social cost of carbon (SCC) and social cost of methane based on a 2.5%, 3%, or 5% discount rate.

Many RIAs also present ranges of estimates. Some may reflect differences in assumptions on the premature mortality dose-response functions for ozone and PM. Some may reflect a range over multiple implementation and compliance scenarios, especially in those cases where states have some discretion on how they implement the rule (e.g., the Regional Haze Regulations, RIN 2060-AF32).

The preceding discussion means that it is challenging to construct a consistent set of benefits and costs that enable true apples-to-apples comparisons across RIAs. In our analysis, we have nevertheless endeavored to create a data set that produces measures of benefits and costs that are as comparable as possible, given the information published in the RIAs. In general, we have opted for a full-implementation, snapshot-year measure of benefits and costs based on a 7% discount rate, where discounting is applied to the extent possible.[12] The SCC and some compliance cost calculations will be exceptions because of the differing rates used in the underlying analysis. Our database includes upper- and lower-bound estimates, but here we report results based on the average of the two, unless otherwise indicated. All values are reported in 2019 dollars, with conversions made using the standard gross domestic product (GDP) deflator.[13]

In some RIAs, the costs represent the amortization of capital and operating costs for complying with the regulation over a specified time horizon. This approach is typically estimated with a 7% discount rate. In other RIAs, the snapshot-year costs are simply the estimated compliance costs for that year, and it is unclear the extent to which these snapshots account for initial investments in pollution control equipment. In a few rules, the underlying model for estimating compliance uses discount rates other than 3% or 7%. For example, the model runs used for the NO_x SIP Call rule are based on a 6% rate.[14]

D. Results of Analysis of EPA CAA RIAs

The EPA regulatory program consistently delivers the greatest monetized benefits and imposes the largest costs of any federal regulatory agency's actions (e.g., OMB 2019). To provide context for an assessment of cobenefits, figure 2 illustrates the net social benefits for the CAA regulations in our database. The median rule has about $4.1 billion in net social benefits, based on the average of the lower and upper bounds of benefits and costs for that regulation's snapshot of a full-implementation year. Every rule has positive net social benefits, with five exceptions: (1) the 1997 NAAQS for ozone (RIN 2060-AE57), with an estimated –$6 billion in net social benefits; (2) the 1997 medical waste incinerator standards (RIN 2060-AC62), with an estimated –$125 million in net social benefits; (3) the 2008 NAAQS for lead (RIN 2060-AN83), with an estimated –$90 million net social benefits;[15] (4) the 2005 mercury power plant rule (RIN 2060-AJ65), with an estimated –$1 billion in net social benefits; and (5) the 2016 NSPS for methane at oil and gas operations (RIN 2060-AS30), with an estimated –$200 million in net social benefits.

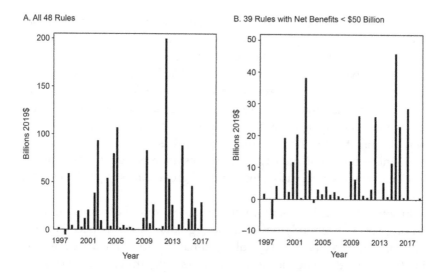

Fig. 2. Net social benefits of Clean Air Act regulatory impact analyses, 1997–2019. The amounts are based on 1-year full-implementation snapshots of monetized benefits and costs. In each panel, regulations are ordered chronologically. Panel A presents results for all 48 regulations in our database, and panel B excludes 9 regulations with net social benefits in excess of $50 billion to better illustrate impacts of rules with smaller net economic effects.

We find that cobenefits account for about 46% of the monetized benefits on average across all RIAs. As figure 3 illustrates, this average masks considerable heterogeneity among the rules. Some rules have no monetized cobenefits, such as the 2013 fine PM NAAQS and the 2014 Tier 3 motor vehicle and emissions standards, which targeted both fine PM and ozone. Other rules, especially several of those focused on HAPs, have zero monetized benefits for the targeted pollutant. In these cases, fine PM pollution reductions are the primary, if not exclusive, source for monetized benefits. For the three joint EPA-NHTSA regulations targeting carbon dioxide emissions and fuel economy (RINs 2060-AP61, 2060-AQ54, and 2060-AS16), we consider reduced fuel costs one of the target benefits of the regulation, given NHTSA's statutory authority. If, however, we were to consider reduced fuel costs a cobenefit from the standpoint of the EPA under its CAA authority, then about $130 billion of benefits over 2011–16 would shift and several of the black bars at the bottom of figure 3 would fall substantially.

The monetized cobenefits in CAA RIAs are primarily a story about fine PM. This has long been acknowledged by the EPA and OMB, the latter in its annual reports to Congress on the benefits and costs of regulation

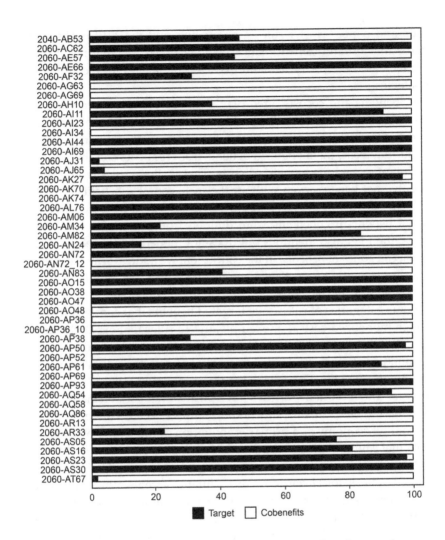

Fig. 3. Relative contribution of target pollutant benefits and cobenefits to total monetized benefits. Regulations are listed by regulation identifier number (RIN) and ordered chronologically from top to bottom spanning 1997–2019. The appendix lists each regulation with its associated RIN.

(e.g., EPA 1997; OMB 2005). In our assessment, the reductions in fine PM identified as cobenefits represent 96% of all monetized cobenefits over 1997–2019. The other categories are visibility (2%) and SO_2, ozone, CO_2, and energy and electricity savings (less than 1% each).

We should also note that in several cases, the EPA estimated cocosts because the regulation would increase emissions of a monetized pollutant. For example, the lower bound of the SO_2 cobenefits in the 1998 pulp and paper "cluster rule" are negative, and the 2010 HAPs standards for Portland cement plants include CO_2 cocosts that result from the increased electricity demand expected under facilities' compliance strategies.

Cobenefits and cocosts often play a pivotal role in determining the sign of net social benefits among the monetized categories of costs and benefits for many CAA regulations. For exactly 50% of the regulations in our database, the monetized benefits from reductions in the targeted pollutant exceed the monetized costs. That is, these rules would show positive net benefits even without the inclusion of cobenefits. The flip side is that half of the rules in our database would have negative net social benefits if cobenefits were omitted from the analysis. In these rules, the EPA also identifies but does not monetize a variety of additional categories of benefits. In the conclusion, we address why the agency may stop counting monetized benefits under the CAA after it has demonstrated positive net benefits.

Some categories of rules have targeted benefits that consistently outweigh monetized costs. For example, the 16 rules that explicitly target fine PM each have positive net social benefits based on an exclusive accounting of monetized benefits associated directly with the targeted pollutant. The joint EPA-NHTSA rules addressing tailpipe CO_2 emissions and fuel economy always have positive net social benefits based only on targeted benefits; this finding follows because of our accounting of fuel economy as a primary motivation of these rules and the sizable fuel savings benefits estimated by the agencies.

In contrast, regulations targeting HAPs—such as the National Emission Standards for Hazardous Air Pollutants—frequently have zero or modest monetized benefits for the targeted pollutant. Most regulations that focused on HAPs, 79% of those in our database, have monetized target benefits less than the monetized costs. In these cases, the monetized cobenefits derive from reductions in fine PM, and in some cases, the regulation explicitly limits PM emissions as a proxy for the HAP. For example, the HAP standard for combustion sources at various pulp mills (RIN 2060-AI34) explicitly notes that the "rule promulgates PM emissions limits as a surrogate for HAP metals" (66 *Federal Register* 3184). Although we classified the PM benefits in this case as cobenefits, these PM emissions limits are explicitly prescribed by the rule. Another reason, at least in the case of the MATS rule, is that the science for and means of economic evaluation for mercury emissions have evolved only recently, whereas the techniques for valuing the health consequences for fine PM are well established (Aldy et al. 2019). The value of monetizing additional benefits based on recent science in the context of RIAs for new air regulations is a topic to which we return later in the article.

Cobenefits and cocosts have been an important part of EPA analysis of its regulations for more than 2 decades. In nearly half the major rules, monetized benefits would not exceed monetized costs without consideration of cobenefits. The EPA's approach was consistent over time, following OMB and EPA guidance set long ago. Despite that, as we described in Section II, EPA rules in the past several years appear to be departing from this long-standing practice. In part, that departure responds to legitimate-sounding questions about the merits of counting untargeted benefits. In the next section, we look at the questions that have arisen, then address them in a simple economic model.

IV.   A Simple Theory of Cobenefits

The previous section demonstrates how the EPA has been considering cobenefits in RIAs for decades. Have they been counted appropriately? Although we do not answer this question on a case-by-case basis, this section describes a simple theoretical framework to help make such determinations. That is, we make the straightforward case for when cobenefits should or should not be fully counted in any BCA. We also address a few of the specific questions that have been raised about including cobenefits: (1) If cobenefits are large, wouldn't regulating them directly be more efficient or cost-effective? (2) How do we count cobenefits if the copollutant is already regulated? And (3) under what circumstances does the inclusion of cobenefits result in double counting?

A.   Decision Criteria

We begin with a discussion about the metrics used to judge the merits of alternative pollution policies. These are important because, as we will show, some of the questions and concerns raised about cobenefits are based on an appeal to different decision-making criteria. The first metric, taught in every Economics 101 course, is efficiency. In this context, efficiency requires that the marginal benefit from abating a unit of each pollutant equal the marginal cost. Though often the focus of conceptual discussions of pollution control policy, efficiency is rarely the metric by which policies are judged in practice. Establishing efficiency is a high bar, as it requires identifying and monetizing the incremental benefits and costs of regulating each pollutant.[16]

A second, less strict metric is cost-effectiveness, which is met when a given policy goal is achieved at least cost. The policy goal might be defined in terms of achieving an arbitrary regulated amount of pollution reduction or in terms of the monetary social benefits of pollution. Either way, cost-effectiveness is a weaker metric than efficiency. All efficient policies are cost-effective, but cost-effective policies are not necessarily efficient. Relative to efficiency, cost-effectiveness is easier to evaluate because it does not require knowing the incremental benefit of abating pollution. OMB (2003) Circular A-4 recommends that cost-effectiveness analysis, in addition to BCA, be used to support major rulemakings.

Finally, the criterion used implicitly by most federal agencies, and the one informed by BCA, is positive net benefits—that is, do the benefits of a policy exceed its costs? Having positive net benefits guarantees neither efficiency nor cost-effectiveness. Although all efficient policies have positive net benefits, policies with positive net benefits are not necessarily efficient. Alternatively, policies can minimize the cost of achieving a policy goal while incurring negative net benefits, or they can have positive net benefits but fail to minimize the costs of achieving a policy goal. We focus on this criterion in our discussion later because agency practice has emphasized this objective. The CAA does not provide an efficiency objective in setting pollutant and emission standards, and the cost-effectiveness objective is permissible under some but not all statutory authorities under the CAA. Moreover, the typical practice of regulatory agencies under EO 12866 has been to demonstrate whether benefits justify costs, which has typically been interpreted as a positive net benefits standard.

B. The Setup

Consider two pollutants, a target pollutant, denoted pollutant 1, and a copollutant, denoted pollutant 2. Pollutant 1 is the direct focus of a particular regulatory action, a policy, and pollutant 2 is secondary.[17] Each pollutant can be reduced through costly investments in abatement (e.g., fuel switching, installing abatement equipment). Abatement functions map investments in abatement into units of pollution reduction. Suppose there are two abatement activities. Let x_i denote investment in abatement activity $i = 1, 2$. The quantity of each pollutant ultimately reduced or the level of abatement, denoted a_1 and a_2, depends on investments in abatement activities. To simplify the intuition (and the math), we denominate the abatement activities x_1 and x_2 in units of pollution abated—the same units as a_1 and a_2.

To capture the idea of cobenefits, we assume that abatement activity 1 is a more direct means of abating pollutant 1, but it has some spillover benefits in the form of reductions in pollutant 2. The reverse is true for abatement activity 2: it is the most direct mechanism for abating pollutant 2 but also abates pollutant 1. We write these abatement functions as

$$a_1 = x_1 + \gamma_2 x_2 \text{ and } a_2 = x_2 + \gamma_1 x_1, \tag{1}$$

where the γs are each less than 1 and greater than 0. A 1-unit increase in x_1 yields 1 fewer unit of pollutant 1 as well as γ_2 fewer units of pollutant 2. Similarly, when x_2 increases by 1 unit, abatement of pollutant 2 increases by 1 unit and abatement of pollutant 1 increases by γ_1 units.

Figure 4 depicts this basic setup. Investments x_1 and x_2 are represented on the two axes. Abatement and benefits are increasing to the northeast, as are costs. An iso-cost curve $C(x_1, x_2)$ shows all the combinations of investments x_1 and x_2 that lead to the same cost, $\bar{C}$. Because we denominate the investments in pollution abated, the marginal costs of abating each pollutant using investments x_1 and x_2 are increasing. This leads to a convex iso-cost curve, as depicted in figure 4.

C. Policies

Now consider a policy that mandates a particular amount of abatement for the target pollutant a_1 at some arbitrary level k_1. In this case, suppose that the regulator implements the target through a performance standard that permits discretion by regulated entities on the choice over pollution control investment so long as they limit their emissions to or below a specified emissions level or rate. Note that the target level of abatement can be achieved entirely by investment in abatement activity 1 ($x_1 = k_1$), entirely by investment in abatement activity 2 ($x_2 = k_1/\gamma_2$), or by some linear combination of the two. The constraint on abatement of the target pollutant imposed by the policy is depicted as the straight line in figure 4, corresponding to the equation $k_1 = x_1 + \gamma_2 x_2$.

The least costly way to comply with the regulation is represented by the lowest iso-cost curve tangent to this line. Depending on the shape

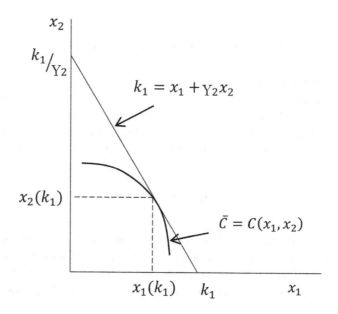

Fig. 4. Cost-effective compliance using two activities (x_1 and x_2) with regulation on one target pollutant ($a_1 \geq k_1$).

of the iso-cost function, that could be at the corner solution using only x_1, at the corner solution using only x_2, or as depicted in the figure at an interior solution using some of both. The least-cost combination $(x_1(k_1), x_2(k_1))$ is by definition cost-effective.

In this example, compliance with regulation of the target pollutant in the least costly way also results in some abatement of the second pollutant. In particular,

$$a_2 = x_2(k_1) + \gamma_1 x_1(k_1). \tag{2}$$

Equation (2) results from plugging the cost-minimizing values of x_1 and x_2 from figure 4 into the abatement function for a_2 in equation (1). The abatement a_2 is a benefit of policy k_1 that targets pollutant 1; it would not have occurred absent the policy. The abatement of pollutant 2 arises from cost-effective compliance with the policy on pollutant 1 through investments in both abatement activities, x_1 and x_2. Note that by equation (2), even with the corner solution at which $x_2(k_1) = 0$, there would still be abatement of a_2 as long as γ_1 is positive.[18] Abatement of the copollutant is a cobenefit only in the semantic sense that the regulatory policy goal was to reduce pollutant 1.

Any policy requiring $a_1 \geq k_1$ that passes a BCA while ignoring those cobenefits would also pass a BCA considering those cobenefits. Nevertheless, some policies that would fail a BCA ignoring cobenefits would pass a BCA once cobenefits are considered. Moreover, in some cases, cobenefits alone may be sufficient for a policy to pass a BCA. Of course, as discussed earlier, passing a BCA does not mean that a policy is efficient or even cost-effective. This raises one of the chief criticisms of counting cobenefits—that if they are important, they should be regulated directly.

D. Targeting Copollutants Directly

Concerns about cobenefits often focus on questions related to cost-effectiveness. For example, when commenting on the MATS rule, Dudley (2012) wrote, "If [PM$_{2.5}$ co-benefits] are legitimate, certainly confronting them directly would achieve PM$_{2.5}$ reductions more *cost-effectively* than going after them indirectly using statutory authority designed to reduce toxic air pollutants" (173, emphasis added). Smith (2011) asserted that "PM$_{2.5}$-related benefits would be more certain and more *cost-effectively* obtained through a different regulation altogether than an air toxics rule" (14, emphasis added).

To address this cost-effectiveness critique, suppose that the regulator considers an alternative policy approach: designing a performance standard to regulate pollutant 2 directly with the target of achieving at least as much abatement as resulted indirectly from the policy targeting pollutant 1 (Sec. IV.C). This approach would require a policy a_2 that satisfies $a_2 \geq k_2 = x_2(k_1) + \gamma_1 x_1(k_1)$ as in equation (2). As earlier, this target level of abatement for pollutant 2 can be met by any linear combination of x_1 and x_2, depicted by the new line added to figure 5, which corresponds to the equation $k_2 = x_2 + \gamma_1 x_1$.

Because the new policy rule is designed to meet the same level of reduction in pollutant 2 achieved by the original policy, it must go through the original cost-minimizing point for compliance with k_1. Note that one way to comply with the new policy is to do exactly the same thing that complied with the original policy. But the slope of the new k_2 policy is less steep than the slope of the original k_1 policy because $-\gamma_1 > -1/\gamma_2$. As shown in figure 5, the line representing the new policy necessarily passes below portions of the iso-cost curve that is tangent to the original k_1 line. This means that a different, lower iso-cost curve, representing smaller

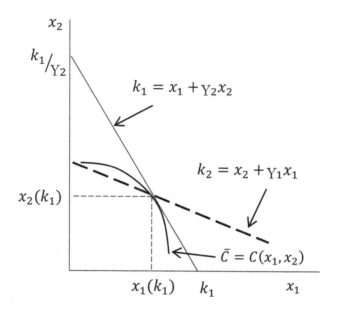

Fig. 5. Cost savings that arise from directly targeting cobenefits but ignoring reductions in originally targeted pollutant.

investments in x_1 and x_2, could achieve the same level of abatement for pollutant 2 at lower cost than $\bar{C}$.

But important, the cost savings do not come for free. The achievement—abating pollutant 2 by an amount equal to the cobenefits from targeting pollutant 1—occurs with an opportunity cost: reduced abatement of pollutant 1. In figure 5, there are no points along the line k_2 where both the original pollutant 1 regulation is met (above k_1) and costs are reduced (below $\bar{C}$). Therefore, the argument against cobenefits ("Wouldn't it be better to target them directly?") works only if we ignore the broader benefits of abating the target pollutant. In this case of the policy targeting pollutant 2, abatement of pollutant 1 arises as a cobenefit due to the same connected abatement activities that resulted in reductions in pollutant 2 originally.

To put it bluntly, the efficiency argument against considering cobenefits holds in general only if we ignore cobenefits. Ultimately, however, it is an empirical question as to whether taking a more cost-effective approach to targeting pollutant 2 results in greater net benefits relative to a counterfactual of targeting pollutant 1. Regulatory decision making is also critically important to a reliance on the cost-effectiveness rationale. The assertion that it would be more cost-effective to regulate pollutant 2 can hold only if the regulator decides to adopt a regulation that targets pollutant 2. As an illustration of how lack of follow-up can come up short, the EPA (2020c) promulgated, on May 22, 2020, its final rule withdrawing the "appropriate and necessary" determination of the MATS rule (Sec. II.D) by excluding consideration of $PM_{2.5}$ benefits. This final rule could have teed up the agency to pursue a new regulatory approach to target $PM_{2.5}$ directly and possibly obtain the associated benefits more cost-effectively. Instead, the EPA (2020d) issued a proposal against setting a more stringent $PM_{2.5}$ NAAQS at effectively the same time (April 30, 2020).

E. Preexisting Policies

We have focused so far on examples in which no preexisting policies regulate either pollutant. With no preexisting policies, benefits are never double counted. Nevertheless, another argument related to the treatment of cobenefits in BCA relates to the potential for double counting in the presence of preexisting policies. For example, Gray (2015, 32) argues that "whenever EPA counts $PM_{2.5}$ or ozone reductions in its cost-benefit analysis for other rules, it is double-counting reductions already mandated."

To examine this concern, we add a preexisting policy targeting pollutant 2, such that abatement must be at least as large as $\bar{k}_2 = \gamma_1 x_1 + x_2$. Figure 6 depicts this case. Note that the preexisting policy can be met with any level of $a_2 \geq \bar{k}_2$ and does not imply a specific level of abatement, as in the previous section. Least-cost compliance with the preexisting policy on a_2 occurs at point A in the figure. The associated cost is $C(x_1(\bar{k}_2), \ x_2(\bar{k}_2))$.

In the presence of the preexisting policy on pollutant 2, consider a new policy that will target pollutant 1. Will this lead to cobenefits or cocosts associated with changes in the abatement of pollutant 2? The answer turns out to depend on the stringency of the new policy, the technology parameters (γ_1 and γ_2), and the cost functions. Figure 6 depicts several possibilities.

The first case is trivial, and arises if the new policy, k'_1 in figure 6, is nonbinding. In this example, compliance with the original policy $\bar{k}_2$ already led to abatement of the first pollutant, a_1, sufficient to comply with the new regulation. There were, in a sense, reverse cobenefits generated from reductions in a_1 due to compliance with the preexisting $\bar{k}_2$ policy, and these reductions were more than sufficient to meet compliance

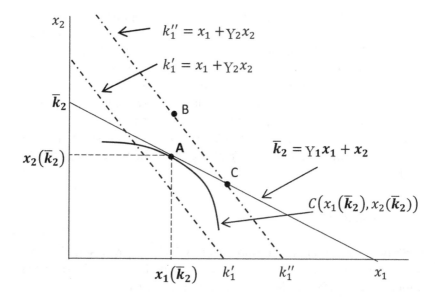

Fig. 6. Effect of preexisting policy on possibility, or lack thereof, of cobenefits.

with the k_1' policy. Polluters therefore need to make no changes, and cost minimization remains at point A in the figure. The new policy k_1' has no benefits or costs.

The more interesting case arises if the new policy binds, as in k_1'' in figure 6. Here compliance with the new policy must increase costs, because the original point A is insufficient to comply with the new policy targeting pollutant 1. In this case there are two possibilities: an interior solution and a corner solution. In the first, depicted as point B, polluters must overcomply with the original policy $\bar{k}_2$ to meet the new k_1'' policy. Compared with point A, abatement of both pollutants is higher at point B, so benefits are also higher. The increase in a_1 generates the target pollutant benefits from the new policy, and the new and additional increase in a_2 represents cobenefits.[19]

In the corner-solution case, represented by point C, there are no cobenefits. Polluters exactly comply with both policies. They comply with the original policy $\bar{k}_2$ in a less cost-effective way, by increasing x_1 and decreasing x_2, but in doing so they comply with the new rule k_1''. Emissions of pollutant 2 simply remain at the level originally mandated under the policy $\bar{k}_2$, reflecting firms' investment adjustments in the two abatement activities. Without accounting for these adjustments, double counting would be a concern. We return to the subject again later, but first we discuss the possibility for the relevant adjustments.

F. Regulatory Rebound

A more nuanced criticism of counting cobenefits on par with benefits associated with the directly targeted pollutant relates to what Fowlie, Rubin, and Wright (2020) call "regulatory rebound." The argument is that when a preexisting regulation limits the level of emissions of pollutant 2, a new policy that indirectly generates reductions in pollutant 2 when it targets reductions in pollutant 1 can induce a regulatory response that permits an increase in the level of pollutant 2 back to the originally mandated level.[20] In the previous discussion, this possibility was unlikely, except in the corner-solution case, because we assumed the two abatement activities generated reciprocal cobenefits; that is, both γ_1 and γ_2 were assumed to be greater than 0. If cobenefits are not reciprocal, then there are two additional possibilities to explore: $\gamma_2 = 0$ or $\gamma_1 = 0$. We start with the first.

Suppose $\gamma_2 = 0$ and $0 < \gamma_1 < 1$ such that investments in abatement activity 1 reduce emissions of pollutant 2 (in addition to pollutant 1) but investments in abatement activity 2 reduce only emissions of pollutant 2.[21] Also suppose there is a preexisting policy on pollutant 2 such that $a_2 \geq \bar{k}_2$. Because $a_2 = \gamma_1 x_1 + x_2$, the policy constraint is just a sloped line as before, depicted in the left panel of figure 7. Cost-minimizing compliance with the $\bar{k}_2$ is depicted as $(x_1(\bar{k}_2), x_2(\bar{k}_2))$. If the regulator now adds a new policy targeting pollutant 1 and denoted as k_1, then the associated constraint can be represented by a vertical line, as in the figure, because $\gamma_2 = 0$. The new policy effectively mandates a minimum level of x_1, investment in abatement activity 1. Complying with the new k_1 policy involves higher costs, less x_2 and more x_1, but no additional abatement of pollutant 2 (i.e., $a_2 = \bar{k}_2$ as before). In this case, there are no cobenefits. Polluters merely comply with the new policy k_1 in a way that increases the cost of meeting the preexisting policy k_2, but that generates the same amount of reduction in pollutant 2. Compliance costs from the new policy k_1 are represented in the graph by the difference between the two cost curves, and the new policy's benefits arise from the increase in a_1. This is 100% regulatory rebound and is a special case of the corner solution depicted as point C in figure 6, which occurs if the new policy k_1 is sufficiently low. If instead the new policy constraint were to the right of the horizontal intercept of $\bar{k}_2$, there would be cobenefits.

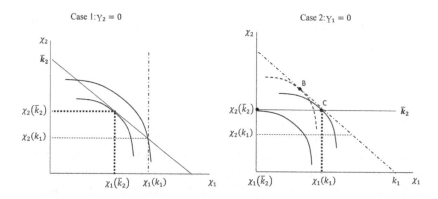

Fig. 7. Special cases with preexisting policies. Case 1 is 100% regulatory rebound with increased costs and no cobenefits; case 2 is increased costs and either cobenefits (point B) or 100% regulatory rebound and no cobenefits.

For completeness, examine the alternative scenario with no cobenefits from the target pollutant to the previously regulated pollutant ($\gamma_1 = 0$), but reverse cobenefits from the previously regulated pollutant to the target pollutant ($0 < \gamma_2 < 1$). This case is depicted in the right-hand panel of figure 7. Here, the preexisting policy $\bar{k}_2$ is represented as a horizontal line; because $\gamma_1 = 0$, the preexisting policy targeting pollutant 2 effectively mandates a minimum level of x_2. Complying with the preexisting policy involves a corner solution, where $x_1 = 0$. When the new policy targeting abatement of pollutant 2 is added such that $a_1 \geq k_1$, then cost-minimizing compliance involves increasing x_1 but not necessarily increasing x_2. First consider point C, which depicts one possibility—cost-minimizing compliance with no increase in x_2 or a_2. This is another special case of the corner solution depicted as point C in figure 6 (Sec. IV.E).

Now consider point B, which represents the cost-minimizing compliance outcome at the tangency between the dashed iso-cost curve and the new policy k_1 (above the $\bar{k}_2$ constraint). In this case, the new policy k_1 yields overcompliance with the preexisting policy $\bar{k}_2$, and therefore cobenefits, as in the interior solution depicted as point B in figure 6. Indeed, figure 7 contains nothing more than two exaggerated examples of what happens in figure 6. In figure 7, as in all the figures, the k_1 policy line is steeper than the $\bar{k}_2$ policy line, by the assumption that $0 < \gamma_1, \gamma_2 < 1$.

In sum, when we add a policy targeting pollutant 1 in the presence of a preexisting policy that targets pollutant 2, there are three possible outcomes. The new policy is (1) moot, and there are no benefits or cobenefits (point A in fig. 6); (2) a corner solution with no cobenefits (point C in fig. 6); or (3) an interior solution with cobenefits (point B in fig. 6). Expanding the analysis in figure 6 by considering extreme values for the cobenefits, as done in figure 7, such that the k_1 line is completely horizontal or the $\bar{k}_2$ line vertical, makes no difference. We still get one of the three possible outcomes.

G.   Double Counting

Returning now to the question: Does considering cobenefits amount to double counting? In some cases, the concern is that the EPA does not follow its own guidelines, which stipulate that baselines for RIAs must assume full compliance with all previously enacted rules, even if those rules have not yet been implemented or complied with (EPA 2014). In other cases, however, critics seem to presume that any consideration of cobenefits would represent double counting.

Our analysis addresses both concerns. Any analysis that ignores a previous policy and assumes that all reductions in pollution stem from compliance with a new policy will double count benefits already counted in a BCA for the original policy. That is why we consider cobenefits to be 0 at points A and C in figure 6, in case 1 in figure 7, and in the corner solution of case 2 in figure 7. In some of these cases, an important mechanism to recognize is the regulatory rebound. Even if the new policy initially reduces a copollutant, adjustments in compliance to a preexisting policy may be such that actual copollutant levels do not change after those adjustments take place. But if the original benefits were already counted, double counting would result.

At the same time, cobenefits represent true benefits when they result in overcompliance with the original rule, as in point B in figure 6 or the dashed interior solution in case 2 in figure 7. Not considering those cobenefits would represent undercounting, not double counting.

V.   Discussion and Conclusion

This article considers the treatment of cobenefits in BCAs, with a particular focus on federal air quality regulations, for which questions and concerns about the role of cobenefits have been gaining momentum. Using a comprehensive data set on all major CAA rules issued by the EPA over the period 1997–2019, we show several trends and patterns. First, cobenefits make up a significant share of the monetized benefits in EPA

RIAs over this period. Second, among the categories of cobenefits, those associated with reductions in adverse health effects due to fine PM are the most significant. Third, the inclusion of cobenefits has been critical in the majority of RIAs for making the determination in prospective analyses that the monetized benefits of the rule exceed the costs.

Are these findings cause for concern? We find that, in general and from a welfare economics perspective, the answer is no. We develop a simple conceptual framework to illustrate a critical point: cobenefits are simply a semantic category of benefits that should be included in BCAs to make an appropriate determination about whether a given policy promotes economic efficiency compared with a baseline status quo. Indeed, this finding is not novel and is covered in standard textbook treatments of best practice for BCAs (e.g., Boardman et al. 2018).[22]

More novel is our consideration of specific questions and concerns about cobenefits that have been raised in the context of CAA rules. First, if cobenefits are large, wouldn't regulating them directly be more efficient or cost-effective? Although a regulator could deliver a given level of cobenefits more cost-effectively by targeting the copollutant directly, such a direct policy is not necessarily a more efficient alternative. In fact, we show that this line of argument against considering cobenefits depends on a tautology, whereby it holds generally only if one starts with the proposition that we should ignore cobenefits. The argument also relies on the questionable starting point that a proposed regulation for one pollutant can be replaced by one for another. Though possible in theory, the idea does not square with the required statutory basis for most CAA regulations.

The second question relates to how we should count cobenefits if the copollutant is already subject to a preexisting regulation. In this case, we show how care needs be taken to measure only those benefits that are the incremental consequence of the policy under consideration. But these challenges are the same as those that arise more generally when regulators are identifying the most appropriate baseline for analysis, and they are not unique to the estimation of cobenefits. In doing so, however, particular attention should be given to the potential for regulatory rebound—that is, the policy under consideration may shift behaviors related to compliance with another policy that targets the copollutant. Taking account of these effects will avoid the possibility for double counting.

By carefully accounting for the cobenefits (and cocosts) of a proposed regulatory action, the EPA can better understand the impacts of the envisioned rule on society and, in theory, use this information to craft a better regulation. Exploiting the full information from a BCA could enable more efficient regulatory design. It may also highlight the potential for greater benefits by targeting both pollutants through regulation. Indeed, there are cases—such as the 1998 pulp and paper cluster rule (RIN 2040-AB53) and the more recent joint EPA-NHTSA tailpipe CO_2/fuel economy standards (RINs 2060-AP61, 2060-AQ54, and 2060-AS16)—where the agencies implemented multiple statutory authorities to realize multiple types of societal benefits.[23]

We conclude with some observations about the political economy underlying why it appears that cobenefits are an increasing topic of debate, notwithstanding how the questions are relatively "settled science" from the perspective of how to conduct BCAs. First, it is important to recognize that in practice, BCAs rarely (if ever) quantify and monetize all the expected benefits and costs of an action. Even as the science and methods of valuation continue to advance, many categories of benefits remain exceedingly difficult or impossible to estimate. Estimating more categories of benefits also takes time and resources, which are often scarce. It is nevertheless sufficient to show that a subset of the benefits, which may arise entirely from cobenefits, are greater than the costs to conclude that a regulation has positive net benefits. This aim in itself can explain why cobenefits are important to BCA of CAA regulations. Research and the development of best practices tend to focus on the impacts that have the greatest value, and the health benefits of reducing fine PM appear to be dramatically larger than the health impacts of cutting other air pollutants. Because the CAA does not require—and in some cases explicitly prohibits consideration of—BCA to inform the setting of air quality standards and regulations, the value of the information in an RIA lies in its communication to the public, stakeholders, and Congress. For many consumers of this information, once the EPA has demonstrated that the monetized benefits exceed the monetized costs, the value of incremental information on other benefits becomes quite low.

Second, the distinction between the quantified, monetized benefits and the true total benefits means that there are two possible interpretations of our findings. It could be that cobenefits truly make up a large part of the actual total social benefits. Alternatively, it could be that cobenefits just happen to be easier for the EPA to monetize, and so make up a large share of the quantified, monetized benefits reported in RIAs.

Finally, let us observe a fundamental tension in the implementation of federal regulatory policy as it pertains to the CAA. As noted earlier, for

4 decades the White House has directed regulatory agencies to adopt rules whose benefits justify or exceed the costs and to pursue, where feasible, regulatory options that maximize net social benefits. Since 2017, however, the Trump administration has focused on the costs of regulations, both through a "regulatory budget" that effectively places limits on the incremental costs new rules can impose on society (regardless of net social benefits) and in its deregulation agenda (CEA 2019). With virtually every CAA regulation since 1997 estimated to deliver monetized benefits in excess of monetized costs (see fig. 2), the removal of any of these rules through deregulatory actions would impose social costs in excess of the benefits.[24] Casting doubt on the applicability or validity of the benefits from reducing fine PM by questioning the appropriateness of including cobenefits could enable a regulator to pursue actions that reduce regulatory costs without appearing to impose net social costs. But for reasons we have discussed, this conclusion would be wrong.

Appendix

Table A1
Major Clean Air Act Regulations, Compiled from Office of Management and Budget Reports to Congress, 1997–2019

RIN	Rule	Date	Federal Register	Monetized Benefits?
2060-AE66	National Ambient Air Quality Standards for Particulate Matter	July 18, 1997	62 FR 38652	Y
2060-AE57	National Ambient Air Quality Standards for Ozone	July 18, 1997	62 FR 38856	Y
2060-AC62	Standards of Performance for New Stationary Sources and Emission Guidelines for Existing Sources: Hospital/Medical/ Infectious Waste Incinerators	September 15, 1997	62 FR 48348	Y
2060-AF76	Control of Emissions of Air Pollution from Highway Heavy- Duty Engines	October 21, 1997	62 FR 54694	N
2040-AB53	National Emission Standards for Hazardous Air Pollutants for Source Category: Pulp and Paper Production; Effluent Limitations Guidelines, Pretreatment Standards, and New Source Performance Standards: Pulp, Paper, and Paper- board Category	April 15, 1998	63 FR 18504	Y
2060-AD33	Emission Standards for Locomotives and Locomotive Engines	April 16, 1998	63 FR 18978	N
2060-AF76_98	Control of Emissions of Air Pollution from Nonroad Diesel Engines	October 1, 1998	63 FR 56968	N
2060-AH10	Finding of Significant Contribution and Rulemaking for Certain States in the Ozone Transport Assessment Group Region for Purposes of Reducing Regional Transport of Ozone	October 27, 1998	63 FR 57356	Y
2060-AE29	Phase 2 Emission Standards for New Nonroad Spark- Ignition Nonhandheld Engines at or below 19 Kilowatts	March 30, 1999	64 FR 15208	N
2060-AH88	Findings of Significant Contribution and Rulemaking on Section 126 Petitions for Purposes of Reducing Interstate Ozone Transport	May 25, 1999	64 FR 28250	N

Continued

Table A1
Continued

RIN	Rule	Date	*Federal Register*	Monetized Benefits?
2060-AF32	Regional Haze Regulations	July 1, 1999	64 FR 35714	Y
2060-AI23	Control of Air Pollution from New Motor Vehicles: Tier 2 Motor Vehicle Emissions Standards and Gasoline Sulfur Control Requirements	February 10, 2000	65 FR 6698	Y
2060-AE29_00	Phase 2 Emission Standards for New Nonroad Spark-Ignition Handheld Engines at or below 19 Kilowatts and Minor Amendments to Emission Requirements Applicable to Small Spark-Ignition Engines and Marine Spark-Ignition Engines	April 25, 2000	65 FR 24268	N
2060-AI12	Control of Emissions of Air Pollution from 2004 and Later Model Year Heavy-Duty Highway Engines and Vehicles; Revision of Light-Duty On-Board Diagnostics Requirements	October 6, 2000	65 FR 59896	N
2060-AI34	National Emission Standards for Hazardous Air Pollutants for Chemical Recovery Combustion Sources at Kraft, Soda, Sulfite, and Stand-Alone Semichemical Pulp Mills	January 12, 2001	66 FR 3180	Y
2060-AI69	Control of Air Pollution from New Motor Vehicles: Heavy-Duty Engine and Vehicle Standards and Highway Diesel Fuel Sulfur Control Requirements	January 18, 2001	66 FR 5002	Y
2060-AI11	Control of Emissions from Nonroad Large Spark-Ignition Engines, and Recreational Engines (Marine and Land-Based)	November 8, 2002	67 FR 68242	Y
2060-AG63	National Emission Standards for Hazardous Air Pollutants for Stationary Reciprocating Internal Combustion Engines	June 15, 2004	69 FR 33474	Y
2060-AK27	Control of Emissions of Air Pollution from Nonroad Diesel Engines and Fuel	June 29, 2004	69 FR 38958	Y
2060-AG52	National Emission Standards for Hazardous Air Pollutants: Plywood and Composite Wood Products; Effluent	July 30, 2004	69 FR 45944	N

Code	Description	Date	FR Citation	
	Limitations Guidelines and Standards for the Timber Products Point Source Category; List of Hazardous Air Pollutants, Lesser Quantity Designations, Source Category List			
2060-AG69	National Emission Standards for Hazardous Air Pollutants for Industrial, Commercial, and Institutional Boilers and Process Heaters	September 13, 2004	69 FR 55218	Y
2060-AL76	Rule to Reduce Interstate Transport of Fine Particulate Matter and Ozone (Clean Air Interstate Rule); Revisions to Acid Rain Program; Revisions to the NOX SIP Call	May 12, 2005	70 FR 25162	Y
2060-AJ65	Standards of Performance for New and Existing Stationary Sources: Electric Utility Steam Generating Units	May 18, 2005	70 FR 28606	Y
2060-AJ31	Regional Haze Regulations and Guidelines for Best Available Retrofit Technology (BART) Determinations	July 6, 2005	70 FR 39104	Y
2060-AM82	Standards of Performance for Stationary Compression Ignition Internal Combustion Engines	July 11, 2006	71 FR 39154	Y
2060-AI44	National Ambient Air Quality Standards for Particulate Matter	October 17, 2006	71 FR 61144	Y
2060-AK70	Control of Hazardous Air Pollutants from Mobile Sources	February 26, 2007	72 FR 8428	Y
2060-AK74	Clean Air Fine Particle Implementation	April 25, 2007	72 FR 20586	Y
2060-AN24	National Ambient Air Quality Standards for Ozone	March 27, 2008	73 FR 16436	Y
2060-AM06	Control of Emissions of Air Pollution from Locomotive Engines and Marine Compression-Ignition Engines Less Than 30 Liters per Cylinder	May 6, 2008	73 FR 25098	Y
2060-AN72	Standards of Performance for Petroleum Refineries	June 24, 2008	73 FR 35838	Y
2060-AM34	Control of Emissions from Nonroad Spark-Ignition Engines and Equipment	October 8, 2008	73 FR 59034	Y
2060-AN83	National Ambient Air Quality Standards for Lead	November 12, 2008	73 FR 66964	Y
2060-AO79	Mandatory Reporting of Greenhouse Gases	October 30, 2009	74 FR 56260	N
2060-AP36	National Emission Standards for Hazardous Air Pollutants for Reciprocating Internal Combustion Engines	March 3, 2010	75 FR 9648	Y
2060-AO38	Control of Emissions of Air Pollution from Category 3 Marine Diesel Engines	April 30, 2010	75 FR 22896	Y

Continued

149

Table A1
Continued

RIN	Rule	Date	*Federal Register*	Monetized Benefits?
2060-AO48	Primary National Ambient Air Quality Standard for Sulfur Dioxide	June 22, 2010	75 FR 35520	Y
2060-AP36_10	National Emission Standards for Hazardous Air Pollutants for Reciprocating Internal Combustion Engines	August 20, 2010	75 FR 51570	Y
2060-AO15	Amendments to the National Emission Standards for Hazardous Air Pollutants and New Source Performance Standards (NSPS) for the Portland Cement Manufacturing Industry	September 9, 2010	75 FR 54970	Y
2060-AP50	Federal Implementation Plans: Interstate Transport of Fine Particulate Matter and Ozone and Correction of SIP Approvals	August 8, 2011	76 FR 48208	Y
2060-AP61	Greenhouse Gas Emissions Standards and Fuel Efficiency Standards for Medium- and Heavy-Duty Engines and Vehicles	September 15, 2011	76 FR 57106	Y
2060-AP52	National Emission Standards for Hazardous Air Pollutants from Coal- and Oil-Fired Electric Utility Steam Generating Units and Standards of Performance for Fossil-Fuel-Fired Electric Utility, Industrial-Commercial-Institutional, and Small Industrial-Commercial-Institutional Steam Generating Units	February 16, 2012	77 FR 9304	Y
2060-AP76	Oil and Natural Gas Sector: New Source Performance Standards and National Emission Standards for Hazardous Air Pollutants Reviews	August 16, 2012	77 FR 49490	N
2060-AN72_12	Standards of Performance for Petroleum Refineries; Standards of Performance for Petroleum Refineries for Which Construction, Reconstruction, or Modification Commenced after May 14, 2007	September 12, 2012	77 FR 56422	Y
2060-AQ54	2017–2025 Light-Duty Vehicle Greenhouse Gas Emission Standards and Corporate Average Fuel Economy Standards	October 15, 2012	77 FR 62624	Y

RIN	Title	Date	FR citation	Modified
2060-AO47	National Ambient Air Quality Standards for Particulate Matter	January 15, 2013	78 FR 3086	Y
2060-AQ58	National Emission Standards for Hazardous Air Pollutants for Reciprocating Internal Combustion Engines; New Source Performance Standards for Stationary Internal Combustion Engines	January 30, 2013	78 FR 6674	Y
2060-AR13	National Emission Standards for Hazardous Air Pollutants for Major Sources: Industrial, Commercial, and Institutional Boilers and Process Heaters	January 31, 2013	78 FR 7138	Y
2060-AQ86	Control of Air Pollution from Motor Vehicles: Tier 3 Motor Vehicle Emission and Fuel Standards	April 28, 2014	79 FR 23414	Y
2060-AP93	Standards of Performance for New Residential Wood Heaters, New Residential Hydronic Heaters and Forced-Air Furnaces	March 16, 2015	80 FR 13672	Y
2060-AR33	Carbon Pollution Emission Guidelines for Existing Stationary Sources: Electric Utility Generating Units	October 23, 2015	80 FR 64662	Y
2060-AP38	National Ambient Air Quality Standards for Ozone	October 26, 2015	80 FR 65292	Y
2060-AP69	NESHAP for Brick and Structural Clay Products Manufacturing; and NESHAP for Clay Ceramics Manufacturing		80 FR 65470	Y
2060-AS30	Oil and Natural Gas Sector: Emission Standards for New, Reconstructed, and Modified Sources	June 3, 2016	81 FR 35824	Y
2060-AS23	Emission Guidelines and Compliance Times for Municipal Solid Waste Landfills	August 29, 2016	81 FR 59276	Y
2060-AS16	Greenhouse Gas Emissions and Fuel Efficiency Standards for Medium- and Heavy-Duty Engines and Vehicles—Phase 2	October 25, 2016	81 FR 73478	Y
2060-AS05	Cross-State Air Pollution Rule Update for the 2008 Ozone NAAQS	October 26, 2016	81 FR 74504	Y
2060-AT67	Repeal of the Clean Power Plan; Emission Guidelines for Greenhouse Gas Emissions from Existing Electric Utility Generating Units; Revisions to Emission Guidelines Implementing Regulations	July 8, 2019	84 FR 32520	Y

Note: RIN = regulation identifier number. Where the Environmental Protection Agency used the same RIN more than once, we have modified the second instance by adding an extension that represents the two-digit year of rule promulgation.

Endnotes

Author email addresses: Aldy (joseph_aldy@hks.harvard.edu), Kotchen (matthew. kotchen@yale.edu). This article was prepared for inclusion in the Environmental and Energy Policy and the Economy conference and publication, sponsored by the National Bureau of Economic Research (NBER). We are grateful to Sofia Caycedo and Tim Bialecki for valuable research assistance while students at Yale. We thank participants at the NBER Environmental and Energy Policy and the Economy conference, Sally Atwater, and Bill Hogan for constructive feedback on an earlier draft. The authors gratefully acknowledge financial support from the NBER and the External Environmental Economics Advisory Committee. For acknowledgments, sources of research support, and disclosure of the authors' material financial relationships, if any, please see https://www.nber.org/books-and-chapters/environmental-and-energy-policy-and-economy-volume-2/co-benefits-and-regulatory-impact-analysis-theory-and-evidence-federal-air-quality-regulations.

1. A major rule is one that has an impact of $100 million or more in at least 1 year. Only a small fraction of final rules are considered major. For example, according to OMB (2019), only 609 of 36,255 final rules published in the *Federal Register* from FY 2007 to FY 2016, or 1.7%, meet the criterion for major designation.

2. The calculation includes four rules jointly promulgated by the EPA and the Department of Transportation (DOT; OMB 2019, table 1-1).

3. We use the term cobenefits throughout the article, though other terms are frequently used as well in the literature and government analyses in reference to the same concept. Impacts may be characterized as "secondary," "indirect," and "ancillary," among others. When referring to cobenefits, we also assume implicitly the possibility for negative benefits—that is, cocosts.

4. In spring 2020, the EPA drafted revisions to its economic guidelines and commissioned their review by a panel convened by the agency's Science Advisory Board (EPA 2020a). The topic of cobenefits (ancillary impacts) and its treatment in the economic guidelines elicited substantial public comment (in writing and during oral remarks in the public comments of the panel meetings) and feedback from panel members. Two coauthors of this article, Aldy and Levinson, are members of that review panel.

5. Refer to Section 2 of the Energy Policy and Conservation Act, Public Law 94-163, December 22, 1975, https://www.govinfo.gov/content/pkg/STATUTE-89/pdf/STATUTE-89-Pg871.pdf.

6. Refer to Sections 102 and 105 of the Energy Independence and Security Act of 2007, Public Law 110-140, December 19, 2007. https://www.govinfo.gov/content/pkg/PLAW-110publ140/pdf/PLAW-110publ140.pdf.

7. Refer to Section 1501 of the Energy Policy Act of 2005, Public Law 109-58, August 8, 2005. https://www.congress.gov/109/plaws/publ58/PLAW-109publ58.pdf.

8. Refer to Section 202 of the Energy Independence and Security Act of 2007.

9. The database and documentation can be accessed at https://doi.org/10.7910/DVN/J2HWDA.

10. Although the RIAs for some rules mention nonmonetized benefits, given the nature of our analysis, we necessarily restrict attention to monetized benefits and costs.

11. We use regulation identifier numbers to identify each regulation we describe in the text. The appendix table lists all regulations with their RINs, publication dates, and *Federal Register* cites that we have compiled for this analysis.

12. We note that the choice of discount rate is less of a concern for this analysis because of the way that benefits and costs are reported for a given snapshot year. There are two categories of exceptions. First, some RIAs present latent fine PM premature mortality risks. These RIAs estimate the present value of these risks over 5 years from the snapshot year. Second, joint EPA-NHTSA regulations addressing fuel economy provide the present value of the benefits from vehicles regulated in the snapshot year.

13. We accessed the GDP Implicit Price Deflator annual series from the St. Louis Federal Reserve Economic Data website on May 11, 2020, https://fred.stlouisfed.org/series/A191RI1Q225SBEA.

14. Refer to table 4-1 in EPA (1998).

15. In the lead NAAQS RIA, the lower-bound benefits exceed the lower-bound costs estimated with a 7% discount rate. Under a 3% discount rate, the lower and upper bounds of the monetized benefits exceed their corresponding scenario's costs.

16. We recognize other potential decision criteria, such as distributional equity, employment, or export promotion. Indeed, some are mentioned explicitly in the executive orders mandating RIAs, and most RIAs include chapters analyzing these other economic outcomes. Our focus here, though, is on whether cobenefits belong in calculations of net benefits.

17. That is, the numbering indicates a pollutant's relative centrality to the particular regulation's intended goal, not necessarily to the timing of regulation. Later in this section, we consider the important case of when copollutant 2 has already been regulated and the EPA is analyzing the net benefits of regulating target pollutant 1.

18. Note that a technology standard—for example, setting $x_1 = k_1$—in lieu of a performance standard would also yield cobenefits in this case.

19. This assumes the benefits can be added together—that is, they are additively separable, which is an implicit assumption typical of EPA regulatory analyses.

20. Fullerton and Karney (2018) evaluate such cobenefit rebounds in a general equilibrium model in which the regulator chooses between tax and cap-and-trade instruments for two pollutants. Also note that this is similar to the overlapping policies problem, where one policy instrument sets a quantitative emissions limit, as described in Levinson (2011) and Goulder and Stavins (2011).

21. For example, consider the relationship between SO_2 (pollutant 1) and CO_2 (pollutant 2). Reducing SO_2 emissions at a coal-fired power plant with a scrubber would yield no CO_2 reductions ($\gamma_2 = 0$), and technically it could result in a modest increase in CO_2 emissions due to the energy penalty associated with operating a scrubber. In contrast, reducing CO_2 emissions by dispatching a natural gas power plant in lieu of the coal-fired power plant would reduce both CO_2 and SO_2 emissions.

22. This finding is common beyond economics. Refer to Castle and Revesz (2019) for a discussion of how federal courts have typically ruled in favor of consideration of ancillary impacts of regulations.

23. Thanks to Don Fullerton and Al McGartland for helpful suggestions on these topics.

24. Refer to Evans et al. (2021) for further discussion of this issue.

References

Aldy, J. 2018. "Promoting Environmental Quality through Fuels Regulations: Lessons for a Durable Energy and Climate Policy." In *Lessons from the Clean Air Act: Building Durability and Adaptability into US Climate and Energy Policy*, ed. A. Carlson and D. Burtaw, 159–99. New York: Cambridge University Press.

Aldy, J., M. Kotchen, M. Evans, M. Fowlie, A. Levinson, and K. Palmer. 2019. "Report on the Proposed Changes to the Federal Mercury and Air Toxics Standards." E-EEAC Committee Report. https://www.e-eeac.org/mats-report.

———. 2020. "Deep Flaws in Mercury Regulatory Analysis." *Science* 368:247–48.

Blackwell, A. G. 2017. "The Curb-Cut Effect." *Stanford Social Innovation Review* Winter:28–30.

Boardman, A. E., D. H. Greenberg, A. R. Vining, and D. L. Weimer. 2018. *Cost-Benefit Analysis: Concepts and Practice.* Cambridge: Cambridge University Press.

Burtaw, D., A. Krupnick, K. Palmer, A. Paul, M. Toman, and C. Bloyd. 2003. "Ancillary Benefits of Reduced Air Pollution in the US from Moderate Greenhouse Gas Mitigation Policies in the Electricity Sector." *Journal of Environmental Economics and Management* 45 (3): 650–67.

Castle, K. M., and R. L. Revesz. 2019. "Environmental Standards, Thresholds, and the Next Battleground of Climate Change Regulations." *Minnesota Law Review* 103:1349–437.

CEA (Council of Economic Advisers). 2019. *The Economic Effects of Federal Dereg-ulation since January 2017: An Interim Report.* Washington, DC: Executive Office of the President. https://www.whitehouse.gov/wp-content/uploads/2019/06 /The-Economic-Effects-of-Federal-Deregulation-Interim-Report.pdf.

Dudley, S. 2012. "Perpetuating Puffery: An Analysis of the Composition of OMB's Reported Benefits of Regulation." *Business Economics* 47 (3): 165–76.

EO (Executive Order) 12291, Federal Regulation, 46 *Federal Register* 13193, February 17, 1981.

EO (Executive Order) 12866, Regulatory Planning and Review, 58 *Federal Register* 51735, October 4, 1993.

EO (Executive Order) 13771, Reducing Regulation and Controlling Regulatory Costs, 82 *Federal Register* 9339, February 3, 2017.

EPA (Environmental Protection Agency). 1973. Regulation of Fuels and Fuel Additives, 38 *Federal Register* 1254, January 10.

———. 1976. Lead National Ambient Air Quality Standard, 41 *Federal Register* 14921, April 8.

———. 1997. The Benefits and Costs of the Clean Air Act, 1970 to 1990. Report to Congress, EPA-410-R-97-002, October. https://www.epa.gov/sites/production /files/2017-09/documents/ee-0295_all.pdf.

———. 1998. Regulatory Impact Analysis for the NOx SIP Call, FIP, and Section 126 Petitions, Volume I: Costs and Economic Impacts. EPA-452/R-98-003, September.

———. 2014. *Guidelines for Preparing Economic Analyses.* May 2014 Update. Washington, DC: EPA/National Center for Environmental Economics. https:// www.epa.gov/sites/production/files/2017-08/documents/ee-0568-50.pdf.

———. 2015. Carbon Pollution Emission Guidelines for Existing Stationary Sources: Electric Utility Generating Units. 80 *Federal Register* 64662, October 23, RIN 2060-AR33. https://www.govinfo.gov/content/pkg/FR-2015-10-23/pdf /2015-22842.pdf.

———. 2018a. Increasing Consistency and Transparency in Considering Costs and Benefits in the Rulemaking Process. 83 *Federal Register* 27524, June 13, RIN 2010-AA12. https://www.govinfo.gov/content/pkg/FR-2018-06-13/pdf/2018-12707.pdf.

———. 2018b. Strengthening Transparency in Regulatory Science. 83 *Federal Register* 18768, April 30, RIN 2080-AA14. https://www.govinfo.gov/content /pkg/FR-2018-04-30/pdf/2018-09078.pdf.

———. 2019a. Oil and Natural Gas Sector: Emissions Standards for New, Reconstructed, and Modified Sources Review. 84 *Federal Register* 185, September 24, RIN 2060-AT90. https://www.govinfo.gov/content/pkg/FR-2019-09-24/pdf /2019-19876.pdf.

———. 2019b. Repeal of the Clean Power Plan; Emission Guidelines for Greenhouse Gas Emissions from Existing Electric Utility Generating Units; Revisions to Emission Guidelines Implementing Regulations. 84 *Federal Register* 32520, July 8, RIN 2060-AT67. https://www.govinfo.gov/content/pkg/FR-2019-07-08 /pdf/2019-13507.pdf.

———. 2020a. *Guidelines for Preparing Economic Analyses.* Review Copy Prepared for EPA's Science Advisory Board's Economic Guidelines Review Panel. April 3. https://yosemite.epa.gov/sab/sabproduct.nsf/0/30D5E59E8DC91C22852 58403006EEE00/$File/GuidelinesReviewDraft.pdf.

———. 2020b. Increasing Consistency in Considering Benefits and Costs in the Clean Air Act Rulemaking Process. 85 *Federal Register* 35612, June 11, RIN 2060-AU51. https://www.govinfo.gov/content/pkg/FR-2020-06-11/pdf/2020-12535.pdf.

———. 2020c. National Emission Standards for Hazardous Air Pollutants: Coal- and Oil-Fired Electric Utility Steam Generating Units—Reconsideration of

Supplemental Finding and Residual Risk and Technology Review. 85 *Federal Register* 31286, May 22, RIN 2060-AT99. https://www.govinfo.gov/content/pkg/FR-2020-05-22/pdf/2020-08607.pdf.

———. 2020d. Review of the National Ambient Air Quality Standards for Particulate Matter. 85 *Federal Register* 24094, April 30, RIN 2060-AS50. https://www.govinfo.gov/content/pkg/FR-2020-04-30/pdf/2020-08143.pdf.

EPA (Environmental Protection Agency) and NHTSA (National Highway Traffic Safety Administration). 2020. The Safer Affordable Fuel-Efficient (SAFE) Vehicles Rule for Model Years 2021–2026 Passenger Cars and Light Trucks. 85 *Federal Register* 24174, April 30, RIN 2060-AU09. https://www.govinfo.gov/content/pkg/FR-2020-04-30/pdf/2020-06967.pdf.

Evans, M., K. Palmer, J. Aldy, M. Fowlie, A. Levinson, and M. Kotchen. 2021. "The Role of Retrospective Analysis in an Era of Deregulation: Lessons from the U.S. Mercury and Air Toxics Standards." *Review of Environmental Economics and Policy* 15 (1), forthcoming.

Fowlie, M., E. Rubin, and C. Wright. 2020. "Declining Power Plant Emissions, Co-Benefits, and Regulatory Rebound." Paper presented at ASSA [sp out] meetings, San Diego, January 4, 2020.

Friedman, L., D. Hedeker, and E. Richter. 2009. "Long-Term Effects of Repealing the National Maximum Speed Limit in the United States." *American Journal of Public Health* 99 (9): 1626–31.

Fullerton, D., and D. H. Karney. 2018. "Multiple Pollutants, Co-Benefits, and Suboptimal Environmental Policies." *Journal of Environmental Economics and Management* 87:52–71.

Goulder, L. H., and R. N. Stavins. 2011. "Challenges from State-Federal Interactions in US Climate Change Policy." *American Economic Review* 101 (3): 253–57.

Gray, C. B. 2015. "EPA's Use of Co-Benefits." *Engage* 16 (2): 31–33.

Hansman, C., J. Hjort, and G. León. 2018. "Interlinked Firms and the Consequences of Piecemeal Regulation." *Journal of the European Economic Association* 17 (3): 876–916.

Karlsson, M., E. Alfredsson, and N. Westling. 2020. "Climate Policy Cobenefits: A Review." *Climate Policy* 20 (3): 292–316.

Kotchen, M., M. Moore, F. Lupi, and E. Rutherford. 2006. "Environmental Constraints on Hydropower: An Ex-Post Benefit-Cost Analysis of Dam Relicensing in Michigan." *Land Economics* 82:389–403.

Levinson, A. 2011. "Belts and Suspenders: Interactions among Climate Policy Regulations." In *The Design and Implementation of US Climate Policy*, ed. D. Fullerton and C. Wolfram, 127–40. Chicago: University of Chicago Press.

Linn, J. 2008. "Technological Modifications in the Nitrogen Oxides Tradable Permit Program." *Energy Journal* 29 (3): 153–76.

Lutter, R., and J. Shogren. 2002. "Tradable Permit Tariffs: How Local Air Pollution Affects Carbon Emissions Permit Trading." *Land Economics* 78 (2): 159–70.

Napolitano, S., G. Stevens, J. Schreifels, and K. Culligan. 2007. "The NOx Budget Trading Program: A Collaborative, Innovative Approach to Solving a Regional Air Pollution Problem." *Electricity Journal* 20 (9): 65–76.

Nichols, A. L. 1997. "Lead in Gasoline." In *Economic Analyses at EPA: Assessing Regulatory Impact*, ed. R. D. Morgenstern, 49–86. Washington, DC: Resources for the Future.

OMB (Office of Management and Budget). 2003. "Circular A-4: Regulatory Analysis." Washington, DC: Executive Office of the President. September 17. https://www.whitehouse.gov/sites/whitehouse.gov/files/omb/circulars/A4/a-4.pdf.

———. 2005. "Validating Regulatory Analysis: 2005 Report to Congress on the Costs and Benefits of Federal Regulations and Unfunded Mandates on State, Local, and Tribal Entities." Executive Office of the President. https://www.whitehouse.gov/sites/whitehouse.gov/files/omb/assets/OMB/inforeg/2005_cb/final_2005_cb_report.pdf.

———. 2017. Memorandum M-17-21, Guidance Implementing Executive Order 13771, Titled "Reducing Regulation and Controlling Regulatory Costs," April 5. https://www.whitehouse.gov/sites/whitehouse.gov/files/omb/memoranda/2017/M-17-21-OMB.pdf.

———. 2019. "Report to Congress on the Benefits and Costs of Federal Regulations and Agency Compliance with the Unfunded Mandates Reform Act." https://www.whitehouse.gov/wp-content/uploads/2019/12/2019-CATS-5885-REV_DOC-2017Cost_BenefitReport11_18_2019.docx.pdf.

Schmalensee, R., and R. Stavins. 2013. "The SO_2 Allowance Trading System: The Ironic History of a Grand Policy Experiment." *Journal of Economic Perspectives* 27 (1): 103–22.

Sigman, H. 1996. "Cross-Media Pollution: Responses to Restrictions on Chlorinated Solvent Releases." *Land Economics* 72: 298–312.

Smith, A. 2011. "An Evaluation of the $PM_{2.5}$ Health Benefits Estimates in Regulatory Impact Analyses for Recent Air Regulations." Final Report NERA Economic Consulting. https://www.nera.com/content/dam/nera/publications/archive2/PUB_RIA_Critique_Final_Report_1211.pdf.

Geographic and Socioeconomic Heterogeneity in the Benefits of Reducing Air Pollution in the United States

Tatyana Deryugina, *University of Illinois and NBER,* United States of America

Nolan Miller, *University of Illinois and NBER,* United States of America

David Molitor, *University of Illinois and NBER,* United States of America

Julian Reif, *University of Illinois and NBER,* United States of America

Executive Summary

Policies aimed at reducing the harmful effects of air pollution exposure typically focus on areas with high levels of pollution. However, if a population's vulnerability to air pollution is imperfectly correlated with current pollution levels, then this approach to air quality regulation may not efficiently target pollution reduction efforts. We examine the geographic and socioeconomic determinants of vulnerability to dying from acute exposure to fine particulate matter ($PM_{2.5}$) pollution. We find that there is substantial local and regional variability in the share of individuals who are vulnerable to pollution both at the county and ZIP code levels. Vulnerability tends to be negatively related to health and socioeconomic status. Surprisingly, we find that vulnerability is also negatively related to an area's average $PM_{2.5}$ pollution level, suggesting that basing air quality regulation only on current pollution levels may fail to effectively target regions with the most to gain by reducing exposure.

JEL Codes: I14, Q53, Q56

Keywords: air pollution, vulnerability, geographic heterogeneity, pollution regulation

I. Introduction

Recent research has found that acute pollution exposure is harmful to health even in areas where ambient pollution levels are generally low, such as in the United States (e.g., Ward 2015; Knittel, Miller, and Sanders 2016; Schlenker and Walker 2016; Deryugina et al. 2019). This research suggests that there may be substantial social benefits to further reductions

Environmental and Energy Policy and the Economy, volume 2, 2021.

in US air pollution. However, additional emissions reductions may require increasingly costly measures, making it crucial to understand where such reductions would be most beneficial.

The benefits of air quality regulation in a region depend on many factors, including the amount by which air pollution is reduced, the vulnerability of the local population to air pollution, local population density, and, if the pollution-damage function is nonlinear, the initial level of pollution. Traditional approaches to air quality regulation have targeted regions that have high levels of pollution. For example, the Clean Air Act requires "nonattainment" areas that fail to meet air quality standards to take action to reduce pollution and to achieve attainment status as soon as possible, whereas areas that meet the standards do not need to take additional actions to further improve air quality. However, if pollution levels are imperfectly or negatively correlated with population vulnerability and density, areas with high pollution levels may not be the most cost-effective places to target for pollution reduction.

We investigate factors that predict elderly vulnerability to fine particulate matter ($PM_{2.5}$) and measure how well they correlate with local $PM_{2.5}$ levels. By improving our understanding of the geographic and socioeconomic characteristics that matter for vulnerability, our results can help policy makers identify the most promising targets for air pollution reduction or for compliance and enforcement efforts.

Deryugina et al. (2019) show that there is substantial heterogeneity in vulnerability to acute $PM_{2.5}$ exposure in the US elderly population. Although acute pollution exposure increases mortality among the elderly overall, a machine-learning-based analysis involving extensive individual and local characteristics estimates that acute $PM_{2.5}$ exposure increases the probability of death for only about 25% of Medicare beneficiaries.

In this paper, we extend Deryugina et al.'s (2019) analysis to identify the geographic and socioeconomic correlates of such vulnerability and investigate the extent to which factors correlated with vulnerability are related to local pollution levels. If, for example, poor areas tend to attract pollution sources, such as factories and traffic, and poor people tend to be in worse health, then targeting pollution regulation at high-pollution areas may be an effective way of protecting individuals who are at the highest risk of pollution-related illness or death. However, if vulnerable populations do not tend to locate in high-pollution areas, then current pollution policy may be poorly targeted. As a result, existing pollution reduction efforts could be adapted to achieve greater increases in health, or similar increases in health could be achieved at lower resource costs.

Although the methods used in the Deryugina et al. (2019) vulnerability prediction are computationally complex, the basic idea is straightforward. Following this approach, we generate two mortality predictions for each elderly individual who was enrolled in Medicare in 2013. The first captures their likelihood of dying based on the experiences of similar people on days when they are exposed to high pollution, whereas the second predicts the likelihood of death based on the experiences of similar people on days when they are not exposed to high pollution. The average difference in the two predictions, which we refer to as the person's vulnerability index, represents the increased likelihood of the person dying on a day due to elevated acute $PM_{2.5}$ exposure.

After identifying those who are most and least vulnerable to death from pollution exposure, we compare the prevalence of various characteristics of individuals who are predicted to be highly vulnerable to $PM_{2.5}$ to individuals who are predicted to have low vulnerability to $PM_{2.5}$. Importantly, we base our predictions on a large set of individual-level measures from Medicare data and ZIP-code-level socioeconomic factors from the US Census and related data sets. These rich data allow us to construct accurate and precise measures of vulnerability.

We find that the individuals identified in our data as most vulnerable to pollution are less healthy than the least vulnerable on a variety of measures, including the presence of chronic conditions such as Alzheimer's disease or related dementia, chronic obstructive pulmonary disease (COPD), lung cancer, chronic kidney disease, and congestive heart failure, as well as measures of health-care use and spending. Geographically, we find that areas with high proportions of vulnerable individuals tend to form an L-shaped pattern, extending south from the Dakotas to Texas and then east along the Gulf Coast states. Areas with high proportions of vulnerable individuals are poorer, are less urban, have a higher prevalence of obesity and smoking and a lower prevalence of exercise, have higher overall elderly mortality rates, and have hotter climates, as measured by the annual number of cooling-degree days.

We also find significant heterogeneity at the county level within states and also at the ZIP code level within counties. Average vulnerability and average $PM_{2.5}$ levels are negatively related even though average $PM_{2.5}$ levels are positively related to the prevalence of an array of adverse health conditions. Finally, the total number of vulnerable individuals in a county is positively but imperfectly correlated with average $PM_{2.5}$ levels.

Overall, these results cast doubt on the presumption that a region's baseline pollution level is sufficient to target pollution reduction efforts—whether through regulation or direct expenditure—on those individuals and communities who will benefit the most. In particular, regulations such as the Clean Air Act, which impose penalties on high-pollution areas but do not require reductions in average pollution or mitigation of pollution spikes in low-pollution areas, may fail to direct resources to their highest-benefit uses. Further, the substantial within-county heterogeneity in vulnerability that we identify suggests broad, geographically defined approaches are also likely to be imprecisely targeted and that additional attention should be paid to policies that account for local population socioeconomic characteristics such as income, education, and health; local amenities such as hospital quality and capacity; and local environmental characteristics.

Whereas Deryugina et al. (2019) focused only on individuals living in counties with pollution monitors (902 counties in total), the sample we use in this paper includes beneficiaries who reside in any county in the conterminous United States (3,101 counties in total), whether or not the county has a pollution monitor. Adding these new beneficiaries allows us to greatly expand our inquiry into geographic heterogeneity, as more than two-thirds of US counties lack pollution monitors.

Our study is not without limitations. Most importantly, our analysis focuses on the elderly, a large vulnerable population likely to benefit from reductions in air pollution, and excludes working-age adults and children. Prior studies have documented significant effects of air pollution on infant mortality, even in developed countries (Chay and Greenstone 2003; Knittel et al. 2016). Although the elderly represent a large and important fraction of the US population, we emphasize that our results are not readily applied to younger age groups.

The rest of the paper is organized as follows. Section II provides a brief background on $PM_{2.5}$ and describes the data we use. Section III summarizes our analytical approach. Section IV presents the results, and Section V concludes.

II. Background and Data

$PM_{2.5}$ is a mixture of various particles with diameters of less than 2.5 μm, including nitrates, sulfates, ammonium, and carbon (e.g., Kundu and Stone 2014). Manmade $PM_{2.5}$ comes from power plant and car emissions and can be carried for hundreds of miles away from where it is emitted. In many parts of the country, particularly the East, regional, rather than local, emissions make up a significant share of local particulate matter (EPA 2004). The extent of pollution transport depends on a host of factors, including wind direction and speed, precipitation, and chemical reactions with other airborne molecules.

Many studies have examined the effect of air pollution on various health outcomes, including mortality. Much of the scientific literature focuses on the health effects of $PM_{2.5}$ because fine particulate matter can penetrate lung tissue and get into the bloodstream. Numerous epidemiological studies have documented a positive correlation between short-term exposure to particulate matter and mortality, especially from cardiovascular and respiratory disease (e.g., Samet et al. 2000; Pope and Dockery 2006; EPA 2011). However, quasi-experimental methodology such as the one we utilize has been argued to be much more reliable than associational studies (Dominici, Greenstone, and Sunstein 2014).

Our health and health-care use data come from Medicare administrative files. To inform our vulnerability index, we use the sample of all elderly beneficiaries aged 65 through 100 enrolled in Medicare in 2001–13. We then focus our analysis on a single cohort: those aged 65–100 who were enrolled in Medicare in 2013. This sample comprises more than 97% of elderly US residents that year.[1] Medicare enrollment files provide verified date of death, age, sex, and county of residence. The Medicare Provider Analysis and Review (MedPAR) file provides data on health-care use and cost for individuals enrolled in traditional fee-for-service Medicare. Detailed data on health-care use are not available for individuals enrolled in Medicare Advantage managed care plans.[2] The MedPAR file, derived from Medicare Part A (facility) claims, provides information on each inpatient stay in a hospital or skilled nursing facility. The MedPAR data include information on the date of admission, length of stay, and total monetary cost of the stay.[3]

Spending on inpatient stays accounted for about 70% of all Medicare Part A costs and about 43% of all Medicare spending (including Parts A, B, and D) on elderly fee-for-service beneficiaries during 1999–2013, the years on which our machine-learning model is trained. We complement this data set with data on outpatient emergency room (ER) visits that do not result in admission to the hospital from Medicare outpatient claims files, although we do not observe the cost of these visits. Because our unit of analysis is the county-day, we aggregate the Medicare data using patients' county of residence and the admission date (for inpatient stays) or the date of service (for outpatient ER visits).

The chronic conditions segment of the Master Beneficiary Summary File provides individual-level indicators for the presence of 27 different chronic conditions, such as heart disease, COPD, diabetes, and depression. These indicators are generated by professional medical coders who infer these conditions from a detailed examination of the claims data. Because they are based on claims data, this information is only available for beneficiaries in fee-for-service Medicare. And because it may take time for the relevant claims to appear in the data, the chronic conditions indicators are most reliable for individuals who have been enrolled in fee-for-service Medicare for several years.

Air pollution levels are correlated with temperature and precipitation, which may have independent effects on mortality. Our analysis therefore controls for these variables to avoid confounding their effects with the effects of pollution. Our temperature and precipitation data come from Schlenker and Roberts (2009) and include total daily precipitation and maximum and minimum temperatures for each point on a 2.5 mile by 2.5 mile grid covering the conterminous United States from 1999 to 2013. The Schlenker and Roberts (2009) data are derived from combining underlying data from PRISM and weather stations.[4] We aggregate to the county-day level by averaging the daily measures across all grid points in the county.

ZIP-code-level characteristics include various income and employment measures (e.g., median income, median home value, fraction of the population below the poverty line, labor force participation rate), measures of overall population health (e.g., the fraction of population with hearing or vision difficulties), and some other characteristics (e.g., travel time to work, prevalence of different heating fuels). These data are taken from the American Community Survey's (ACS) 2007–11 5-year estimates. Health-related variables such as disability and health coverage come from the 2008–12 ACS, the first years that this information was included in the ACS.

Similarly, our county-level characteristics, which we correlate with the vulnerability index, come from a variety of sources, including Medicare administrative records, the US Census, the Behavioral Risk Factor Surveillance System (BRFSS), and variables used and constructed by Chetty and Hendren (2018) in their study of neighborhood impacts on intergenerational mobility. Characteristics we consider include average income; average Medicare spending; population health indicators such as the rate of smoking, exercise, and obesity; average temperatures; the crime rate; and measures of intergenerational income mobility. These characteristics are intended to capture an area's key environmental, economic, and public health conditions.

III. Empirical Strategy

We are interested in estimating the causal effect of air pollution on mortality. Quantifying this effect in nonexperimental data is complicated because air pollution is correlated with many other factors that matter for health. For example, traffic jams increase both pollution levels and stress, and low-income individuals are more likely to reside in high-pollution areas. Moreover, air pollution is not well measured: even monitored counties typically have only a few Environmental Protection Agency (EPA) pollution monitors. But an individual's air pollution exposure likely depends on finer measures of geography—such as which side of a highway the person lives on. Such measurement errors can lead to biased estimates of the effect of air pollution even in settings where the variation in air pollution is as good as random.

To overcome these difficulties, our empirical strategy builds on Deryugina et al. (2019), who exploit quasi-random transport of $PM_{2.5}$ by the wind to estimate the mortality costs of acute air pollution exposure. Because changes in daily wind direction are unlikely to be related to other factors that affect health (such as traffic levels), this approach is likely to capture health effects attributable solely to air pollution. This approach also addresses measurement error concerns because it employs variation in air pollution that is blown in from far away and affects an entire area.

The amount of transported pollution is significant (Zhang et al. 2017). For example, the EPA estimates that most of the $PM_{2.5}$ in the eastern United States was transported from hundreds of miles away (EPA 2004). Deryugina et al. (2019) exploit this variation by instrumenting for daily $PM_{2.5}$ with the local wind direction. Their study shows that local wind direction is strongly predictive of changes in local $PM_{2.5}$, even after conditioning on extensive controls for other atmospheric conditions and a host of fixed effects.

Deryugina et al.'s (2019) analysis focuses on areas with EPA monitors, which include 902 counties covering about 70% of the national elderly population. Their instrumental variables design estimates that, on average, a 1-unit increase in $PM_{2.5}$ (about 10% of the daily mean) increases same-day mortality by approximately 0.36 deaths per million beneficiaries in their sample. To estimate heterogeneity in the vulnerability to dying from acute air pollution exposure, they then apply a recently developed machine-learning method (Chernozhukov et al. 2018) to the rich set of characteristics available in the Medicare data. Chernozhukov et al.'s method demonstrates how to estimate heterogeneous treatment effects using machine-learning techniques in the context of a binary treatment variable.

To form a binary treatment variable, Deryugina et al. (2019) assign a person-day observation to the "treatment" group if the local wind direction on that day is associated with an above-median level of $PM_{2.5}$, as measured in their first-stage specification. Otherwise, the observation is assigned to the "control" group. They then train a gradient-boosted decision tree algorithm (Chen and Guestrin 2016) to predict one-day mortality, $Died_{it}$, as a function of various measures of weather conditions, Census division fixed effects, local economic conditions, and individual-level characteristics, all denoted by Z_{it}. The model is estimated separately for observations in the treatment and control groups, resulting in two mortality prediction models.

In this paper, we apply the models estimated by Deryugina et al. (2019) to the 2013 Medicare cohort (i.e., all individuals 65 and older who were alive and enrolled in Medicare at some point in 2013). Notably, our sample includes beneficiaries who reside in counties without pollution monitors and who were thus not included in Deryugina et al. (2019). The addition of these new beneficiaries allows us to greatly expand our inquiry into geographic heterogeneity, as about two-thirds of US counties lack pollution monitors. We can include these beneficiaries in our vulnerability analysis because, as we explain below, pollution data are not required to calculate the vulnerability index. ($PM_{2.5}$ data are required only to estimate the model, which has already been done in Deryugina et al. 2019.)

To ensure that we have reliable chronic condition indicators, we restrict our attention to beneficiaries who have been continuously enrolled in fee-for-service Medicare for at least 2 years.[5] We create an observation for each day such an individual is alive and then predict their daily mortality probabilities using both the treatment group and control group prediction models.[6] The difference between these two predictions, $\hat{S}_{it}(Z_{it})$, represents the change in the observation's predicted likelihood of death due to being exposed to a high-pollution wind direction, and it is referred to as a proxy predictor of the (true) conditional average treatment effect, $s_0(Z_{it})$. We then take the person-level average of these daily proxy predictors to calculate a single proxy predictor for each beneficiary, $\bar{S}_i(Z_{it})$.

$\hat{S}_{it}(Z_{it})$ and, by extension, $\bar{S}_i(Z_{it})$ can be used to infer where in the distribution of treatment effects an observation lies. Deryugina et al. (2019) estimate average treatment effects for various percentiles of the proxy predictor in their sample and conclude that about 25% of the Medicare population is vulnerable to acute fluctuations in $PM_{2.5}$. Given this finding, we focus our analysis on individuals whose average proxy predictors place them in the top 25% of the overall distribution of $\bar{S}_i(Z_{it})$ in the

2013 Medicare cohort. We hereafter refer to these individuals as "vulnerable to acute $PM_{2.5}$ exposure."

IV. Results

A. *The Geographic Distribution of Air Pollution Vulnerability*

Table 1 compares the characteristics of 2013 elderly Medicare beneficiaries who are vulnerable to acute $PM_{2.5}$ exposure to the characteristics of those who are not vulnerable. On average, those who are vulnerable are almost 4.5 years older and are 4 percentage points more likely to be male. They are more than twice as likely to suffer from Alzheimer's or related dementia, lung cancer, and congestive heart failure and are almost twice as likely to have chronic kidney disease or COPD. Consistent with their poor health indicators, beneficiaries who are vulnerable to acute $PM_{2.5}$ exposure also have substantially higher medical spending and are much more likely to have experienced various medical events, such as dialysis and hospice stays.

Figure 1 shows the geographic distribution of elderly who are vulnerable to acute $PM_{2.5}$ exposure as a percentage of the overall number of elderly Medicare beneficiaries in a given county.[7] Values below 25% indicate that a county's beneficiaries are, on average, less vulnerable than the average fee-for-service beneficiary in the nation, whereas values above 25% indicate a disproportionately vulnerable population. As is readily apparent in figure 1, there is a great deal of dispersion in this measure of vulnerability: some counties have less than 10% of their beneficiaries classified as vulnerable, whereas others have more than 50% classified as vulnerable. In addition, there is substantial local variation in this measure, with some adjacent counties having very different scores. Although some of this variation may be due to noise, county-level variation can also be due to variation in factors like income and urbanity, which can vary discontinuously from one county to the next.

The counties shaded light gray or gray have between 20% and 30% of beneficiaries in the top 25% of vulnerability, which is near the 25% that would be expected if the county were representative of Medicare as a whole. Counties in lighter shades of gray and darker shades of gray and black represent counties where there are substantial deviations from the average of 25%. These deviations could be due to differences between the health or socioeconomic characteristics of the beneficiaries in that county and in Medicare overall, or they could be due to differences between

Table 1

Summary Statistics for the Medicare Beneficiaries Most and Least Affected by Pollution in 2013

	(1)	(2)	(3)
Outcome	Bottom 75%	Top 25%	Difference
Demographics:			
Age (years)	75.3	79.7	4.42**
			(.00435)
Male	.421	.461	.0408**
			(.000294)
Chronic conditions:			
Alzheimer's or dementia	.0946	.239	.144**
			(.000197)
Chronic kidney disease	.176	.343	.166**
			(.000241)
COPD	.197	.386	.189**
			(.00025)
Heart failure	.192	.412	.219**
			(.00025)
Lung cancer	.00965	.0251	.0155**
			(.0000685)
Medical spending (dollars):			
Durable medical equipment	160	333	173**
			(.438)
Hospice	148	394	245**
			(1.69)
Hospital outpatient	1,177	2,246	1,068**
			(2.63)
Part B drug	277	637	360**
			(3.11)
Part B other	118	264	146**
			(.710)
Medical events:			
Dialysis	.0522	.153	.101**
			(.00073)
Durable medical equipment	2.17	4.27	2.10**
			(.00399)
Hospice stays	.00626	.0163	.010**
			(.0000553)
Part B drug	2.54	3.90	1.36**
			(.00404)
Part B evaluation and management	4.25	8.86	4.61**
			(.00828)

Notes: Column 1 presents means for person-day observations predicted to have a below-median treatment effect. Column 2 presents means for those in the top 25%. Column 3 reports the difference between columns 2 and 1. Medical spending and medical events are measured over the calendar year prior to the date of the observation. Hospice stays are defined as the number of unique admissions. For all other medical events, the event is defined as each line item on the insurance claim that contains the relevant service. COPD stands for chronic obstructive pulmonary disease. Standard errors, clustered by county, are reported in parentheses.
***$p < .001$.

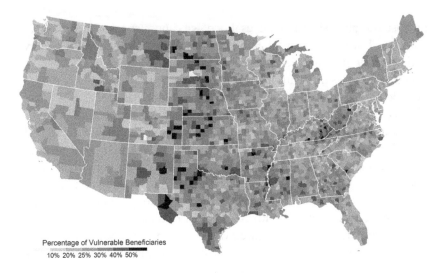

Percentage of Vulnerable Beneficiaries
10% 20% 25% 30% 40% 50%

Fig. 1. The map shows the fraction of Medicare beneficiaries in each county who were vulnerable to acute $PM_{2.5}$ exposure (i.e., were in the top 25% of the acute $PM_{2.5}$ vulnerability index) in 2013.

characteristics of the county (e.g., health-care infrastructure, baseline pollution, etc.) and those of the typical county where Medicare beneficiaries live. Our analysis below will identify some of these associations and illustrate the potential importance of both types of factors.

Figure 1 reveals several important patterns. First, areas with the highest concentration of vulnerable people tend to be concentrated in an L-shaped band running south from the Dakotas to Texas and then east through the Gulf Coast states. An additional group of counties with high concentrations of vulnerable people runs through eastern Kentucky and West Virginia. Second, there are marked differences in average vulnerability across states. For example, the West Coast states tend to have the lowest fraction of vulnerable people, whereas New England is in the middle, and Nebraska and West Virginia have high levels of vulnerability. Third, although many states, such as those along the Pacific Coast, are fairly uniform in terms of vulnerability, there are a number of states where there is significant within-state variation in vulnerability. For example, counties in western Kentucky tend to have lower concentrations of vulnerable people than eastern Kentucky, the Florida Panhandle has more vulnerability than the southern part of the state, and the Upper Peninsula of Michigan is more vulnerable than most of the Lower Peninsula.

Given the substantial amount of county-level heterogeneity in vulnerability depicted in figure 1, a natural question is what drives this vulnerability.

Because our analysis is not a causal one, we cannot speak directly to that question. But we can investigate the association between vulnerability and an array of county-level characteristics.

Figure 2 shows the relationship between the county-level share of vulnerable beneficiaries and various county-level characteristics. We emphasize that these relationships are descriptive and should not be interpreted causally. Some of these characteristics will be directly correlated with ZIP-code-level variables that were used in constructing the mortality models underlying our vulnerability index (e.g., median income and home value). Other characteristics are not used directly in constructing the vulnerability index (e.g., share urban, percentage obese) but may nonetheless be correlated with characteristics that were included.

Each estimate reported in figure 2 was obtained from a separate county-level regression where the outcome variable was the share of vulnerable beneficiaries in a county and the independent variable was a county characteristic. We consider one county characteristic at a time because some characteristics are highly correlated; in such cases, including multiple characteristics in the same regression can lead to a loss of precision and misleading conclusions. To make the results directly comparable to each other, we report coefficients and confidence intervals scaled by the interdecile range of a given characteristic (i.e., the difference between the 90th and 10th percentiles in our sample of counties). Thus, the results can be interpreted as the change in the share of the population that is vulnerable (in percentage points) when comparing a county in the 90th percentile of the distribution of a particular characteristic to a county in the 10th percentile of that distribution.

The associations shown in figure 2 illustrate that vulnerability tends to be negatively related to health. Healthy behaviors, such as exercising, significantly decrease vulnerability, although in our elderly sample exercising may be acting primarily as an indicator of baseline health. In contrast, obesity and smoking prevalence are positively correlated with vulnerability, although this association may arise because obesity and smoking are correlated with other comorbidities rather than suggesting a causal effect on vulnerability. This possibility is supported by the fact that a high mortality rate is positively related to vulnerability. Indicators of high socioeconomic status are generally negatively related to vulnerability. High-income and high-median home values are both associated with low vulnerability, whereas a high poverty rate is positively related to vulnerability.

The climate variables, cooling degree days and heating degree days, are also related to vulnerability. Cooling degree days (which are high

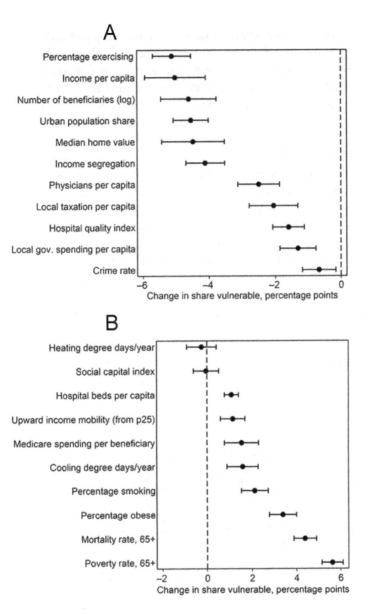

Fig. 2. The figure shows correlations between the share of beneficiaries who were vulnerable to acute PM$_{2.5}$ exposure (i.e., in the top 25% of the acute PM$_{2.5}$ vulnerability index) in 2013 and county-level characteristics. Each estimate is from a separate county-level regression of the share vulnerable on the given characteristic.

in generally hot places) are positively related to vulnerability, whereas heating degree days (which are high in generally cold places) are not significantly related to vulnerability. This result is somewhat surprising because studies have shown that both very hot and very cold days increase overall elderly mortality. The fact that heat interacts with vulnerability to air pollution in a way that cold does not suggests that different mechanisms likely underlie these two phenomena.

In addition to identifying areas with a high proportion of vulnerable people, optimal policy might also depend on identifying where the most vulnerable people live for a few reasons. First, although approximately 25% of the US elderly population are vulnerable to acute $PM_{2.5}$ exposure in the sense that they have a higher expected probability of death on polluted days than on clean days, for some of these people the increased risk is small, and thus it may be more effective to target air quality regulation at areas where the potential benefits of pollution reduction are large. Second, focusing on the top 25% of vulnerability may mask heterogeneity in the proportion of individuals who are most vulnerable to pollution exposure. To investigate these issues, we next turn to an analysis of geographic heterogeneity in this extremely vulnerable group.

Figure 3 shows the geographic distribution of beneficiaries who are extremely vulnerable to acute $PM_{2.5}$ exposure: those who are in the top

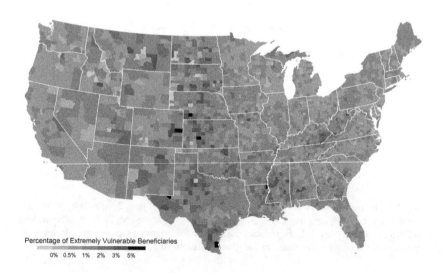

Percentage of Extremely Vulnerable Beneficiaries

0%   0.5%   1%   2%   3%   5%

Fig. 3. The map shows the fraction of Medicare beneficiaries in each county who were extremely vulnerable to acute $PM_{2.5}$ exposure (i.e., were in the top 1% of the acute $PM_{2.5}$ vulnerability index) in 2013.

1% of the distribution of the proxy predictor $\bar{S}_i(Z_{it})$. The patterns are over-all similar to those depicted in figure 1, with areas with a high proportion of extremely vulnerable people falling along an L-shaped band from the Dakotas to Texas and then east along the Gulf Coast states.

Figures 1 and 3 illustrate the geographic distribution of vulnerable and "extremely" vulnerable populations, respectively. To quantify how correlated these two measures are, we estimate a population-weighted regression of the county-level share of vulnerable beneficiaries on the county-level share of extremely vulnerable beneficiaries. The R-squared from this regression is .61, indicating that considering the share of bene-ficiaries who are in the top 1% of the vulnerability index is highly but not perfectly informative about those who are in the top 25%.[8] An advantage of employing the broader (top 25%) definition of vulnerability is that it is subject to less measurement error in less populated areas, so we focus on the top 25% for the remainder of the paper. There are, however, some dif-ferences in the patterns that we will briefly remark upon here. For exam-ple, at the southern tip of Texas, there are areas where the proportion of individuals in the top 1% of vulnerability is very high (black) relative to other counties but the proportion of individuals in the top 25% is more moderate. The opposite is also true, with there being counties where the relative frequency of individuals in the top 1% is low but the frequency of individuals in the top 25% is moderate.

We next turn to a ZIP-code-level analysis to illustrate heterogeneity at a very granular level. Figure 4 shows the geographic distribution of vul-nerable beneficiaries (those in the top 25% of the $\bar{S}_i(Z_{it})$ distribution) at the ZIP code level. To comply with disclosure rules, we do not show ZIP codes that have fewer than 100 Medicare beneficiaries in 2013. We observe 32,331 ZIP codes in our data, 21,506 of which have at least 100 Medicare beneficiaries.

Comparing the ZIP-code-level map in figure 4 to the county-level map in figure 1 reveals the existence of significant within-county hetero-geneity. For example, the northern part of the lower peninsula of Mich-igan appears to have low vulnerability in figure 1's county-level map, but figure 4 reveals several highly vulnerable ZIP codes. Similarly, seen at the county level, Maine appears to be uniformly moderately vulner-able, whereas the ZIP-code-level analysis reveals a mix of high- (black) and low- (gray) vulnerability ZIP codes. Although some of this variation may be due to noise, many of the important correlates of vulnerability identified in figure 2, such as income, are known to vary within counties.

To illustrate the degree of ZIP-code-level variability in the share of vulnerable beneficiaries, figures A3–A7 display ZIP-code-level maps

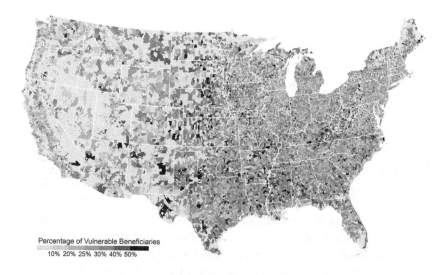

Fig. 4. The map shows the fraction of Medicare beneficiaries in each ZIP code tabulation area (ZCTA) who were vulnerable to acute $PM_{2.5}$ exposure (i.e., in the top 25% of the acute $PM_{2.5}$ vulnerability index) in 2013. Lightest gray areas indicate regions not in a ZCTA or with fewer than 100 beneficiaries.

of five commuting zones, some of which exhibit a lot of variability and some of which have very little variability.[9] To quantify the amount of within-versus across-county variation more systematically, we regress the ZIP-code-level share of vulnerable beneficiaries (including ZIP codes with less than 100 beneficiaries) on county fixed effects, weighting by the number of beneficiaries in that ZIP code. The R-squared in this regression is .33, suggesting that the majority (67%) of the ZIP-code-level variation depends on within-county differences. We perform a similar exercise using the share of beneficiaries who are extremely vulnerable (top 1%) and find that 76% of the ZIP-code-level variation depends on within-county differences.

B. Vulnerability and Pollution Levels

Given the high degree of geographic variation in vulnerability, it is natural to investigate whether that variation is correlated with variation in underlying pollution levels. For example, it may be that a given pollution shock is more deadly in regions that already have high pollution levels. Indeed, this hypothesis is at least consistent with the idea that pollution regulation should be targeted at locations with high pollution levels.

To give a sense of the geographic distribution of pollution, the map in figure 5 shows the average annual $PM_{2.5}$ level for each US county in 2013. $PM_{2.5}$ pollution tends to be highest in California and in the Rust Belt states ranging from Illinois to Pennsylvania and lowest along the Rocky Mountains.

Figure 6*A* shows the county-level relationship between the share of elderly beneficiaries who are vulnerable and 2013 $PM_{2.5}$ levels, with a population-weighted trend line drawn to aid in visualizing the statistical relationship between the two. Perhaps surprisingly, less polluted counties tend to have a higher share of vulnerable beneficiaries: for each 1-unit increase in average $PM_{2.5}$ levels, the share of vulnerable beneficiaries decreases by 0.83 percentage points. Although this correlation could be coincidental (e.g., sub urban areas may be less polluted and attract more frail elderly because of superior medical care), another potential explanation is that those who are vulnerable to air pollution explicitly avoid more polluted areas. Indeed, residential sorting on the basis of air pollution levels has been documented in numerous prior studies (see Banzhaf, Ma, and Timmins 2019 for a review). In addition, if we were to interpret this relationship causally, it suggests that reducing average pollution levels makes individuals more vulnerable to pollution spikes and vice versa.

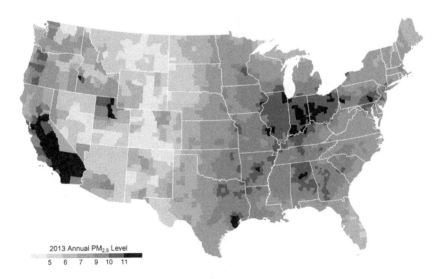

2013 Annual $PM_{2.5}$ Level

5   6   7   9   10   11

Fig. 5.   The map shows county-level annual $PM_{2.5}$ in 2013. The $PM_{2.5}$ measure is provided by the Centers for Disease Control and Prevention's (CDC) National Environmental Public Health Tracking Network and was created using monitor data when available and modeled estimates for days or counties that do not have monitor data.

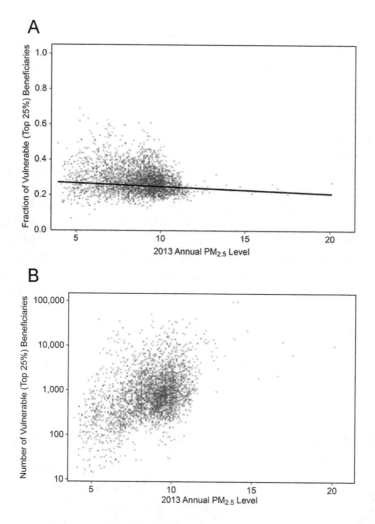

Fig. 6. Each dot plots the 2013 county-level average ambient concentration of $PM_{2.5}$ in micrograms per cubic meter ($\mu g/m^3$) against the fraction of that county's 2013 Medicare beneficiaries who were vulnerable to acute $PM_{2.5}$ exposure (panel A) or the number of 2013 Medicare beneficiaries in that county who were vulnerable to acute $PM_{2.5}$ exposure (panel B).

Figure 6B shows the county-level relationship between the number of elderly beneficiaries who are vulnerable (on a log scale) and 2013 $PM_{2.5}$ levels.[10] In this case, less polluted counties tend to have fewer vulnerable beneficiaries. However, because the relationship is far from perfect, targeting counties based on pollution levels would still be less effective in reaching vulnerable individuals than targeting based on vulnerability. For example, targeting the 406 counties that are at or above the 75th population-weighted percentile of 2013 $PM_{2.5}$ levels (above 10.3 $\mu g/m^3$) would reach 26.5% of all vulnerable beneficiaries. By contrast, a policy targeting the same number of counties based on how many vulnerable beneficiaries live there would reach 60.9% of all vulnerable beneficiaries. Overall, figure 6 lends additional support to the idea that targeting regulation at highly polluted areas may be less beneficial for population health than simple intuition would suggest.

As shown in table 1, the Medicare beneficiaries who are most vulnerable to air pollution are less healthy than the average beneficiary. If beneficiaries in good general health are more likely to reside in areas with high levels of air pollution, then this might explain why we find an inverse relationship between a county's pollution levels and its average vulnerability.

We investigate that possibility by estimating the correlations between $PM_{2.5}$ levels and the other predictors of vulnerability we identified in table 1. Figure 7 displays scatterplots of annual $PM_{2.5}$ levels against the county-level share of beneficiaries with a particular chronic condition. Although overall vulnerability is negatively correlated with $PM_{2.5}$ levels, more polluted counties, on average, have a higher share of beneficiaries with congestive heart failure (panel A), stroke (panel B), and Alzheimer's/dementia (panel E). More polluted counties also have higher average Medicare spending (panel F). However, we do not detect a significant relationship between ambient pollution levels and COPD (panel C) or lung cancer (panel D). Overall, these results suggest that the negative relationship between ambient $PM_{2.5}$ and vulnerability is not driven by chronic condition or average total Medicare spending.

The lack of a significant relationship between background pollution levels and COPD is particularly interesting because the harmful effects of the small particulates comprising $PM_{2.5}$ are thought to arise when the particles are inhaled and irritate the lungs. The fact that we do not find increased incidence of COPD in areas with high pollution levels is consequently surprising. This null result could be due to the presence of confounders that are correlated with $PM_{2.5}$ levels. Alternatively, the impact of high pollution levels on the lungs could manifest in some way that is not classified as COPD. In either case, this issue warrants further study.

V.   Conclusion

This paper has explored the socioeconomic and geographic correlates of vulnerability to acute $PM_{2.5}$ exposure in the United States. Building on

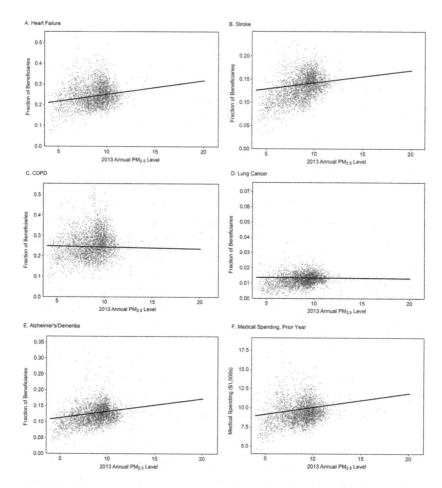

Fig. 7. Each dot indicates the annual average ambient concentration of $PM_{2.5}$ in micrograms per cubic meter $(\mu g/m^3)$ and the fraction of Medicare beneficiaries with certain chronic conditions or average Medicare spending in a county, in 2013. *A*, Heart failure; *B*, Stroke; *C*, COPD; *D*, Lung cancer; *E*, Alzhemier's/dementia; *F*, Medical spending, prior year.

the analysis in Deryugina et al. (2019), we apply the model from that paper to the 2013 Medicare cohort. Whereas Deryugina et al. (2019) was restricted to 902 counties containing pollution monitors, our sample includes all Medicare beneficiaries living in the conterminous United States (3,101 counties in total), which permits a detailed investigation of geographic heterogeneity. Our paper computes a proxy indicator for the conditional average treatment effect for each individual in our data and uses that to classify individuals as vulnerable or not vulnerable to acute air pollution.

As one might expect, we find that vulnerability is positively and significantly associated with a range of health indicators. Individuals in the top quartile of vulnerability are older, more likely to be male, and more likely to exhibit chronic conditions such as Alzheimer's disease or related dementia, chronic kidney disease, COPD, congestive heart failure, or lung cancer. Highly vulnerable individuals are also likely to spend more on health care and to consume more health-care services.

We aggregate across individuals within a particular geographic area to investigate geographic heterogeneity. At the county level, we find a large degree of variation in the share of individuals in the top quartile of vulnerability, ranging from below 5% to above 50%. The areas with the highest proportion of individuals in the vulnerable category lie in an L-shaped band that ranges from the Dakotas south to Texas and then eastward through the Gulf Coast states toward Georgia and Northern Florida. An additional group of areas with large shares of vulnerable elderly falls in eastern Kentucky and West Virginia. In contrast, many of the counties in New England and Pacific Coast states have lower-than-expected shares of vulnerable residents.

Given the large amount of county-level heterogeneity, we next turn toward investigating the geographic and socioeconomic correlates. As might be expected from the individual-level analysis, we find that vulnerability and health tend to be positively correlated at the county level as well. Counties with high shares of individuals who report exercising have low shares of vulnerable individuals, whereas counties with high levels of smoking, obesity, and elderly mortality rates have high shares of vulnerable individuals. The relationship between health-care infrastructure and vulnerability tends to be more mixed, with high numbers of physicians per capita and high hospital quality correlating with low vulnerability, whereas having a high number of hospital beds per capita and high Medicare spending per beneficiary are both correlated with higher vulnerability. The reasons for this discrepancy are not obvious, although reverse causation likely plays a role: areas with more vulnerable people will tend to have higher Medicare spending and higher mortality.

Turning to socioeconomic indicators, counties with high average income and home values have lower shares of vulnerable individuals, whereas counties with high poverty levels have higher shares. Having a large population and a high proportion of individuals living in urban areas are associated with lower vulnerability. Interestingly, areas with high levels of government services, as measured by local government spending per capita and local taxation per capita, tend to have lower shares of vulnerable elderly.

Somewhat surprisingly, we find that the share of vulnerable individuals within a county is negatively related to baseline pollution, although it is positively related to various measures of poor health. Although the exact mechanism underlying this pattern is beyond the scope of this paper, it suggests that using high pollution as a basis for targeting air pollution efforts, as is done under the Clean Air Acts and other environmental regulations, may lead to misallocation of resources.

Although our study sheds substantial light on the geographic and socioeconomic heterogeneity in vulnerability to air pollution, some caveats are in order. First, as we have stated throughout the paper, our analysis is not causal. Nevertheless, the correlational patterns we identify in the paper may provide inspiration for future causal investigations. Second, our study is limited to the elderly. Although there is substantial evidence that the elderly are particularly vulnerable to pollution shocks, pollution has also been shown to increase infant mortality. To the extent that patterns of infant mortality differ from those of the elderly, these differences should also be taken into account by policy makers seeking to direct resources toward pollution reduction. Finally, although our analysis is based on a large sample of elderly Medicare beneficiaries from across the United States, our vulnerability computations are based only on a single year (2013). If vulnerability changes over time, then our 2013 analysis may not generalize to current (or future) vulnerability.

Appendix

Table A1
Summary of County-Level Characteristics

	10th Percentile	Median	Mean	90th Percentile
Heating degree days/year	1,459	4,600	4,361	6,904
Cooling degree days/year	471.1	1,181	1,421	2,836
Hospital quality index	.709	.782	.779	.856
Hospital beds per capita	.930	2.925	3.406	5.938
Physicians per capita	.576	1.965	2.349	4.474
Urban population share	.229	.741	.675	.992
Poverty rate, 65+	5.577	8.753	10.11	17.04
Percentage exercising	67.05	74.34	74.30	81.49
Percentage obese	15.56	20.32	20.78	26.60
Percentage smoking	16.86	21.68	21.94	27.04
Crime rate	2.801	6.786	6.981	11.23
Social capital index	−1.714	−.350	−.315	1.060
Local government spending per capita (1,000s)	1.364	2.191	2.320	3.375
Local taxation per capita (1,000s)	.346	.727	.795	1.347
Income segregation	.006	.046	.051	.100
Upward income mobility (from p25)	−.528	.029	.033	.582
Median home value (1,000s)	58.70	95.80	113.2	195.8
Income per capita (1,000s)	15.18	19.79	20.73	27.91
Number of beneficiaries (log)	7.639	9.124	9.215	10.84
Medicare spending per beneficiary	9.219	10.91	11.16	13.39
Mortality rate, 65+	.049	.053	.053	.058

Note: The table shows the population-weighted 10th percentiles, medians, means, and 90th percentiles of county-level characteristics used in the analysis. p25 = 25th percentile.

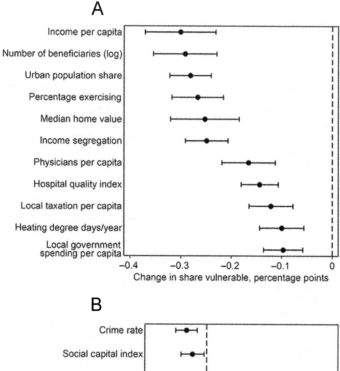

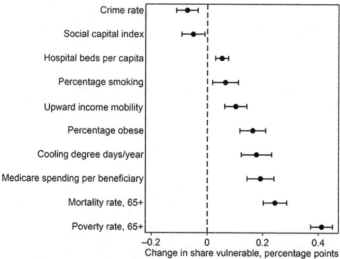

Fig. A1. The figure shows correlations between the share of beneficiaries who were extremely vulnerable to acute $PM_{2.5}$ exposure (i.e., in the top 1% of the acute $PM_{2.5}$ vulnerability index) in 2013 and county-level characteristics. Each estimate is from a separate county-level regression of the share extremely vulnerable on the given characteristic.

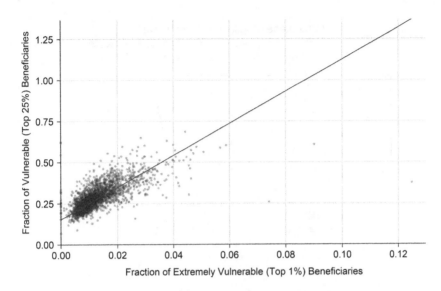

Fig. A2. Each dot represents a county and indicates the fraction of Medicare beneficiaries who were in the top 1% of the acute PM$_{2.5}$ vulnerability index ("extremely vulnerable") and the fraction of beneficiaries who were in the top 25% of the vulnerability index ("vulnerable") in 2013.

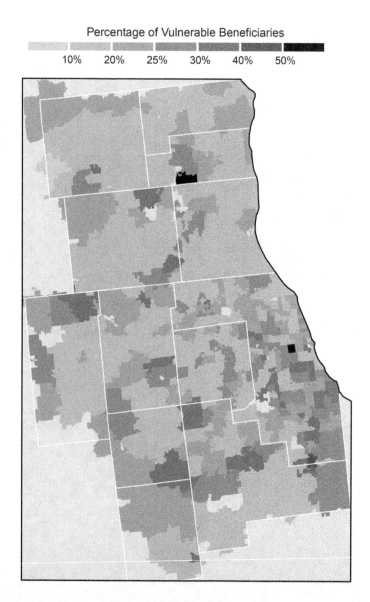

Fig. A3. The map reports ZIP-code-level vulnerability to acute $PM_{2.5}$ exposure for all counties in the commuting zone containing the Chicago-Naperville-Joliet, IL Metropolitan Division. ZIP code shading indicates the fraction of Medicare beneficiaries in each ZIP code who were vulnerable to acute $PM_{2.5}$ exposure (i.e., in the top 25% of the acute $PM_{2.5}$ vulnerability index) in 2013. White lines correspond to county borders. Lightest gray areas indicate ZIP codes where the majority of the population lives outside of the commuting zone or ZIP codes with fewer than 100 beneficiaries.

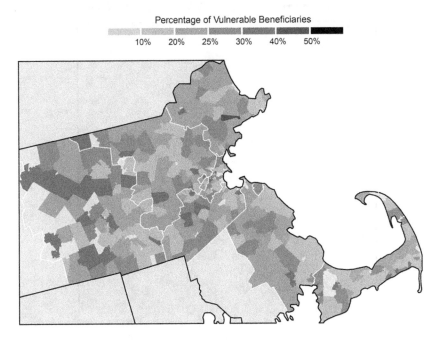

Fig. A4. The map reports ZIP-code-level vulnerability to acute $PM_{2.5}$ exposure for all counties in the commuting zone containing the Boston-Quincy, MA Metropolitan Division. ZIP code shading indicates the fraction of Medicare beneficiaries in each ZIP code who were vulnerable to acute $PM_{2.5}$ exposure (i.e., in the top 25% of the acute $PM_{2.5}$ vulnerability index) in 2013. White lines correspond to county borders. Lightest gray areas indicate ZIP codes where the majority of the population lives outside of the commuting zone or ZIP codes with fewer than 100 beneficiaries.

Fig. A5. The map reports ZIP-code-level vulnerability to acute PM$_{2.5}$ exposure for all counties in the commuting zone containing the Champaign-Urbana, IL Metropolitan Statistical Area. ZIP code shading indicates the fraction of Medicare beneficiaries in each ZIP code who were vulnerable to acute PM$_{2.5}$ exposure (i.e., in the top 25% of the acute PM$_{2.5}$ vulnerability index) in 2013. White lines correspond to county borders. Lightest gray areas indicate ZIP codes where the majority of the population lives outside of the commuting zone or ZIP codes with fewer than 100 beneficiaries.

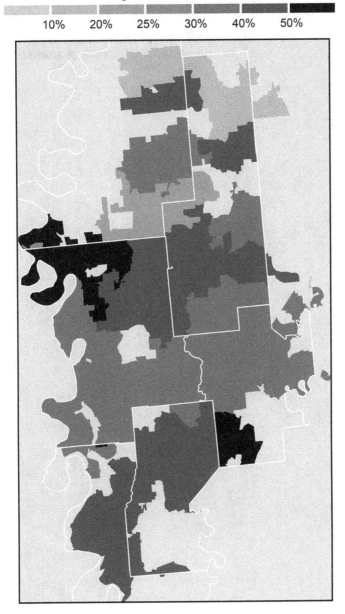

Fig. A6. The map reports ZIP-code-level vulnerability to acute PM$_{2.5}$ exposure for all counties in the commuting zone containing the Greenville, MS Micropolitan Statistical Area. ZIP code shading indicates the fraction of Medicare beneficiaries in each ZIP code who were vulnerable to acute PM$_{2.5}$ exposure (i.e., in the top 25% of the acute PM$_{2.5}$ vulnerability index) in 2013. White lines correspond to county borders. Lightest gray areas indicate ZIP codes where the majority of the population lives outside of the commuting zone or ZIP codes with fewer than 100 beneficiaries.

Fig. A7. The map reports ZIP-code-level vulnerability to acute PM$_{2.5}$ exposure for all counties in the commuting zone containing the Oakland-Fremont-Hayward, CA Metropolitan Division. ZIP code shading indicates the fraction of Medicare beneficiaries in each ZIP code who were vulnerable to acute PM$_{2.5}$ exposure (i.e., in the top 25% of the acute PM$_{2.5}$ vulnerability index) in 2013. White lines correspond to county borders. Lightest gray areas indicate ZIP codes where the majority of the population lives outside of the commuting zone or ZIP codes with fewer than 100 beneficiaries.

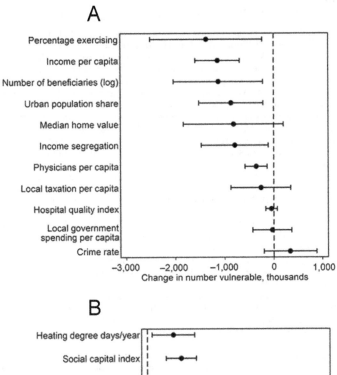

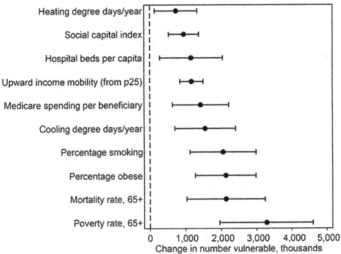

Fig. A8. The figure shows correlations between the number of beneficiaries who were vulnerable to acute $PM_{2.5}$ exposure (i.e., in the top 25% of the acute $PM_{2.5}$ vulnerability index) in 2013 and county-level characteristics. Each estimate is from a separate county-level regression of the number vulnerable on the given characteristic. p25 = 25th percentile.

Endnotes

Author email addresses: Deryugina (deryugin@illinois.edu), Miller (nmiller@illinois.edu), Molitor (dmolitor@illinois.edu), Reif (jreif@illinois.edu). We thank Matt Kotchen, James Stock, Catherine Wolfram, and participants in the 2nd Annual NBER Environmental and Energy Policy and the Economy Conference for helpful comments. Research reported in this publication was supported by the National Institute on Aging of the National Institutes of Health under award numbers P01AG005842 and R01AG053350. The content is solely the responsibility of the authors and does not necessarily represent the official views of the National Institutes of Health. For acknowledgments, sources of research support, and disclosure of the authors' material financial relationships, if any, please see https://www.nber.org/books-and-chapters/environmental-and-energy-policy-and-economy-volume-2/geographic-and-socioeconomic-heterogeneity-benefits-reducing-air-pollution-united-states.

1. Focusing on a single cohort ensures that each individual who was alive in 2013 appears in our data only once.

2. In 2013, 28% of all Medicare beneficiaries were enrolled in Medicare Advantage plans.

3. Our measure of cost is the total allowed charges due to the provider and includes all monetary costs of the stay, consisting of payments made by Medicare, the beneficiary, and/or another payer.

4. See http://www.prism.oregonstate.edu/ for the original PRISM data set and http://www.columbia.edu/~ws2162/links.html for a detailed description of the daily data. Accessed February 26, 2020.

5. There were 43.5 million Medicare beneficiaries in 2013 (Deryugina et al. 2019). After excluding individuals without sufficient health history information and those individuals used to train the Deryugina et al. (2019) prediction algorithm, we are left with 14.9 million beneficiaries to inform our analysis of the geographic and socioeconomic characteristics of the vulnerable.

6. The mortality models from Deryugina et al. (2019) include controls for two leads and two lags of the treatment indicator. Because we cannot determine treatment status for observations in counties without pollution monitors, we omit these controls from this paper. Omitting these high-level controls is unlikely to have any meaningful impact on our individual-level vulnerability index.

7. Recall that we define an individual as "vulnerable" if our model predicts that individual to be in the top 25% of the vulnerability distribution.

8. Analogous to figure 2, figure A1 shows the correlation between various county-level characteristics and the share of beneficiaries in the top 1% of vulnerability. Figure A2 presents a scatterplot between the county-level share of beneficiaries in the top 25% of vulnerability and the share of beneficiaries in the top 1% of vulnerability.

9. Commuting zones are geographies similar to Metropolitan Statistical Areas (MSAs) that group nearby areas based on commuting patterns. For our purposes, commuting zones are preferred due to their superior coverage of rural areas and the fact that they are defined at the supracounty level.

10. Analogous to figure 2, figure A8 shows the relationship between the *number* of vulnerable beneficiaries and various county-level characteristics. Although a few county-level characteristics—such as median home value, local taxation, and local government spending—cease to be significant predictors of vulnerability, the ranking of characteristics by the magnitude of the correlation is virtually identical to figure 2.

References

Banzhaf, Spencer, Lala Ma, and Christopher Timmins. 2019. "Environmental Justice: The Economics of Race, Place, and Pollution." *Journal of Economic Perspectives* 33 (1): 185–208.

Chay, Kenneth, and Michael Greenstone. 2003. "The Impact of Air Pollution on Infant Mortality: Evidence from Geographic Variation in Pollution Shocks Induced by a Recession." *Quarterly Journal of Economics* 118 (3): 1121–67.

Chen, Tianqi, and Carlos Guestrin. 2016. "XGBoost: A Scalable Tree Boosting System." https://arxiv.org/abs/1603.02754.

Chernozhukov, Victor, Mert Demirer, Esther Duflo, and Ivan Fernandez-Val. 2018. "Generic Machine Learning Inference on Heterogenous Treatment Effects in Randomized Experiments." Working Paper no. 24678, NBER, Cambridge, MA.

Chetty, Raj, and Nathaniel Hendren. 2018. "The Impacts of Neighborhoods on Intergenerational Mobility II: County-Level Estimates." *Quarterly Journal of Economics* 133 (3): 1163–228.

Deryugina, Tatyana, Garth Heutel, Nolan Miller, David Molitor, and Julian Reif. 2019. "The Mortality and Medical Costs of Air Pollution: Evidence from Changes in Wind Direction." *American Economic Review* 109 (12): 4178–219.

Dominici, Francesca, Michael Greenstone, and Cass Sunstein. 2014. "Particulate Matter Matters." *Science* 344 (6181): 257–59.

EPA (Environmental Protection Agency). 2004. *The Particle Pollution Report. Current Understanding of Air Quality and Emissions through 2003*. Washington, DC: US Environmental Protection Agency.

———. 2011. *The Benefits and Costs of the Clean Air Act from 1990–2020*. Washington, DC: US Environmental Protection Agency.

Knittel, Christopher, Douglas Miller, and Nicholas Sanders. 2016. "Caution, Drivers! Children Present: Traffic, Pollution, and Infant Health." *Review of Economics and Statistics* 98 (2): 350–66.

Kundu, Shuvashish, and Elizabeth A. Stone. 2014. "Composition and Sources of Fine Particulate Matter across Urban and Rural Sites in the Midwestern United States." *Environmental Science: Processes and Impacts* 16 (6): 1360–70.

Pope, C. Arden, and Douglas Dockery. 2006. "Health Effects of Fine Particulate Air Pollution: Lines That Connect." *Journal of the Air and Waste Management Association* 56 (6): 709–42.

Samet, Jonathan, Francesca Dominici, Frank Curriero, Ivan Coursac, and Scott Zeger. 2000. "Fine Particulate Air Pollution and Mortality in 20 US Cities, 1987–1994." *New England Journal of Medicine* 343 (24): 1742–49.

Schlenker, Wolfram, and Michael J. Roberts. 2009. "Nonlinear Temperature Effects Indicate Severe Damages to US Crop Yields under Climate Change." *Proceedings of the National Academy of Sciences of the United States of America* 106 (37): 15,594–98.

Schlenker, Wolfram, and W. Reed Walker. 2016. "Airports, Air Pollution, and Contemporaneous Health." *Review of Economic Studies* 83 (2): 768–809.

Ward, Courtney. 2015. "It's an Ill Wind: The Effect of Fine Particulate Air Pollution on Respiratory Hospitalizations." *Canadian Journal of Economics* 48 (5): 1694–732.

Zhang, Qiang, Xujia Jiang, Dan Tong, Steven Davis, Hongyan Zhao, Guannan Geng, Tong Feng, et al. 2017. "Transboundary Health Impacts of Transported Global Air Pollution and International Trade." *Nature* 543 (7647): 705–9.

Do Conservation Policies Work? Evidence from Residential Water Use

Oliver R. Browne, *The Brattle Group,* United States of America
Ludovica Gazze, *University of Chicago,* United States of America
Michael Greenstone, *University of Chicago and NBER,* United States of America

Executive Summary

In response to the historic 2011–17 California drought, local governments enacted a raft of conservation policies, and little is known about which ones explain the sharp decline in residential water consumption. To answer this question, we use a novel data set of hourly water consumption data for more than 82,300 households in Fresno, California, where water consumption declined by nearly a third, and have three main findings. First, we estimate the price elasticity of demand for water to be 0.16 for marginal rates and 0.39 for average rates. Second, reducing the number of days where outdoor watering is allowable from 3 to 2 substantially decreases water use, despite the availability of opportunities to substitute between permitted and nonpermitted hours, days, and seasons. Third, "bully pulpit" pronouncements about the water crisis increased public awareness of drought conditions but did not contribute to water savings. Overall, higher water prices explain 40%–44% of the changes in residential water use observed during our sample period in Fresno, and reductions in the number of days when outdoor watering is allowable explain 45%–51% of these changes. However, the absence of experimental or quasi-experimental variation in these policies means that we interpret this associational evidence cautiously.

JEL Codes: Q2, Q5, H4, L95

Keywords: conservation policies, drought, outdoor watering restrictions

I. Introduction

Environmental goals, such as resource conservation, can be achieved through a range of price and nonprice instruments. However, during crises, policy makers may be forced to adopt multiple policy changes simultaneously to induce urgent behavior change and achieve policy goals. Simultaneous policy changes make it challenging to estimate the effect of

Environmental and Energy Policy and the Economy, volume 2, 2021.
© 2021 National Bureau of Economic Research. All rights reserved. Published by The University of Chicago Press for the NBER. https://doi.org/10.1086/711310

individual actions ex post. As a result, it is unclear what mix of policies most effectively change behavior under such conditions. Although economic analysis may favor using prices to manage demand, price instruments may be untenable for political and equity considerations (Olmstead and Stavins 2009).

We study this issue in the context of water conservation. It is vital for utilities to understand which policies effectively induce water conservation, especially as climate change is expected to increase the frequency and severity of droughts in arid regions worldwide. Moreover, these droughts will likely be exacerbated by growing populations and increased costs of developing new supply. Between 2011 and 2017, California experienced an unprecedented drought, by some measures the worst in more than 1,200 years (Griffin and Anchukaitis 2014). As shown in figure 1, the US Department of Agriculture (USDA) measured a record 78% of the state to be in either "Extreme" or "Exceptional" drought.[1] In an attempt to reduce residential water consumption, utilities deployed a range of policies: they raised water rates, introduced or tightened outdoor water use restrictions, and funded public awareness campaigns. Further, California governor Jerry Brown declared a state of emergency in January 2014,

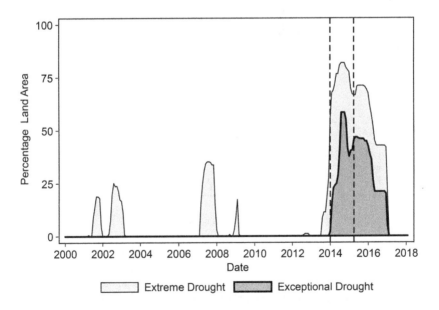

Fig. 1. California drought severity

Note: Using data from the US Drought Monitor, this figure shows the percentage of California in moderate to severe drought from January 2000 to February 2018.

which culminated in an April 2015 mandate that utilities reduce water use by 25% relative to a 2013 baseline. The policies adopted by the utilities were surprisingly successful in achieving their stated goals: 43% of Californian utilities achieved their state-mandated conservation goal, but there is little, if any, systematic evidence on which policy levers were most effective at reducing water consumption and their relative efficiency.

This article seeks to answer this question by disentangling the effect different state and municipal policies had on residential water use in the 2011–17 California drought. We use hourly water use data from more than 82,300 single-family households in Fresno, California, between 2013 and 2016. Fresno is one of the very few large cities that has universally adopted advanced metering infrastructure or "smart meters" that communicate continuously with the utility. Hourly data from these meters allow us to estimate the differential effects of policies across different hours of the day, which is crucial to study compliance with regulations

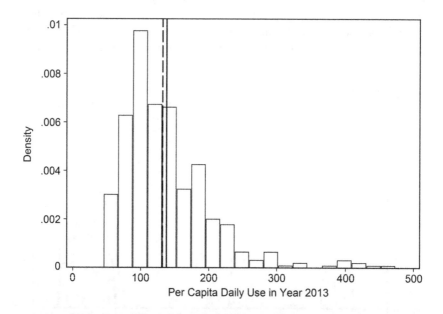

Fig. 2.   Per capita daily residential water use in California in 2013

Notes: In this graph, the dashed line represents the average for Fresno (132 gal/day) whereas the solid line represents the average for all utilities in California (138 gal/day).

Source: California State Water Resources Control Board, https://www.waterboards.ca.gov /water_issues/programs/conservation_portal/conservation_reporting.html. These data include all residential households, whereas the analysis in this article includes only single-family households.

that schedule when outdoor water use is permitted. Figure 2 shows that water use in 2013 in Fresno was comparable to California as a whole (per capita consumption of 132 gal/day for Fresno versus 138 gal/day statewide), suggesting that Fresno can offer a useful case study to learn about water conservation policies elsewhere in California. We link these data with city-level weather and precipitation data to control for daily variation in temperatures and precipitation that could affect water use.

Our 4-year sample period is an appealing period to study the efficacy of water conservation policies in Fresno. In this period, Fresno implemented a suite of water conservation policies, including six rate changes and a reduction in the number of days that households could use water outdoors. Specifically, marginal rates increased twice between January 2013 and August 2014. The second rate increase sparked backlash among customers, leading the city to temporarily reduce both marginal and fixed rates. After a new rate-setting process, marginal rates were increased again, fixed rates decreased, and further annual increases to both rates were planned into the future. At the end of 2016, fixed rates were similar to those at the beginning of 2013, whereas marginal rates had more than doubled. The backlash against the rate increase in August 2014 suggests that these rate changes were salient. Further, two state-level regulatory announcements related to the drought occurred in this period: the state of emergency declaration in January 2014 and the April 2015 mandate requiring all utilities to reduce water use by 25% relative to a 2013 baseline. Importantly, per household water consumption in Fresno declined by 136 gallons per day or 32.8% between 2013 and 2016.

Water use is highly seasonal, peaking in summer as outdoor irrigation increases. From 2013 to 2015, water use decreases year on year in Fresno, a trend that stops in 2016 as the drought eased (fig. 3). This seasonality coupled with the simultaneity of the policies implemented to reduce water use makes it challenging to disentangle the policies' individual effects. Our empirical analysis controls for seasonality using week-of-year fixed effects and weather controls. Our preferred specification does not include year fixed effects, because, given our relatively short time frame, the fixed effects absorb important variation in outcomes necessary to identify the effects of the policies of interest. The absence of year fixed effects means that we interpret the results with some caution; however, we also report estimates from specifications that include year fixed effects.[2]

There are three main findings. First, we find a 0.16 elasticity with respect to marginal price and a 0.39 elasticity with respect to average price. Rate changes account for 40%–44% of household water savings in Fresno

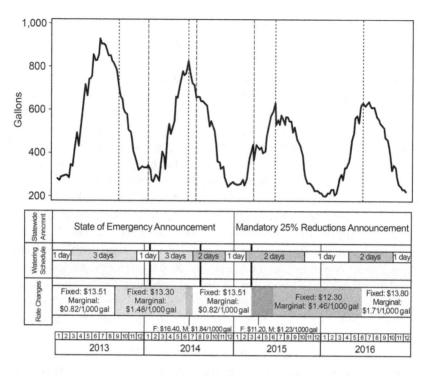

Fig. 3. Average daily water use and policy changes in Fresno, 2013–2016
Notes: The top panel of this figure shows average daily water use. The bottom panel shows all of the policy changes we analyze. Dashed lines in the figure correspond to when each statewide announcement was introduced. Dotted lines correspond to each rate change.

between the first half of 2013, before any change in policy occurred, and the year 2016. It is noteworthy that our estimated price elasticity of demand of water is consistent with the previous literature on the elasticity of demand for water and electricity (Olmstead, Hanemann, and Stavins 2007; Olmstead 2009; Nataraj and Hanemann 2011; Baerenklau, Schwabe, and Dinar 2014; Jessoe and Rapson 2014; Klaiber et al. 2014; Labandeira, Labeaga, and López-Otero 2017). Further, our findings also accord with recent literature estimating larger elasticities with respect to average rather than marginal prices (Ito 2013, 2014; Wichman 2014).

Second, we study a change in the outdoor water schedule regulations that reduced the number of days that outdoor water use was permitted during the summer. After adjustment for all other policies, we find that summer water consumption significantly declined after the summer restrictions went into place. The estimated summer decline in water use associated with the schedule change accounts for 45%–51% of the total water savings between the first half of 2013 and the year 2016. However, we note that there is also a decline in winter water use in the same period, although the winter outdoor watering policy was unchanged.[3] Without experimental or even quasi-experimental variation in the policy, we cannot decisively determine whether the decline in winter water consumption is due to persistent behavior changes such as lawn replacements or reflects confounding factors such as secular trends that also explain the summer reduction.

Our unique hourly water use data allow us to shed light on the effects of nonprice instruments like watering restrictions on times when the restrictions do and do not bite. On the one hand, we find evidence of spillover effects on unrestricted times, in line with evidence suggesting that restrictions increase the salience of conservation behavior (Pratt 2019). On the other hand, we document that intertemporal substitution of water use reduces the environmental benefits of the restrictions. These findings parallel the mixed evidence on the effect of automobile driving restrictions based on license plate numbers due to substitution across times and vehicles (Davis 2008; Viard and Fu 2015; Zhang, Lawell, and Umanskaya 2017). Despite the high implied disutility associated with the restrictions, which may result in lower overall welfare (Baumol 1988; Hensher, Shore, and Train 2006; Grafton and Ward 2008; Mansur and Olmstead 2012), mandated restrictions can effectively reduce water use, depending on the information content and enforcement strength (Michelsen, McGuckin, and Stumpf 1999; Renwick and Green 2000; Kenney, Klein, and Clark 2004; Halich and Stephenson 2009; Castledine et al. 2014; Wichman, Taylor, and von Haefen 2016; Pratt 2019).

Third, we observe that, after the "state of emergency" and "mandated reductions" announcements, interest in the California drought increases, as measured by a Google search index for the keyword "drought." However, this increased awareness does not appear to have contributed substantially to the realized water savings in Fresno during our sample period. Although nonprice instruments such as behavioral nudges, social norms, and moral persuasion may help correct mistakes and improve welfare under imperfect information (Ferraro and Price 2013; Asensio and Delmas 2015; Allcott 2016; Ito, Ida, and Tanaka 2018), our findings complement research showing that targeted marketing campaigns can raise public awareness of an issue yet may not change behavior (Syme, Nancarrow, and Seligman 2000). Moreover, our findings contrast with previous literature on social norms and water use that shows, for example, that peer comparisons and injunctive messaging effectively reduce resource use

(Allcott 2011; Ferraro, Miranda, and Price 2011; Allcott and Rogers 2014; Brent, Cook, and Olsen 2015; Bhanot 2018; Jessoe et al. forthcoming).

This article analyzes the relative effectiveness of different conservation policies at reducing water use. The breadth of the data that we collected is rare and allows for this analysis. Our hourly water meter data stand in stark contrast to the data collected by most utilities, which consist of a single meter reading every month or quarter. We also constructed a comprehensive timeline of all water conservation policies announced and adopted by the City of Fresno and the State of California during our sample period. The concurrence of several policies at one time reflects the messy detail of how policies are often implemented during a crisis, in a piecemeal fashion and simultaneously, with the hope that something sticks. In this article, we take a step forward in disentangling the relative effectiveness of these policies.

The article proceeds as follows: Section II describes the data. Section III examines the effect of each water policy adopted in Fresno on patterns of water use individually. Section IV estimates the effect of conservation policies simultaneously and discusses the extent to which each policy explains the observed changes in water use during our sample period. Section V concludes

II. Data and Background

We observe hourly water use between 2013 and 2016 for the universe of single-family households in Fresno, one of the five largest cities in California. In cleaning the data, we drop all newly constructed houses, abandoned houses, and households with a change of address during our sample period. We also drop all hours when smart-meter transmission malfunctions lead to implausible estimates of water use more than 4 standard deviations away from the city's average. This process leaves us with around 31,400 hourly observations for more than 82,300 households. We link these data with daily temperature and precipitation data from the National Centers for Environmental Information within the National Oceanic and Atmospheric Administration.

To measure changes in public awareness of the drought over our sample period, we collect Google Trends data showing the relative popularity of Google searches related to "drought" between 2013 and 2016 at the weekly level in the Fresno-Visalia region. Our query returns a "Drought Interest" index between 0 and 100. The index takes a value of 100 at its peak number of searches in a given week and 50 when the term is half as popular. A score of 0 means that the number of weekly searches was less than 1% of the peak. We use this index to explain changes in water consumption as a result of public awareness of drought conditions.

Figure 3 documents changes in average daily water use relative to the range of water conservation policies adopted in Fresno during our sample period. Water rates changed six times, with monthly fixed rates ranging between $11.20 and $16.40 and marginal rates varying between $0.82 and $1.84 per 1,000 gallons. Moreover, in August 2014, Fresno reduced the number of days households were allowed to use water outdoors in the summer months from 3 to 2. Finally, we note two public announcements during our sample period. On January 17, 2014, Governor Jerry Brown declared California to be in a state of emergency as a result of the drought. This declaration allowed the state to access federal disaster relief funds and gave the state additional jurisdiction over local water institutions to manage water supply. On April 1, 2015, the state imposed unprecedented mandatory water use reductions, requiring all local water utilities to reduce water use by 25% relative to 2013.

Table A1 compares demographic and climate characteristics, as well as average water use, in Fresno with the top 100 water utilities in California. Figure A1 maps the average maximum temperature and rainfall across all of California. Fresno is quite populous, albeit poorer than the rest of urban California. It ranks toward the middle third among the top 100 utilities for baseline water use, and it registers rainfall and low temperatures that are close to the average for the state, although its daily high temperatures are among the highest. In general, Fresno offers a reasonable case study for other cities in California and the US South.

III.   Empirical Estimates of Water Conservation Policies on Consumption

This section considers the effect of water conservation policies implemented in Fresno individually and separately estimates their effects on household water use. Specifically, we study the effect of (1) rate changes, (2) a reduction in the number of outdoor watering days, and (3) statewide regulatory announcements. In Section IV, we pool all of these policies together to estimate their simultaneous impact.

To evaluate each policy, we employ different empirical approaches depending on the identifying variation generated by its implementation. In general, we use an event-time framework, controlling for week-of-year fixed effects to partial out seasonal variation. In this framework, the treatment effect is identified by the change in water use relative to the average water use in a given week in the other 3 years of the sample. Our use of week-of-year fixed effects is likely conservative: part of the effect of any policy change will be absorbed by these fixed effects given the small number of years in our sample. When additional variation is available, we adopt a difference-in-differences design to compare households differentially affected by a given policy. In a difference-in-differences design, the estimated treatment effect is the change in water use between households affected by a treatment at a given time (such as the prohibition on outdoor water use) and similar households that are not. Unless noted otherwise, the standard errors are clustered at the household and sample month level to account for serial correlation and city-level shocks.

A. Rate Changes

This section estimates the effect of rate changes on household water use. Figure 4 shows the timeline and magnitude of six different rate changes in our sample for marginal, fixed, and average rates separately. Between

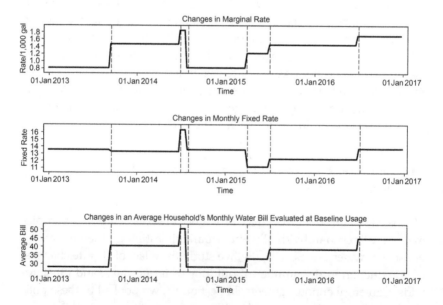

Fig. 4.   Rate changes between 2013 and 2016

Notes: The top, middle, and bottom figures show changes in the marginal, fixed, and average rates, respectively, charged throughout the sample period. Fixed rates shown only for 1″ sized water meter. Average rates are calculated based on the household's monthly water use at the beginning of the sample period.

the beginning and end of this period, marginal rates increased in Fresno. Yet some rate changes reduced both marginal and fixed rates: notably, in August 2014 the city reversed previous rate increases under political pressure from ratepayers, only to increase rates again the next year after approving a new rate-setting process. This episode emphasizes the degree to which rate changes were salient to households during our sample period.

Because rate changes hit all households in the city simultaneously, the estimates are identified from time-series variation. Specifically, we compare water use within the same week across the four sample years when different rates are in place. We estimate the following equation:

$$y_{it} = f(\text{Rates})_{it} + \gamma_{\text{woy}} + \gamma_i + X_t\theta + \varepsilon_{it}, \tag{1}$$

where y_{it} is a function of household i's average daily water use in week t, in gallons, and $f(\text{Rates})_{it}$ is a function of either marginal, fixed, or average water rate at week t, depending on the specification. Our preferred specification uses the inverse hyperbolic sine (IHS) of water use and of rates to estimate elasticities because of its robustness to the inclusion of observations with zero water use, 0.96% of our daily data set, but we also report estimates using the logarithm.[4] γ_{woy} and γ_i are week-of-year and household fixed effects, X_t includes weather and seasonal controls.[5] Our preferred specification does not include year fixed effects because they would absorb any persistent effects of the policies we study.

Table 1 presents our estimates. Columns 1 and 2, which include year fixed effects, appear to suggest customers are not very sensitive to prices when comparing within-year water use. By contrast, columns 3 and 4, which do not include year fixed effects, estimate an elasticity of 0.18 with respect to marginal prices and 0.43 with respect to average prices.[6] Columns 5 through 8, which specify the outcome variable as the log of average daily water use plus 1 rather than the IHS, find similar results to columns 1 through 4. These estimates do not take into account the fact that the city and the state both introduced other policies throughout our sample period; we account for these other factors in our price elasticity estimates in Section IV.

These estimates are consistent with the literature documenting that customers respond more strongly to average rather than marginal prices for water. Specifically, Ito (2013) finds that households in Orange County display a short-run elasticity to average water rates of 0.097–0.13, versus an elasticity with respect to marginal rates of close to 0.[7] However, unlike Orange County, Fresno does not have increasing block rates; thus

Table 1
Elasticity of Average Daily Use

	IHS of Average Daily Use (Gallons)				Log of (1 + Average Daily Use [Gallons])			
Dependent Variable	(1)	(2)	(3)	(4)	(5)	(6)	(7)	(8)
	A. Regression Coefficients							
Fixed rate	.945**		1.379**		.761**		1.180**	
	(.189)		(.157)		(.137)		(.131)	
Marginal rate per gallon	.043		−.185**		.033		−.191**	
	(.037)		(.067)		(.031)		(.060)	
Average rate per gallon		−.108		−.425**		−.037		−.373**
		(.107)		(.150)		(.076)		(.124)
	B. Implied Elasticities							
Marginal rate per gallon	.04		−.18		.03		−.19	
Average rate per gallon		−.11		−.43		−.04		−.37
Year fixed effects	X	X			X	X		
Observations	17,017,841	17,017,841	17,017,841	17,017,841	17,017,841	17,017,841	17,017,841	17,017,841

Note: The independent variables are inverse hyperbolic sine (IHS) of fixed rates (FR), marginal rates (MR), and average rates (AR), respectively, in columns 1–4, and are logarithms of FR/MR/AR, respectively, in columns 5–8. Standard errors in parentheses are two-way clustered at household and sample-month levels. All regressions include weather controls, an indicator for whether summer watering schedule is in place, household fixed effects, and fixed effects in week of year. Average rate per gallon is evaluated at household baseline usage. We compute elasticities using the following formula derived by Bellemare and Wichman (2020): $\xi_{yx} = \hat{\beta} \cdot \left(\frac{\bar{x} \cdot \sqrt{\bar{x}^2 + 1}}{\bar{y} \cdot \sqrt{\bar{x}^2 + 1}} \right)$, where $\bar{x}$ is the mean of our independent variable and $\bar{y}$ is the mean of our dependent variable.
**p < .01.

we rely only on time-series variation to identify the simultaneous effects of changes in marginal and fixed rates. For this reason, we do not find the coefficient estimates on fixed rates to be credible. Nonetheless, cross-sectional variation in baseline water use combined with time-series variation in fixed rates generates variation that allows us to identify the effect of average rates.

B. Reducing the Number of Allowed Outdoor Watering Days

Next, we evaluate nonprice policies, starting with time-of-day and day-of-week restrictions on outdoor water use. These restrictions are ubiquitous throughout California among other drought-prone states and typically target lawn irrigation, the single largest end use of residential water (Hanak and Davis 2006). Seventy percent of Californians were already subject to some restrictions on outdoor water use, even before drought regulations made them mandatory.[8] Typically these policies restrict outdoor water use to only nights and evenings, when less water is lost to evaporation, and also limit the number of days in a week households can use water outdoors. During our sample period, outdoor water use violations in Fresno were subject to a $45 fine. A small team of utility representatives patrolled the city, often at night, targeting customers with a history of high water use during banned hours and issuing fines to customers caught violating water use regulations. First-time violators had the option of having the fine waived if they agreed to a household water audit.

This section exploits a watering schedule change in August 2014 that reduced the number of permitted watering days during summer months from 3 to 2 days per week. Ex ante, it is not clear whether this schedule change will reduce aggregate water use. On the one hand, this policy could update households' beliefs about the frequency with which they need to irrigate their lawns, thus preventing over-irrigation. On the other hand, this policy change does not limit total water use, as households can substitute between hours or days. We start by exploring how water use patterns change with this policy within a day, a week, and even a year. This analysis allows us to document that the policy effects spill over to times when the policy does not bind. We speculate that these spillovers may be due to intertemporal substitution as well as to physical (e.g., swapping out lawns) or mental (e.g., reconsideration of how much water was necessary) capital stock changes. Yet without experimental or quasi-experimental variation in the policy, we cannot decisively rule out that

confounding factors such as secular trends may drive the estimated policy effects. Then, we examine the net effects of all of these adjustments.

To reduce the load on the stormwater system, houses with odd- and
even-numbered addresses are allowed to use water outdoors on different
days of the week. During summers prior to August 2014, even-numbered
houses were permitted to use water outdoors on Wednesdays, Fridays,
and Sundays and odd-numbered houses were permitted to use water
outdoors on Tuesdays, Thursdays, and Saturdays. Beginning in August
2014, all customers were also prohibited from using water outdoors on
Thursdays and Fridays, reducing the number of days. On Mondays, all
households in Fresno are banned from using water outdoors. Table 2
summarizes these summer watering schedule rules before and after this
change.

We exploit the fact that even- and odd-numbered households are allowed to water outdoors on different days of the week to estimate the
net effect of the schedule restriction in a difference-in-differences design.
For example, we can compare the behavior of two neighbors living on the
opposite side of the street, at numbers 1 and 2, on different days of the
week. Household 1 was never allowed to water on Fridays and can serve
as a control group for Household 2, who is newly prohibited from watering

Table 2
Outdoor Water Use Schedule before and after August 2014

| | | Odd | | | | Even | | | |
| | | Summer | | Winter | | Summer | | Winter | |
Day	Type of Day	Before	After	Before	After	Before	After	Before	After
Monday	Always banned								
Tuesday	Always allowed summer day	X	X						
Wednesday	Always allowed summer day					X	X		
Thursday	Banned after August 01, 2014	X							
Friday	Banned after August 01, 2014					X			
Saturday	Always allowed	X	X	X	X				
Sunday	Always allowed					X	X	X	X
	Total watering days	3	2	1	1	3	2	1	1

Note: This table shows which days each household is permitted to use water outdoors
both before and after the schedule change based on whether their house is odd- or even-
numbered. On permitted days, marked with an X, households may use water outdoors but
only before 9 a.m. in the morning or after 6 p.m. in the evening.

on Fridays starting in August 2014, and vice versa on Thursdays. If we assume that all households comply with the watering schedule, then the difference between even-numbered and odd-numbered household water use on different days would be entirely accounted for by outdoor water use. To the extent that some households do not comply with this regulation, by using differences in water use of households with different watering schedules, we likely underestimate true outdoor water use and consequent savings from this policy restriction. Specifically, we estimate the following equation separately for each hour of the day and different days of the week on the sample of summer months, when outdoor water restrictions are in place:[9]

$$y_{bnt} = \beta_1 \text{BannedDay}_{nt} + \beta_2 \text{AlwaysPermitted}_{nt}$$
$$+ \beta_3 \text{PostBan}_t + \beta_4 \text{BannedDay}_{nt} \times \text{PostBan}_t \qquad (2)$$
$$+ \beta_5 \text{AlwaysPermitted}_{nt} \times \text{PostBan}_t$$
$$+ \gamma_b + \gamma_n + \gamma_{\text{dow}} + \gamma_{\text{woy}} + \gamma_{\text{yr}} + \varepsilon_{bnt}.$$

where y_{bnt} is the IHS of the average daily water use, in gallons, on week t by the average household in block group b with house number in group $n \in \{\text{odd}, \text{even}\}$. BannedDay$_{nt}$ is an indicator for the days that become banned in August 2014, that is, Thursdays for odd-numbered homes and Fridays for even-numbered homes. AlwaysPermitted$_{nt}$ is an indicator for days when outdoor watering is allowed both before and after August 2014.[10] The omitted category includes days when outdoor watering is not permitted either before or after August 2014.[11] PostBan$_t$ equals 1 for weeks after the change in the outdoor watering schedule. Thus, the coefficient β_3 estimates the effect of the ban on water use, y_{bnt}, during days when outdoor use was never permitted. The sum of $\beta_3 + \beta_4$ and $\beta_3 + \beta_5$ estimates the effect of the ban on water use on days that become banned and are always permitted, respectively. We control for fixed effects at the block group level (y_b), fixed effects for odd- and even-numbered houses (y_n), and fixed effects for the day of week (y_{dow}), week of year (y_{woy}), and year (y_{yr}). As such, coefficients in these regressions are identified by the comparison between an even-numbered house that is permitted to water outdoors and an odd-numbered house in the same census block group that is not, and vice versa. Standard errors are clustered at the block group and month level.

We find that intertemporal substitution of water use to days when outdoor watering is still allowed undoes some of the water savings occurring during days when the schedule change binds. Figure 5 presents

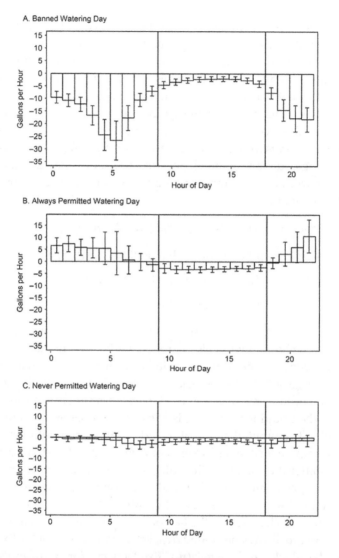

Fig. 5. Water use after outdoor schedule change, by hour of day and day type

Notes: This figure shows coefficients from hour-by-hour regressions of water use on indicator variables for whether outdoor water use for a household on that day of the week was either banned after the policy change (panel A), always permitted (panel B), or never permitted (panel C). Each regression includes indicators for the day of the week, an indicator for post-schedule change, and interactions between indicators for "post-schedule change," "banned day," and "always permitted day." The regression also controls for whether households live in even-numbered homes, census block group fixed effects, and fixed effects for the day of week, week of year, and year. Each regression is weighed by number of households in the census block group. Standard errors are two-way clustered at census block group and sample-month levels. Vertical lines delimit daytime hours (9 a.m.–6 p.m.) when outdoor use is never permitted.

the hour-by-hour estimates of these regressions on banned, always-permitted, and never-permitted days, respectively. The vertical lines in the figure delimit daytime hours (9 a.m.–6 p.m.) when outdoor use is never permitted. Panel A shows that on the day that becomes banned, water use decreases across all hours of the day by a total of 256 gallons, with 87% of this decrease (223 gallons) occurring at night during hours when irrigation became banned. However, Panel B shows that households offset 37% of these reductions by substituting 94 gallons per week of irrigation from the night that is now banned to the two nights that remain permitted.

All panels in figure 5 show a puzzling reduction in daytime water use, when outdoor watering is never permitted, either before or after the schedule change. Indeed, summing up changes in water use over all days of the week, figure 6 shows that despite the substitution of water use from newly banned to permitted times, net water use decreases virtually during all hours, adding up to 333 gallons per week, 10% of average weekly

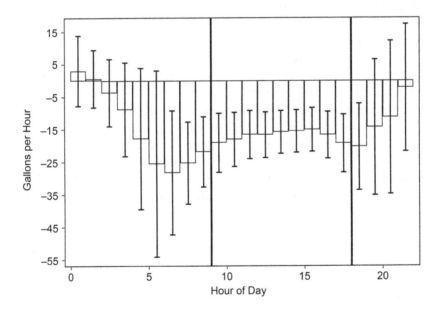

Fig. 6. Average effect of schedule change on use, by hour

Notes: This figure calculates the average hour-by-hour effect of schedule change on weekly water use. The averages are calculated from the regression coefficients in figure 5. The estimates are weighted given that after the schedule change, each week has 1 day that became banned, 2 days that were always permitted, and 4 days that were never permitted. The vertical lines delimit daytime hours (9 a.m.–6 p.m.) when outdoor use is never permitted.

consumption. Importantly, daytime savings represent 52% of all savings. This reduction could reflect higher compliance with the watering schedule, perhaps in fear of heightened enforcement, or increased conservation along other dimensions associated with publicity about the schedule change.

To gauge the persistence of the policy effects, table 3 estimates the total effect of the schedule change by net of both direct and indirect effects over our entire sample period. Specifically, we estimate the following equation:

$$y_{it} = \beta_1 I_t^{\text{Post-Schedule Change}} + \beta_2 I_t^{\text{Post-Schedule Change}}$$
$$\times I_t^{\text{Summer}} + \gamma_{\text{woy}} + \gamma_i + X_t\theta + \varepsilon_{it}, \tag{3}$$

where y_{it} is the IHS of household i's average daily water use in week t and $I_t^{\text{Post-Schedule Change}}$ is an indicator for week t being after the schedule change, γ_i and γ_{woy} are household and week-of-year fixed effects, and X_t includes weather controls, including a summer indicator. Column 1 of table 3 constrains β_1 to be 0, because the outdoor watering schedule did not change in winter months. Column 2 constrains β_2 to be 0, that is, it constrains the effect of the schedule change to be constant year-round. Columns 4–6 also include year fixed effects.

Table 3 shows that water use declines by about a third after the schedule change, with little difference across summer and winter months.[12] One potential explanation for this year-round decrease in water use is that the change in the schedule led to persistent behavior change.[13] Alternatively, households may have responded to changes in enforcement and city services coinciding with the tightening of the outdoor water regulations. Figure A3 shows that enforcement actions and city services such as water audits and timer tutorials are few and far between, suggesting that these factors cannot have a large effect on aggregate water use. Still, without experimental or even quasi-experimental variation in outdoor watering restrictions, we cannot decisively determine whether the decline in winter water consumption is due to persistent behavior changes or reflects confounding factors such as secular trends that also explain the summer reduction.

C.   Increasing Public Awareness

Many environmental programs appeal to moral values to induce behavioral change, yet it is not clear that they are effective (Egebark and Ekström 2016). This section examines the extent to which two key policies

Table 3
Effect of Schedule Change on Water Consumption

	(1)	(2)	(3)	(4)	(5)	(6)
			IHS of Average Daily Use (Gallons)			
1(Post-schedule change)	−.338**	−.317**	−.255**		−.173**	−.112*
	(.033)	(.027)	(.033)		(.035)	(.053)
1(Post-schedule change) × 1(Summer)			−.083⁺	−.144**		−.080
			(.048)	(.035)		(.051)
Year fixed effects				X	X	X
Observations	17,017,841	17,017,841	17,017,841	17,017,841	17,017,841	17,017,841

Note: This table shows coefficients from regressing the inverse hyperbolic sine (IHS) of average daily water use on an indicator that equals 1 in weeks after schedule change. Columns 1 and 4 further restrict this indicator to equal 1 only when the summer outdoor watering schedule is in place. Columns 3 and 6 allow for the effect of the schedule change to be different during the summer. The regression includes weather controls, a control for whether summer watering schedule is in place, household fixed effects, and fixed effects in week of year. Year fixed effects are included where specified. Standard errors in parentheses are two-way clustered at household and sample-month levels.

⁺p < .10.
*p < .05.
**p < .01.

enacted by the State of California affected public awareness of the drought
using Google Trends data: the state of emergency declaration and the introduction of mandatory water use reductions. We then investigate whether
the increased drought awareness during our sample period also led to
changes in water use.

First, on January 17, 2014, Governor Jerry Brown declared the whole of
California to be in a state of emergency as a result of the drought. This
declaration allowed the state to access federal disaster relief funds and
gave the state additional jurisdiction over local water utilities to manage
the water supply. The governor lifted the state of emergency after the
end of our sample period, on April 7, 2017, for most of the state, although
some counties remained under it for longer. Second, on April 1, 2015,
the state imposed unprecedented mandatory water use reductions on all
local water utilities. Requirements included reporting water use monthly
to the state as well as 25% reductions in water use relative to 2013.[14]

Because these policies were one-time announcements that affected all
households simultaneously, we exploit time-series variation by estimating a regression of water use on a sequence of event-time dummy variables while controlling for secular trends, seasonality, and individual fixed
effects. In other words, we estimate the following equation:

$$y_t = \sum_{s=-13}^{13} \beta_s I_t^{\text{Weeks Post-Announcement}} + \gamma_{\text{woy}} + \gamma_{\text{yr}} + X_t \theta + \varepsilon_t, \qquad (4)$$

where y_t is a measure of drought awareness, $I_t^{\text{Weeks Post-Announcement}}$ is an
indicator for week t being s weeks before or after the announcement,
γ_{yr} and γ_{woy} are year and week-of-year fixed effects, and X_t includes
weather controls.[15]

First, we examine the effect of these policies on drought awareness.
We use Google Trends to construct a weekly index of the number of
searches within Fresno containing the word "drought." Figure 7 plots
the coefficients from equation (4) where y_t is the drought awareness
index.[16] Both policy announcements, and especially the state of emergency
announcement, appear to increase awareness of the drought as measured
by our index. By contrast, the change in the outdoor watering schedule
does not appear to increase drought awareness.

Next, we ask whether this increase in awareness translates to a decrease in water use. Figure 8 plots this measure of drought interest against
water use after removing seasonal patterns. Average water use and interest
in the drought move in opposite directions, with a correlation coefficient

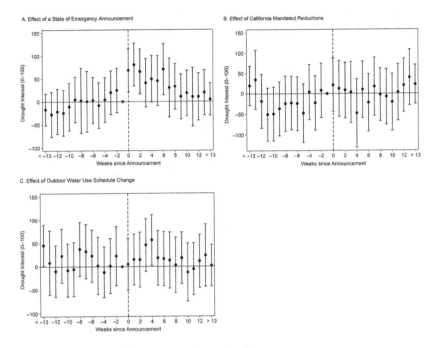

Fig. 7. Event-time estimates—the effect of announcements on drought interest

Notes: This figure shows week-by-week event-time coefficients from regressing our drought interest measure obtained from Google searches on indicators for each week relative to the emergency state announcement (panel A), the state-mandated reductions (panel B), and the schedule change (panel C). Each regression includes weather controls, a control for whether summer watering schedule is in place, household fixed effects, and fixed effects in year and week of the year. Standard errors are two-way clustered at household and sample-month levels. Graphs show coefficient estimates and the 95% confidence intervals.

of −.498. To further explore this pattern, we estimate the following event-study equation:

$$y_{it} = \sum_{s=-13}^{13} \beta_s I_t^{\text{Weeks Post-Announcement}} + \gamma_{\text{woy}} + \gamma_{\text{yr}} + \gamma_i + X_t \theta + \varepsilon_{it}, \qquad (5)$$

where y_{it} is the IHS of household i's average daily water use in week t and $I_t^{\text{Weeks Post-Announcement}}$ is an indicator for week t being s weeks before or after the announcement.[17] Also, γ_i, γ_{yr}, and γ_{woy} are household, year, and week-of-year fixed effects, and X_t includes weather controls.

Figure 9 plots the coefficients from equation (5), suggesting that both announcements are associated with declines in water use. We interpret these results as indicating that drought awareness is negatively correlated with water consumption and explore the robustness of this finding

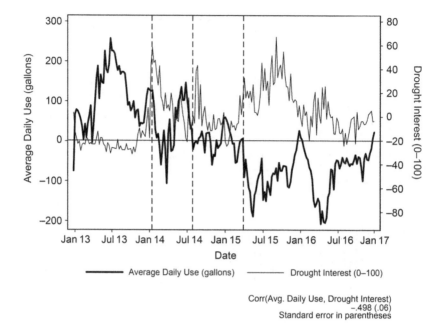

Fig. 8. Drought interest and water use over time

Notes: This figure plots a weekly time series of de-seasoned average daily water use and drought interest. The drought interest measure is computed from Google searches for the word "drought." Vertical lines indicate dates of the state of emergency announcement, the outdoor watering schedule change, and the mandated restrictions.

to controlling for the other policies that were in force in this period in the next section.

IV.   The Policies' Effect on Total Water Conservation

In this section, we use a unified linear regression framework to estimate the effect of the policies discussed independently in Section III. This unified framework enables us to account for the simultaneous introduction of different policies and to estimate the contribution of each policy to total water conservation. Specifically, we estimate the following equation:

$$
\begin{aligned}
y_{it} = \ &\beta_1 \mathrm{IHS}(\mathrm{Rate})_{it} \\
&+ \beta_2 I_t^{\mathrm{PostScheduleChange}} \times I_t^{\mathrm{Summer}} \\
&+ \beta_3 \mathrm{DroughtInterest}_t \\
&+ \gamma_i + \gamma_{\mathrm{woy}} + f(\mathrm{Weather}_t) + \varepsilon_{it},
\end{aligned}
\tag{6}
$$

A. Effect of State of Emergency Announcement

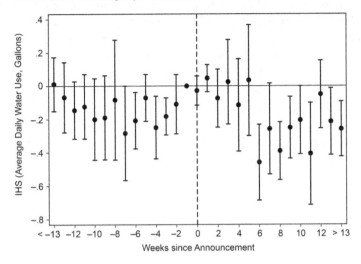

B. Effect of California Mandated Reductions

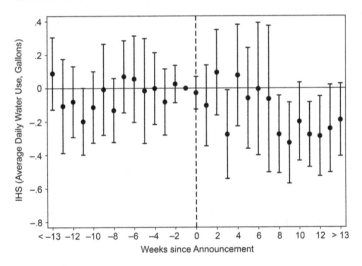

Fig. 9. Event-time estimates—the effect of statewide conservation announcements on water use

Notes: This figure shows week-by-week event-time coefficients from regressing the inverse hyperbolic sine (IHS) of average daily water use on indicators for each week relative to Jerry Brown's January 17, 2014, announcement that the drought had placed California in a state of emergency (panel A) and California's announcement on April 1, 2015, that all municipalities would be collectively required to reduce water use by 25% (panel B). Each event-time estimate includes weather controls, a control for whether summer watering schedule is in place, household fixed effects, and fixed effects in year and week of the year. Standard errors are two-way clustered at household and sample-month levels. Graphs show coefficient estimates and the 95% confidence intervals.

where y_{it} is the IHS of household i's average daily use during week t, IHS(Rate)$_{it}$ is alternatively the IHS of the average rate or the IHS of marginal and fixed rates, $I_t^{\text{PostScheduleChange}}$ is an indicator that equals 1 after the schedule change, and DroughtInterest$_t$ is our measure of Google searches related to the drought. We report versions of this specification that do and do not include year fixed effects, where the latter are more susceptible to confounding factors but enable estimation of long-run effects (instead of limiting identification to the year of implementation). Table 4 presents estimates from this regression with marginal and fixed rates in columns 1–2 and average rates in columns 3–4.

Table 4
Simultaneous Effect of Citywide Conservation Policies and Drought Interest on Water Use

	IHS of Average Daily Use (Gallons)			
Dependent Variable	(1)	(2)	(3)	(4)
	A. Regression Coefficients			
IHS of fixed rate	.563**	.810**		
	(.205)	(.203)		
IHS of marginal rate per gallon	−.164**	−.038		
	(.035)	(.044)		
IHS of average rate per gallon			−.388**	−.367**
			(.085)	(.133)
1(Post-schedule change) × 1(Summer)	−.288**	−.121**	−.329**	−.253**
	(.030)	(.039)	(.032)	(.057)
Drought interest	.006	.018	−.001	.028$^+$
	(.015)	(.013)	(.017)	(.016)
	B. Implied Elasticities			
Marginal rate per gallon	−.16	−.04		
Average rate per gallon			−.39	−.37
Year fixed effects		X		X
Observations	17,017,841	17,017,841	17,017,841	17,017,841

Note: Each column presents regression estimates of the effect of city-level policies on the inverse hyperbolic sine (IHS) of average daily water use. Columns 1 and 2 include marginal and fixed rates, whereas columns 3 and 4 include average rates. Regressions include weather controls, household, and week-of-year fixed effects. Columns 2 and 4 include year fixed effects. Standard errors in parentheses are two-way clustered at household and sample-month levels. We compute elasticities using the following formula derived by Bellemare and Wichman (2020): $\xi_{yx} = \hat{\beta} \cdot \left(\bar{x} \cdot \sqrt{\bar{y}^2 + 1} \middle/ \bar{y} \cdot \sqrt{\bar{x}^2 + 1} \right)$, where $\bar{x}$ is the mean of our independent variable and $\bar{y}$ is the mean of our dependent variable.
$^+ p < .10$.
$^{**} p < .01$.

When simultaneously estimating the effect of the policies, these regressions estimate similar policy effects to those identified separately in Section III. First, table 4 estimates a price elasticity of water demand of 0.16 with respect to marginal rates, and of 0.39 with respect to average rates, both very similar to the estimates in table 1. It is also apparent that the price elasticities are smaller in the specifications that include year fixed effects, but we do not emphasize these specifications because they do not take advantage of all of the identifying variation. Second, we find substantial long-term effects of the schedule change during the summer, on the order of 29%–33%, similar to those estimated in table 3. It is noteworthy that the winter effect remains even when conditioning on the price and drought variables (see table A2). Finally, we estimate no effect of drought awareness on water conservation after controlling for the other policies. This finding suggests that awareness has no additional explanatory power after accounting for the effect of the other policies.[18]

Next, we decompose the total water savings we observe in Fresno between 2013 and 2016 into components attributable to each of the policies analyzed in table 4. First, we calculate "Actual Changes" in water use each year relative to a baseline before any policy changes in the first half of 2013. Then, we compute "Policy-Induced Changes" by predicting water use each year based on the coefficients estimating policy effects in each column of table 4. Specifically, we compute the following equation for each year $t \in 2014$–2016:

$$\text{Policy Induced Changes} = \sum_{i=1}^{3} \widehat{\beta}_i(\text{Policy}_{it} - \text{Policy}_{i0}). \qquad (7)$$

Table 5 reports the results of this exercise year by year using estimates including marginal and fixed rates (columns 1–3) and average rates (columns 4–6). Specifically, rate changes appear to explain 40%–44% of the water savings in 2016 compared with 2013, whereas the schedule change explains 45%–51% of those savings, and drought interest explains at most 2% of the savings, depending on which measure of rates we use.

We caveat this analysis by noting that the results from this exercise are sensitive to how we interpret the effects of the schedule change in the winter. When we include the effects of this policy in all months of the year as opposed to only the summer months when the schedule change is binding, table A4 shows that our analysis overpredicts water

Table 5
Policies' Contributions to Water Conservation

	Estimates Use Marginal/ Fixed Rate Changes			Estimates Use Average Rate Changes		
	Year 2014	Year 2015	Year 2016	Year 2014	Year 2015	Year 2016
	(1)	(2)	(3)	(4)	(5)	(6)
	A. Outcome: IHS of Water Use					
Actual change	−.101	−.307	−.323	−.101	−.307	−.323
Policy-induced change	−.143**	−.306**	−.270**	−.193**	−.296**	−.309**
	(.023)	(.023)	(.025)	(.023)	(.027)	(.034)
Policy-induced change/ actual change	141.6%	99.7%	83.6%	191.1%	96.4%	95.7%
	B. % Actual Change Explained by Each Policy					
Marginal and fixed rate changes	50.30**	39.53**	39.99**			
	(12.29)	(7.89)	(7.45)			
Average rate changes				77.00**	23.75**	43.93**
				(16.82)	(5.19)	(9.60)
1(Post-schedule change) × 1(Summer)	98.48**	63.30**	45.10**	112.40**	72.24**	51.47**
	(10.26)	(6.60)	(4.70)	(10.92)	(7.02)	(5.00)
Drought interest	−7.48	−3.26	−1.51	1.17	.51	.24
	(20.45)	(8.92)	(4.12)	(23.23)	(10.13)	(4.68)

Note: The top panel of this table shows the actual and predicted policy-induced change in the inverse hyperbolic sine (IHS) of average daily water use each year relative to the beginning of the sample period in the first semester of 2013. The policy-induced change is computed using the regression coefficients in column 1 of table 4 for estimates using marginal/fixed rates and column 3 of table 4 for estimates using average rates. The bottom panel shows the contribution of each citywide policy to the total actual change. Standard errors in parentheses are two-way clustered at sample-month and household levels.
**$p < .01$.

savings. Without data from control cities, or even better from a randomized trial, we cannot say whether the policy effects we estimate when the policy was not in effect are due to persistent behavior changes such as lawn replacements or to confounding factors such as secular trends that might also explain the effect in the summer.

V. Conclusion

Resource conservation is one of the common challenges that societies face. Climate change is likely to make crises, such as droughts, more common, putting policy makers under more frequent pressure to adopt conservation policies. By trying to disentangle the effect of different policies on water conservation, this article aims to provide a tool kit for policy makers to reduce resource use. To do so, we take different approaches to assessing the effects of different policies depending on the identifying variation available in the data.

The article's primary contribution is to simultaneously estimate the effect of aggregate policies such as outdoor watering restrictions, rate changes, and policies aimed at increasing drought awareness. First, we find that increasing water rates explain 40%–44% of the water conservation experienced in Fresno between 2013 and 2016. Our analysis abstracts from political economy considerations that marginal rate increases can be viewed as punitive, disproportionally affect low-income customers (Wichman et al. 2016), and divorce revenues from the cost structure of utilities, thus increasing risk. Second, we find that tightening summer outdoor watering restrictions decreased summer water use despite intertemporal substitution to permitted times. However, we also find a decline in winter use that complicates the interpretation of these results. Indeed, using only time-series variation in Fresno, we cannot decisively conclude whether the policy effects we estimate when the policy was not in effect are due to persistent behavior changes or to confounding factors such as secular trends that might also explain the effect in the summer. Moreover, we cannot quantify the welfare effects of the schedule change as we lack data on the disutility it imposes on households. Third, we do not find evidence that increased drought awareness due to state-level announcements leads to long-term water conservation. However, identifying the effect of conservation and media campaigns remains an open and crucial question for demand management policy going forward.

We also have data on take-up of rebates for water-efficient appliances and conservation services offered by the city through programs that did not change over our sample period. In analysis not reported in the article, we find that installing water-efficient toilets and drought-resistant lawns reduces household water use, as does receiving timer tutorials and water use audits. However, the aggregate effects of these rebates and customer services are negligible due to low take-up rates. Most water utilities in California offer rebates for water-efficient appliances on top of rebates offered by the state through the "Save Our Water" program, despite mixed evidence on the effectiveness of resource-efficient appliances at reducing use due to rebound effects (Davis 2008; Lee, Tansel, and Balbin 2011, 2013; Bennear, Lee, and Taylor 2013; Gillingham et al. 2013). Anecdotally, most households redeem both city- and state-offered rebates, meaning rebates could cover the total cost of a toilet and up to 40% of the cost of a new washer. Similarly, virtually all utilities in California enforce outdoor water use restrictions and offer services such as water audits and timer tutorials. Thus, we believe that further research is warranted to study the scalability and cost-effectiveness of these policies, given that there likely are many inframarginal takers.

Understanding what works in managing resource use during crises is paramount to navigate the challenges posed by climate change. Answering this question requires sorting out the effects of policies that are often enacted simultaneously. Importantly, this simultaneity also raises questions of the complementarity or substitutability of these policies, which will affect the external validity of our findings. This article provides novel associational evidence, but decisive evidence of the effects of multiple policies and their interactions requires experimental or valid quasi-experimental variation in them. We are especially optimistic about opportunities to implement randomized controlled trials (Browne et al. 2020).

Appendix

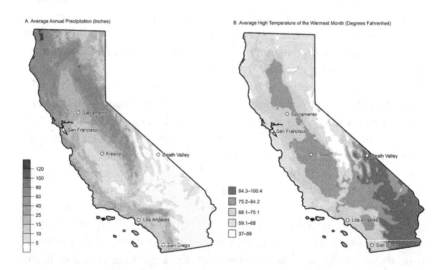

Fig. A1.   Precipitation and high temperature in Fresno and California *A*, Average annual precipitation (inches). *B*, Average high temperature of the warmest month (degrees Fahrenheit).

Note: Source of map is the California Coastal Commission (https://www.coastal.ca.gov /coastalvoices/resources/Biodiversity_Atlas_Climate_and_Topography.pdf).

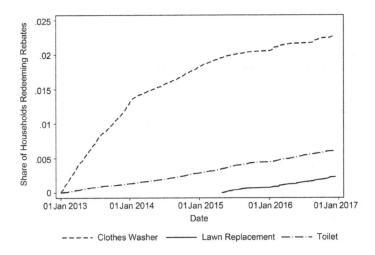

Fig. A2. Rebate adoption over time

Notes: This plot shows the cumulative share of sample households issued a clothes washer, lawn replacement, or toilet rebate over the sample period. Lawn replacement rebates were introduced in 2015.

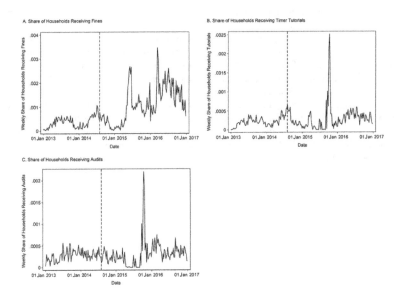

Fig. A3. Fines, timer tutorials, and audits issued in Fresno. *A*, Share of households receiving fines. *B*, Share of households receiving timer tutorials. *C*, Share of households receiving audits.

Notes: Panels A, B, and C respectively show the weekly share of households in our sample that received fines, timer tutorials, and audits issued in Fresno throughout the sample period. The vertical line is the date of the schedule change on August 1, 2014.

Table A1

Summary Statistics

	California	Fresno	Rank in California
Demographics:			
Population	35,984,596	506,132	5
Average household income	$88,595	$58,219	90
Median household income	$61,933	$41,455	96
Fraction of bachelor's degree or more	30.43%	20.10%	69
Average household size	3.04	3.10	43
Fraction of homeowners	54.69%	46.06%	80
Average per capita residential water use (gal/day):			
Year 2013	145	140	27
Year 2014	129	122	34
Year 2015	98	105	22
Year 2016	97	120	13
Climate Characteristics (2013–16):			
Average precipitation (in/day)	.0529	.0367	36
Average daily high temperature (°F)	76.00	80.94	7
Average daily low temperature (°F)	53.10	53.69	50

Note: This table shows summary statistics on demographics, average water use, and climate in California and Fresno. It also shows Fresno's rank within the 100 largest water utilities in California with regard to water use and its rank among the 100 largest census locations with regard to demographics and weather. Demographics data are from 2014 American Community Survey 5-year estimates. Income-related statistics are in 2014 inflation-adjusted dollars. Average per capita daily water use data are from California State Water Resources Control Board (https://www.waterboards.ca.gov/water_issues/programs /conservation_portal/conservation_reporting.html). Most weather data before October 2014 are imputed. Aggregate California weather estimates are averaged across the 100 most populous census places, accounting for 59.6% of the state's population over 2013–16. Climate characteristics are from NOAA National Climatic Data Center (https://www.ncdc.noaa .gov/cdo-web/search).

Table A2

Simultaneous Effect of Citywide Conservation Policies and Drought Interest on Water Use, Year-Round Schedule Change Effects

Dependent Variable	IHS of Average Daily Use (Gallons)			
	(1)	(2)	(3)	(4)
	A. Regression Coefficients			
IHS of fixed rate	.399*	.344*		
	(.157)	(.158)		
IHS of marginal rate per gallon	−.165**	−.388**		
	(.028)	(.070)		
IHS of average rate per gallon			−.401**	−1.346**
			(.071)	(.243)
1(Post-schedule change)	−.266**	−.529**	−.288**	−.974**
	(.032)	(.091)	(.039)	(.148)
1(Post-schedule change) × 1(Summer)	−.017	.011	−.028	.056
	(.043)	(.040)	(.050)	(.042)
Drought interest	−.009	.003	−.012	−.007
	(.009)	(.012)	(.012)	(.013)
	B. Implied Elasticities			
Marginal rate per gallon	−.17	−.39		
Average rate per gallon			−.40	−1.35
Year fixed effects		X		X
Observations	17,017,841	17,017,841	17,017,841	17,017,841

Note: Each column presents regression estimates of the effect of city-level policies on the inverse hyperbolic sine (IHS) of average daily water use. Columns 1 and 2 include marginal and fixed rates, whereas columns 3 and 4 include average rates. Regressions include weather controls and household and week-of-year fixed effects. Columns 2 and 4 include year fixed effects. Standard errors in parentheses are two-way clustered at household and sample-month levels. We compute elasticities using the following formula derived by Bellemare and Wichman (2020): $\xi_{yx} = \hat{\beta} \cdot \left(\frac{\bar{x} \cdot \sqrt{\bar{y}^2+1}}{\bar{y} \cdot \sqrt{\bar{x}^2+1}} \right)$, where $\bar{x}$ is the mean of our independent variable and $\bar{y}$ is the mean of our dependent variable.
*$p < .05$.
**$p < .01$.

Table A3

Simultaneous Effect of Citywide Conservation Policies and Drought Interest on Log Water Use

Dependent Variable	Log of (1 + Average Daily Use[Gallons])			
	(1)	(2)	(3)	(4)
Log of fixed rate	.422**	.555**		
	(.145)	(.148)		
Log of marginal rate per gallon	−.183**	−.052		
	(.025)	(.035)		
Log of average rate per gallon			−.351**	−.242*
			(.057)	(.093)
1(Post-schedule change) × 1(Summer)	−.292**	−.144**	−.322**	−.218**
	(.024)	(.036)	(.026)	(.044)
Drought interest	.017	.011	.008	.013
	(.013)	(.010)	(.014)	(.012)
Year fixed effects		X		X
Observations	17,017,841	17,017,841	17,017,841	17,017,841

Note: This table calculates the same results as table 4, except using the log(1 + average daily water use) rather than the inverse hyperbolic sine. Each column presents regression estimates of the effect of city-level policies on the log of average daily water use. Columns 1 and 2 include marginal and fixed rates, whereas columns 3 and 4 include average rates. Regressions include weather controls and household and week-of-year fixed effects. Columns 2 and 4 include year fixed effects. Standard errors in parentheses are two-way clustered at household and sample-month levels.

*$p < .05$.

**$p < .01$.

Table A4
Policies' Contributions to Water Conservation, Year-Round Schedule Change Effects

	Estimates Use Marginal/ Fixed Rate Changes			Estimates Use Average Rate Changes		
	Year 2014	Year 2015	Year 2016	Year 2014	Year 2015	Year 2016
	(1)	(2)	(3)	(4)	(5)	(6)
	A. Outcome: IHS of Water Use					
Actual change	−.101	−.307	−.323	−.101	−.307	−.323
Policy-induced change	−.189**	−.399**	−.407**	−.234**	−.404**	−.459**
	(.017)	(.021)	(.027)	(.016)	(.023)	(.034)
Policy-induced change/actual change	187.1%	130%	126%	231.7%	131.6%	142.1%
	B. % Actual Change Explained by Each Policy					
Marginal and fixed rate changes	52.59**	34.45**	38.40**			
	(10.23)	(5.34)	(5.50)			
Average rate changes				79.60**	24.55**	45.42**
				(14.16)	(4.37)	(8.08)
Schedule change	122.20**	90.61**	85.17**	135.00**	99.79**	93.35**
	(10.06)	(7.03)	(6.56)	(10.31)	(7.36)	(7.26)
1(Post-schedule change)	116.2**	86.79**	82.45**	125.50**	93.69**	89.00**
	(13.94)	(10.41)	(9.89)	(17.01)	(12.70)	(12.06)
1(Post-schedule change) × 1(Summer)	5.95	3.82	2.72	9.50	6.11	4.35
	(14.59)	(9.38)	(6.68)	(17.03)	(10.94)	(7.80)
Drought interest	11.61	5.07	2.34	16.40	7.16	3.30
	(12.40)	(5.41)	(2.50)	(16.47)	(7.18)	(3.31)

Note: The top panel of this table shows the actual and predicted policy-induced change in the inverse hyperbolic sine (IHS) of average daily water use each year relative to the beginning of the sample period in the first semester of 2013. The policy-induced change is computed using the regression coefficients in column 1 of table A2 for estimate using marginal/fixed rates and column 3 of table A2 for estimates using average rates. The bottom panel shows the contribution of each citywide policy to the total actual change. Standard errors in parentheses are two-way clustered at sample-month and household levels.
**$p < .01$.

Endnotes

Authors' email addresses: Browne (oliver.browne@berkeley.edu), Gazze (lgazze@uchicago.edu), Greenstone (mgreenst@uchicago.edu). We thank Laura Grant, Matt Kotchen, Casey Wichman, and participants at the EPIC Lunch seminar, AERE, ASSA, and NBER EEPE conferences for helpful comments. We also thank Bridget Pals, Iris Song, and Jackson Reimer, who provided excellent research assistance. This article would not have been possible without the endless support from our partners in Fresno to help us understand their programs; in particular we thank Tommy Esqueda, Bud Tickel, Cheryl Burns, and Nora Laikam. All remaining errors are our own. For acknowledgments, sources of research support, and disclosure of the authors' material financial relationships, if any, please see https://www.nber.org/books-and-chapters/environmental-and-energy-policy-and-economy-volume-2/do-conservation-policies-work-evidence-residential-water-use.

1. "Extreme drought" and "Exceptional drought" are the two most extreme of the five levels of drought classification measured by the USDA drought monitor. An area experiences "Extreme drought" when major crop areas and pasture losses are common, fire risk is extreme, and widespread water shortages can be expected. An "Exceptional drought" is the most severe category of water shortage that, in addition to the traits of Extreme drought, result in water emergencies.

2. A better research design might compare changes in water consumption in Fresno to another city that did not change its watering schedule on the same date. We attempted to secure data from comparable cities with different policies, but we were unable to do so.

3. When the total reduction in water use throughout the year is treated as the effect of the change in summer water schedule regulations, then the policy appears to explain 92% of the observed water savings and the sum of the savings explained by each policy becomes larger than the total water savings observed over our sample period. Because the decrease in winter consumption is comparable to the summer decline, we would conclude that the reduction in outdoor watering days did not explain any of the observed water savings if both are due to a confounder.

4. Following Bellemare and Wichman (2020), we multiply the argument of the IHS transformations by a large number, 100,000,000, to include observations where the arguments are 0. Algebraically, the multiplicative constant does not affect the regression estimates. Water meter readings of 0 may be due to a weeklong vacation, meter malfunctions, or water access being shut off to the household on a given day.

5. Controls include a summer indicator as well as the following indicators constructed at the daily level and averaged over the days d in each week t: nine indicators for any precipitation, precipitation more than 0.2 inches, and precipitation more than 0.5 inches on day d, day $d - 1$, and days $d - 2$ to $d - 7$, each interacted with the summer indicator, and six indicators for maximum temperature above 95°F and above 100°F on day d, $d - 1$, and days $d - 2$ to $d - 7$.

6. We compute elasticities using the following formula derived by Bellemare and Wichman (2020): $\xi_{yx} = \hat{\beta} \cdot \left(\bar{x} \cdot \sqrt{\bar{y}^2 + 1} \middle/ \bar{y} \cdot \sqrt{\bar{x}^2 + 1} \right)$ where $\bar{x}$ is the mean of our independent variable and $\bar{y}$ is the mean of our dependent variable.

7. Ito (2014) documents similar results in the electricity sector.

8. Authors' calculation based on State Water Resource Control Board data on Conservation Reporting.

9. Due to limitations of computation power, we estimate this equation at the block group-odd/even level, weighting by number of households per block group.

10. These days are Tuesdays and Saturdays for odd-numbered homes and Wednesdays and Sundays for even-numbered homes.

11. These days are Mondays, Wednesdays, Fridays, and Sundays for odd-numbered homes and Mondays, Tuesdays, Thursdays, and Saturdays for even-numbered homes. See table 2.

12. The estimates appear roughly halved when introducing year fixed effects.

13. A wide range of behavior changes may lead to persistent declines in water use, including saving water in daily activities and installing water efficient appliances. To explore the investment channel, we have limited data on city-level take-up of rebates for clothes washers and low-flow toilets, available in Fresno since 2006, as well as rebates for lawn replacements, available since 2015. Figure A2 shows no evidence of any discontinuous increase in rebate take-up for clothes washer and toilet rebates. Furthermore, the relatively low take-up of rebates implies that they cannot explain trends in aggregate water use.

14. In addition, this regulation instituted a temporary, statewide consumer rebate program to replace old appliances with water- and energy-efficient models; required

campuses, golf courses, cemeteries, and other properties with large green spaces to make significant cuts in water use; prohibited new home developments from irrigating with potable water; prohibited irrigation of street medians; prohibited the serving of tap water in restaurants unless asked for by customers; and prohibited irrigation in days following rainfall.

15. Indicators for weeks −13 and 13 include also weeks before and after the window, respectively.

16. Because the drought awareness index is constructed at the city level, this specification does not include household fixed effects.

17. Indicators for weeks −13 and 13 include also weeks before and after the window, respectively.

18. Table A3 shows that our estimates are robust to using logarithm transformations of the outcome and the rate variables instead of the IHS transformation.

References

Allcott, Hunt. 2011. "Social Norms and Energy Conservation." *Journal of Public Economics* 95 (9–10): 1082–95.

———. 2016. "Paternalism and Energy Efficiency: An Overview." *Annual Review of Economics* 8:145–76.

Allcott, Hunt, and Todd Rogers. 2014. "The Short-Run and Long-Run Effects of Behavioral Interventions: Experimental Evidence from Energy Conservation." *American Economic Review* 104 (10): 3003–37.

Asensio, Omar I., and Magali A. Delmas. 2015. "Nonprice Incentives and Energy Conservation." *Proceedings of the National Academy of Sciences* 112 (6): E510–E515.

Baerenklau, Kenneth A., Kurt A. Schwabe, and Ariel Dinar. 2014. "The Residential Water Demand Effect of Increasing Block Rate Water Budgets." *Land Economics* 90 (4): 683–99.

Baumol, William J. 1988. *The Theory of Environmental Policy.* Cambridge: Cambridge University Press.

Bellemare, Marc F., and Casey J. Wichman. 2020. "Elasticities and the Inverse Hyperbolic Sine Transformation." *Oxford Bulletin of Economics and Statistics* 82 (1): 50–61.

Bennear, Lori S., Jonathan M. Lee, and Laura O. Taylor. 2013. "Municipal Rebate Programs for Environmental Retrofits: An Evaluation of Additionality and Cost-Effectiveness." *Journal of Policy Analysis and Management* 32 (2): 350–72.

Bhanot, Syon P. 2018. "Isolating the Effect of Injunctive Norms on Conservation Behavior: New Evidence from a Field Experiment in California." *Organizational Behavior and Human Decision Processes.* https://doi.org/10.1016/j.obhdp.2018.11.002.

Brent, Daniel A., Joseph H. Cook, and Skylar Olsen. 2015. "Social Comparisons, Household Water Use, and Participation in Utility Conservation Programs: Evidence from Three Randomized Trials." *Journal of the Association of Environmental and Resource Economists* 2 (4): 597–627.

Browne, Oliver R., Ludovica Gazze, Michael Greenstone, and Olga Rostapshova. 2020. "Enforcement and Deterrence with Certain Detection: An Experiment in Water Conservation Policy." Mimeograph.

Castledine, A., K. Moeltner, M. K. Price, and S. Stoddard. 2014. "Free to Choose: Promoting Conservation by Relaxing Outdoor Watering Restrictions." *Journal of Economic Behavior and Organization* 107:324–43.

Davis, Lucas W. 2008. "Durable Goods and Residential Demand for Energy and Water: Evidence from a Field Trial." *RAND Journal of Economics* 39 (2): 530–46.

Egebark, Johan, and Mathias Ekström. 2016. "Can Indifference Make the World Greener?" *Journal of Environmental Economics and Management* 76:1–13.

Ferraro, Paul J., Juan Jose Miranda, and Michael K. Price. 2011. "The Persistence of Treatment Effects with Norm-Based Policy Instruments: Evidence from a Randomized Environmental Policy Experiment." *American Economic Review* 101 (3): 318–22.

Ferraro, Paul J., and Michael K. Price. 2013. "Using Nonpecuniary Strategies to Influence Behavior: Evidence from a Large-Scale Field Experiment." *Review of Economics and Statistics* 95 (1): 64–73.

Gillingham, Kenneth, Matthew J. Kotchen, David S. Rapson, and Gernot Wagner. 2013. "Energy Policy: The Rebound Effect Is Overplayed." *Nature* 493 (7433): 475.

Grafton, R. Quentin, and Michael B. Ward. 2008. "Prices versus Rationing: Marshallian Surplus and Mandatory Water Restrictions." *Economic Record* 84:S57–S65.

Griffin, Daniel, and Kevin J. Anchukaitis. 2014. "How Unusual Is the 2012–2014 California Drought?" *Geophysical Research Letters* 41:9017–23.

Halich, Greg, and Kurt Stephenson. 2009. "Effectiveness of Residential Water-Use Restrictions under Varying Levels of Municipal Effort." *Land Economics* 85 (4): 614–26.

Hanak, Ellen, and Matthew Davis. 2006. "Lawns and Water Demand in California." *California Economic Policy* 2 (2): 1–22.

Hensher, David, Nina Shore, and Kenneth Train. 2006. "Water Supply Security and Willingness to Pay to Avoid Drought Restrictions." *Economic Record* 82 (256): 56–66.

Ito, Koichiro. 2013. "How Do Consumers Respond to Nonlinear Pricing? Evidence from Household Water Demand." Working paper, University of Chicago.

———. 2014. "Do Consumers Respond to Marginal or Average Price? Evidence from Nonlinear Electricity Pricing." *American Economic Review* 104 (2): 537–63.

Ito, Koichiro, Takanori Ida, and Makoto Tanaka. 2018. "Moral Suasion and Economic Incentives: Field Experimental Evidence from Energy Demand." *American Economic Journal: Economic Policy* 10 (1): 240–67.

Jessoe, Katrina, Gabriel Lade, Frank Loge and Edward Spang. Forthcoming. "Spillovers from Behavioral Interventions: Experimental Evidence from Water and Energy Use." *Journal of the Association of Environmental and Resource Economists.*

Jessoe, Katrina, and David Rapson. 2014. "Knowledge Is (Less) Power: Experimental Evidence from Residential Energy Use." *American Economic Review* 104 (4): 1417–38.

Kenney, Douglas S., Roberta A. Klein, and Martyn P. Clark. 2004. "Use and Effectiveness of Municipal Water Restrictions During Drought in Colorado." *JAWRA Journal of the American Water Resources Association* 40 (1): 77–87.

Klaiber, H. Allen, V. Kerry Smith, Michael Kaminsky, and Aaron Strong. 2014. "Measuring Price Elasticities for Residential Water Demand with Limited Information." *Land Economics* 90 (1): 100–113.

Labandeira, Xavier, José M. Labeaga, and Xiral López-Otero. 2017. "A Meta-Analysis on the Price Elasticity of Energy Demand." *Energy Policy* 102:549–68.

Lee, Mengshan, Berrin Tansel, and Maribel Balbin. 2011. "Influence of Residential Water Use Efficiency Measures on Household Water Demand: A Four Year Longitudinal Study." *Resources, Conservation and Recycling* 56 (1): 1–6.

———. 2013. "Urban Sustainability Incentives for Residential Water Conservation: Adoption of Multiple High Efficiency Appliances." *Water Resources Management* 27 (7): 2531–40.

Mansur, Erin T., and Sheila M. Olmstead. 2012. "The Value of Scarce Water: Measuring the Inefficiency of Municipal Regulations." *Journal of Urban Economics* 71 (3): 332–46.

Michelsen, An M., J. Thomas McGuckin, and Donna Stumpf. 1999. "Nonprice Water Conservation Programs as a Demand Management Tool." *JAWRA Journal of the American Water Resources Association* 35 (3): 593–602.

Nataraj, Shanthi, and W. Michael Hanemann. 2011. "Does Marginal Price Matter? A Regression Discontinuity Approach to Estimating Water Demand." *Journal of Environmental Economics and Management* 61 (2): 198–212.

Olmstead, Sheila M. 2009. "Reduced-Form Versus Structural Models of Water Demand Under Nonlinear Prices." *Journal of Business and Economic Statistics* 27 (1): 84–94.

Olmstead, Sheila M., W. Michael Hanemann, and Robert N. Stavins. 2007. "Water Demand Under Alternative Price Structures." *Journal of Environmental Economics and Management* 54 (2): 181–98.

Olmstead, Sheila M., and Robert N. Stavins. 2009. "Comparing Price and Nonprice Approaches to Urban Water Conservation." *Water Resources Research* 45 (4): W04301.

Pratt, Bryan. 2019. "A Fine Is More Than a Price: Evidence from Drought Restrictions." Mimeograph.

Renwick, Mary E., and Richard D. Green. 2000. "Do Residential Water Demand Side Management Policies Measure Up? An Analysis of Eight California Water Agencies." *Journal of Environmental Economics and Management* 40 (1): 37–55.

Syme, Geoffrey J., Blair E. Nancarrow, and Clive Seligman. 2000. "The Evaluation of Information Campaigns to Promote Voluntary Household Water Conservation." *Evaluation Review* 24 (6): 539–78.

Viard, V. Brian, and Shihe Fu. 2015. "The Effect of Beijing's Driving Restrictions on Pollution and Economic Activity." *Journal of Public Economics* 125:98–115.

Wichman, Casey J. 2014. "Perceived Price in Residential Water Demand: Evidence from a Natural Experiment." *Journal of Economic Behavior and Organization* 107:308–23.

Wichman, Casey J., Laura O. Taylor, and Roger H. von Haefen. 2016. "Conservation Policies: Who Responds to Price and Who Responds to Prescription?" *Journal of Environmental Economics and Management* 79:114–134.

Zhang, Wei, C.-Y. Cynthia Lin Lawell, and Victoria I. Umanskaya. 2017. "The Effects of License Plate-Based Driving Restrictions on Air Quality: Theory and Empirical Evidence." *Journal of Environmental Economics and Management* 82:181–220.